Saskatchewan

The Traveller's Canada

Saskatchewan

Edward McCourt

Toronto / Macmillan of Canada

First published 1968
First paperback 1977

ISBN 0-7705-1618-1

Printed in Canada for
The Macmillan Company of Canada Limited,
70 Bond Street, Toronto, Ontario   M5B 1X3

For Michael, Brenda, and Sean

Contents

Illustrations

Maps

Photographs *between pages 114 and 115*

Preface

It is my hope that this book may help the visitor to Saskatchewan to choose roads to travel over, places to visit, and things to see that will most effectively acquaint him with the nature and variety of the land and with the history and character of its people.

Some communities may feel annoyed because I haven't mentioned them; others, perhaps, because I have. Let me say to any whom I may have offended – and this not by way of apology but of justification – that what I have written here about the land and the people of Saskatchewan I have written never out of malice, occasionally out of anger, and always out of affection.

I would like to thank my wife for the splendid companionship and support she gave me during our wanderings; and to insist that since I have borrowed freely of her observations on people and places she must assume some responsibility for the contents of this book.

University of Saskatchewan   *Edward McCourt*

Saskatchewan

Prologue

The Land and the People

The Rock Mistaseni was once, so the story goes, a shrine of the Plains Cree. Until only a few years ago the isolated granite boulder, lying humped like a stranded leviathan on the bank of the South Saskatchewan River a few miles above the site of the recently built South Saskatchewan River Dam, was looked upon as no more than a mildly interesting freak of nature; but the discovery of an extraordinary number of artifacts at its base, allied with the time-blurred recollections of aged Indians, excited the interest of anthropologists and archeologists; and shortly before the time set by the Dam authorities for flooding that part of the river valley in which the Rock lay, the cry went up to save from submersion one of the few remaining relics of the culture of the Cree Indians.

The 'Save Mistaseni' campaign was conducted with enormous vigour and enthusiasm – even to the point where it was proposed to bring in from the Egyptian Aswan Dam project engineers skilled in the transplanting of huge ancient statues, to whom moving the Rock would be merest child's play. True, a few voices were raised to oppose the project. Fundamentalists contended that whatever money might be collected should be spent on converting the Indians from Rock-worship to Christianity, humanitarians that it be used to feed and clothe them. One newspaper correspondent urged – by way of preserving the Rock without going to the expense of moving it – that it be surmounted by a totem pole complete with platform at the top from which the faithful might be summoned to prayer. But such voices, however strident, were lost in the all but unanimous shout of approval that greeted the project. Local radio stations and newspapers gave the Rock lavish publicity; balladeers told the Mistaseni story in song – indeed helped to create it; professors pleaded for the preservation of the Rock in the interests of science; opposition members of the Legislature demanded that it be made a ward of the provincial government, members of the provincial government that it be moved at federal expense; people from all walks of life offered freely of their time, energy, and ideas – of everything, in fact, except the money needed to pay a contractor to move the Rock to high ground.

Only the Indians remained indifferent to the fate of Mistaseni. The inevitable came to pass. The Rock ceased after a time to be the object of a new crusade, became instead an irritant, a reproach to those who would not or could not save it. The newspaper stories dropped to a back page and then out of sight; the tumult and the shouting died away – even the ballad singers at last fell silent. Meanwhile the waters rose in the river valley, crept close to the base of the Rock. At which point a government agency, in a move explicable only as an inexpensive sop to a not wholly quiescent public conscience, blasted the Rock with dynamite and carried off a few bits and pieces from which to make a monument to a dismembered and submerged relic of native culture.

A pity Mistaseni could not have been saved. Few people have left behind them scantier evidences of their culture than the Indians of the great plains. 'They left no arts, no tradition, no buildings or roads or laws,' Rupert Brooke wrote in his *Letters From America*: 'only a story or two, and a few names, strange and beautiful.' These and a scattering of primitive artifacts, here and there a medicine wheel, a few pictographs on rock faces, and that is all.

There is really no evidence to show that the Plains Cree ever attached much religious significance to the big Rock. It was probably primarily important to them as a landmark and meeting-place; and perhaps it reminded the first comers of their earlier habitat, the rock-ridden Shield country lying north-east towards James Bay. But the fact that it achieved any kind of importance at all is what interests the anthropologist; North American Indian religious beliefs ordinarily attached little significance to inanimate objects.

The Indians, and after them the white men, came late to the great central plains area of Canada which today forms the southern part of the province of Saskatchewan. Their reluctance to establish a permanent home on the naked plains will not surprise visitors to Saskatchewan, particularly if they make their visit in the dead of winter; indeed they may be moved to agree whole-heartedly with the embittered early homesteader who expressed his distaste for his surroundings in a verse-portrait of a lady neither sweet nor fair:

> *Saskatchewan, you always seem to me*
> *A woman without favour in your face,*
> *Flat-breasted, angular, devoid of grace.*
> *Why do men woo you? naught is fair to see*
> *In that wide visage with thin unkempt hair,*
> *And form that squarely stands, feet splayed apart.*

The lines express what is in fact a common misconception; the truth is that the Saskatchewan landscape is never barren (except in times of prolonged drought) and in few places flat. The great southern plains are seamed deep by gullies and creek beds and frequently ridged by low hills which at a distance appear bathed in a romantic blue-green haze; two hundred miles north of the border the plains merge into pleasant, rolling parkland which in turn yields after another two hundred miles or more to a vast forest-lake-and-muskeg belt impinging on the subarctic terrain of the barren lands. And everywhere there are things to be seen and felt that exalt or soothe the sensitive spirit: crocuses spreading a mauve mist along railway embankments before the last patch of dirty grey snow has melted; wheatfields merging into a wave-surfaced green or golden ocean, unbounded save for an incredibly remote horizon rim at times indistinguishable from the sky itself; autumn days when the wind is miraculously quiet and premonitions of winter-death impel a man to look on a landscape of muted greys and browns with the passionate intensity of a lover parting from his beloved; mid-winter hoar-frost hanging on fence and telephone wires like strung popcorn; and the occasional vista – from the top of a ridge or butte or even a grain elevator – when a man sees all the kingdoms of the earth stretched out at his feet and feels himself a creature of utter insignificance in the sum of things or else the very centre of the universe.

But in spite of her very considerable scenic variety Saskatchewan is likely to impress the stranger with an awareness of encompassing natural forces more hostile than benevolent. This to a far greater degree than does either of her sister provinces. For Manitoba is only halfway plains country; great forests line her eastern flank, northward her land surface is engulfed by inland fresh-water seas; and her heart – so many truculent true-blue westerners affirm – yearns towards Ontario. West of Saskatchewan amply endowed Alberta floats on a lake of oil and snuggles comfortably into the protective embrace of the Rockies; and even her most exposed parts feel from time to time the caress of the genial chinook. But Saskatchewan stands defenceless, no forest belt or mountain range along her flanks to hold the wind at bay. Nowhere else in the west does the stranger feel himself more exposed to the wrath of the gods and the fury of the elements than in the middle of the Saskatchewan prairie.

Even though he may be sheltered behind walls. A sign in each unit of a Maple Creek motel reads thus: *When the wind blows please hang on to the door.*

The wind blows almost without intermission. The Earl of Southesk, in 1859 struggling through 'the glittering white intensity of the cold', reported gloomily that 'our fate seems to be that to which prophecy dooms a certain ancient family,

"The Tracies
Shall always have the wind in their faces." '

And a writer of more recent date, Anne Marriott, has encompassed within a poet's lines the frustration and heartbreak experienced by men and women battered by the searing winds of the dust-bowl years when the lamp at noon was the symbol of a wind-and-drought-tormented wasteland:

> *God, will it never rain again? What about*
> *those clouds out west? No, that's just dust, as thick and stifling*
> *now as winter underwear.*
> *No rain, no crop, no feed, no faith, only*
> *wind.*

Any attempt to explain why the Saskatchewan man differs to a noticeable degree in personality and outlook from the Albertan or Manitoban who should logically be his counterpart must take into account the consequences, both physical and psychological, of the dust-bowl years. The world-wide economic depression that began in 1929 affected all of Canada; Saskatchewan bore an additional and dreadful burden – nine successive years of drought and crop failure. 'The people of Saskatchewan have suffered a reduction of income during the last decade which has probably been unparalleled in peacetime in any other civilized country,' the Royal Commission on Dominion-Provincial Relations reported in 1939. (Incredibly, the net agricultural incomes for 1931 and 1932 were reported in *minus* figures.) 'The land was a landscape of almost incredible desolation,' a Regina newspaper reporter wrote after driving through southern Saskatchewan in the midsummer of 1934, 'as lifeless as ashes, and for miles there was scarcely a thing growing to be seen. . . . Gaunt cattle and horses with little save their skins to cover their bones stalked about the denuded acres, weakly seeking to crop the malign Frenchweed which seemed to be maintaining some sickly growth. When the miserable animals moved it seemed as if their frames rattled. The few people in evidence in the little towns appeared haggard and hopeless.'

At first Saskatchewan was an object of concern and charity to her sister provinces, most notably Ontario; but as the long years continued to weave the unvarying tragic design with no end in sight the charitable impulse weakened – as it always does over the long stretch – and government relief alone kept many Saskatchewan people alive. Captain John Palliser had been right, it seemed, when he reported in 1859 that the southern plains area of the North-west was unfit for cultivation, and there was talk in eastern Canada of moving the Saskatchewan farm population to the northern Ontario bush.

The year 1937 brought the worst disaster of all. No rain fell, the wind blew what little topsoil remained in the fields into roadside ditches; dust-clouds – black, sinister, shot through here and there with eerie shafts of light – wavered all day and every day between earth and sky, and the heat was appalling. In Weyburn on a July day the temperature rose to 114 degrees above zero – a record which still stands. On the Moose Mountain Indian Reserve old Chief Sheepskin, nominally a Christian, summoned his braves to perform a rain dance. He died shortly afterwards, no doubt confirmed in the faith of his fathers, for the day before he died a heavy shower fell on Moose Mountain. In Regina, bathers in Wascana Lake found themselves unable to reach the bath-houses from the water without being coated with dust and in the end went home to scrape the mud off themselves in their own bath-tubs; and in a small town near by, a baseball player – now an archetypal dust-bowl figure – lost his way running round the bases and was later found three miles out on the prairie.

The wheat crop that year averaged two and one half bushels to the acre.

But there was little thought of quitting – and none at all of moving to the Ontario bush. The bewilderment and despair of the earlier years had by 1937 given way to a sterner emotion, and the people now took a kind of defiant pride in showing the world their strength to endure, without flinching, the worst that nature could do to them. 'The country is dismal, scorched, smashed,' the mayor of Assiniboia said, 'but the people are magnificent.' He was right. No one could survive nine years of hell without courage. Nor without faith – not in a benevolent god but in one's own capacity to endure.

Nor without scars. The rains fell at last and the erstwhile desert rejoiced and blossomed like the rose; but no amount of rainfall could ever wash away dreadful memories of the agonizing struggle to survive. For the people of Saskatchewan that nine years' sojourn in a dust-darkened wilderness was a genuinely traumatic experience which has left its mark not only on those who actually lived through the Dirty Thirties but to some degree on their descendants.

The Saskatchewan man has thus been shaped by a sterner physical environment than that of most Canadians. Having been compelled to adapt himself to that environment, he has made his own rules for survival and looks with suspicion on traditional values cherished in softer lands. He tends to take a less optimistic view of life than do his neighbours, particularly those who live in Alberta. He is less ebullient and more independent. To the stranger, Saskatchewan cities may appear dull and colourless, and in many respects they are, but at least what character they do possess is honestly their own. (In this they are to be distinguished from Calgary, now an outpost of Texas, and from Edmonton, striving frenetically to become a suburb of Dawson City.) The Saskatchewan man is politically-minded but distrustful of all political parties, remembering that no government did more than keep him barely alive during his time of greatest need – hence his willingness to indulge in far-out political and social experiments and his refusal to conform to any voting pattern that makes sense to the orthodox outsider. What, after all, is one

to make of an electorate which for twenty years returned a socialist government to power, supported the introduction of Medi-
care, replaced the socialists with a government of Liberals led by
an ex-socialist, and at the same time sent a solid phalanx of
Tories to Ottawa?

No doubt the political scientist and the sociologist can explain
such goings-on in their own peculiar terms; but whenever any
friend of mine from eastern Canada remarks on the multiplicity
of political parties spawned on the prairies and the maverick
tendencies of many of the party constituents, I am content to tell
him the story of Mr. Portingale.

In the old homesteading days of more than half a century ago,
Mr. Portingale was a near neighbour of ours. He was a scruffy
little Englishman born, according to the nomenclature of his
time, into the lower middle class. Mr. Portingale was a staunch
imperialist and devout church-goer; he knew his place in the
scheme of things and until he took to homesteading in the middle
of the prairie was content to keep it. A meek little man (but
with no hope of inheriting the earth or any part thereof), he
never dreamt of calling into question the wisdom and rectitude
of either God or the government.

Not, that is, until he had lived – but only barely – through
part of a prairie winter. One day in mid January of his first year
on the homestead he borrowed my father's team and sleigh and
hauled a load of grain to town, thirty miles away. He spent the
night in the hotel and next morning, in defiance of warnings
from weather-wise old-timers, started for home. Ten miles out, a
blizzard met him head on. Fortunately the horses, grizzled old
veterans of many a winter storm, took charge of Mr. Portingale
and dragged him several hours later into our yard. My father
dug him out from under about two feet of snow, unwound him
from the horse-blankets he had thoughtfully wrapped himself
in, and half-dragged, half-carried him into our kitchen.

Mother superintended the thawing-out operations. She placed
one end of Mr. Portingale in a tub of cold water (his feet were
badly frost-bitten) and after first clearing a channel through the
icicles festooning his scraggy moustache poured into the other
end about a gallon of hot tea generously laced with ginger.

Within fifteen minutes Mr. Portingale was thawing out all
right and suffering the tortures of the damned. His feet were

immersed in a tub of flaming coals and the tea had peeled most of the skin off the roof of his mouth. In the ordinary way Mr. Portingale was the humblest, least aggressive of men, his voice an appropriate piping treble, and the strongest expletive any of us had heard him use – and then only when greatly moved – was 'Gryte Scott!' But now those of us gathered in the kitchen were seeing something vastly more significant than the mere restoration of Mr. Portingale's circulatory system to its more or less normal channels; we were awe-stricken witnesses to a striking spiritual phenomenon peculiar to the prairies. For of a sudden, Mr. Portingale was no longer a humble sheep content to follow the bell-wether of the flock – he was the Stag at Bay. He glared at us out of red-rimmed bloodshot eyes and flung bloated pin-cushion hands aloft.

'The bloodiest absolutely bloodiest climate on the fice of the bloody earth!' Mr. Portingale bawled. 'And by God something's bloody well got to be done abaat it!'

Saskatchewan teems with Mr. Portingales. Men who, lapped in an enervating cloak of eastern smog or rendered soft and pliable by the eternal West Coast rain, would pass through life in meek unquestioning obedience to those placed in authority over them, develop, after a brief spell of prairie living, affinities with the Mau Mau or the I.R.A. Scorched by sun and battered by wind three months of the year and confined in a deep freeze for six, the prairie dweller is soon afflicted by a kind of nervous irritability which impels him to flail out in all directions. Being, as a rule, a religious man – intimate association with nature at its most awesome inclines to make him so – he hesitates to blame the Almighty for his miseries. The next authority – human, fallible, vulnerable – is the government. And something, by God, has got to be done about it!

It is also a matter of common observation that the man who survives the prairie weather for any length of time is likely to develop, in addition to a chronic irritability, an alarming measure of self-confidence. By the very fact of surviving he has proved himself a man fit to whip his weight in wildcats. (Mr. Portingale's battle against the elements assumed, in later years, the proportions of an epic drama in which Mr. Portingale led his floundering, bewildered horses to safety over twenty storm-battered miles of prairie.) Moreover, the Saskatchewan farmer's determination, once he takes action, to get something done in a hurry may be directly attributable to weather-conditioning. Out-door plumbing in below-zero temperatures is conducive to hustle.

The self-confidence and energy thus created by climatic condi-tions do not weaken with the passing of time, for they are sustained and nurtured by the very air the prairie dweller breathes. The C.P.R. publicity pamphlets which flooded the country about the turn of the century – designed to encourage prairie settlement and by all odds the richest, purplest fiction ever written about the Canadian west – never tired of emphasiz-ing the wine-like quality of prairie air. Its stimulative power, in certain peculiarly favoured localities, was freely compared to that of the best vintage champagne. No wonder Nicholas Flood Davin, editor of the old Regina *Leader* and one of the Grand Old Men of prairie journalism (who incidentally preferred to absorb his alcohol through the stomach rather than the lungs), looked into the future of Saskatchewan with the eye of a prophet and recorded his vision in the words of a poet:

> All the charms that belong to youth, hope, energy, are found in the North-West; and the bracing influence of the new free land on mind and character is very remarkable. The climate is akin to that which nurtured the warrior hordes, the Goths and the Vandals, who became the terror and ultimately the destroyers of the Roman Empire, and whose magnificent physique has been described by graphic pens made eloquent by fear.

It is a pity Mr. Davin did not live to see the fulfilment of his implied prophecy in the descent of the prairie Goths and Vandals – thinly disguised as Progressives, Independents, C.C.F.ers, Dief-enbaker Tories – upon the beleaguered capital of the Dominion.

The proliferation of political parties in the Canadian west, astonishing to those who have never endured the rigours of the prairie climate – and particularly that of Saskatchewan – is thus seen to be not only logical but inevitable. The 'typical' west-erner, whatever his racial origin or the social status of his fore-bears, is a man toughened by climate, inside and out, to the texture of old cowhide. He is proud of his strength, confident of his cunning, and drunk on air all the year round. Is it con-ceivable that such a man will be content to tag along meekly in the wake of a traditional political machine controlled from afar? In good years he will tolerate the machine's existence, make no overt move to throw a monkey-wrench into the works. But let the chill winds of winter blow just a little colder, let the sun scorch the earth a little browner, and the heavens are filled with denunciations, the meeting-houses with trigger-happy Jacquerie, and a new political party is born. Grass-roots movements always flourish when the grass stops growing.

The Saskatchewan farmer's down-east counterpart is, by comparison, a sedate and conservative fellow who, like the unconverted Mr. Portingale, knows his place and keeps it. Occasionally a prolonged rainy spell, a fall in market prices, or a rise in income tax may tempt him to timid protest, but the most drastic positive steps he ever takes to improve his lot are to replace the Tories with the Liberals or vice versa. In purely material terms his lot is probably worse than that of the prairie farmer, but he never experiences those alternating expansions and contractions induced by extremes of heat and cold which – because they create a kind of friction, both physical and spiritual – impel the sufferer to explosive action.

I speak of the 'typical' westerner in the present tense, but the sad truth is that he is in danger of becoming extinct. Natural-gas heating, T.V., improved road transportation, school buses, and indoor plumbing are sapping his vitality, may shrink him spiritually to the size of his eastern counterpart. Our farms, it seems, are getting bigger all the time and our farmers smaller.

The passing of the old breed must be, for those of us who knew it at its maverick best, a cause of bitter regret. The west in its Golden Age produced more than its share of stout-hearted, strong-lunged rebels – godlike Prometheans ready to challenge at the drop of a sombrero the wisdom and authority of an all-ruling Liberal or Tory Zeus. But never let us forget that behind the Prometheans, inspiring them, propping them up, stood (and let us hope still stands) that unsung Atlas of the prairies – Mr. Portingale.

The Great Plains

1. First Comers

Troy town rose and fell ten times on the hill Hissarlik above the Hellespont; the Indian village sited a few miles west of Moose Jaw went Troy three better — thirteen distinct cultural levels have been uncovered in the Mortlach 'midden', first stumbled upon by a local farmer who observed an unusual number of arrowheads in a pasture cowpath. The materials thus far brought to light range from pottery and tools of the kind in common use when the white man first reached the plains country to the primitive scrapers, fireplace ash, and bones of a stone-age people. None of the levels suggests anything more than transient occupation of the site; it was a convenient stopping-place for nomadic tribesmen and hunting parties, but at no time a settlement of long duration.

Carbon counts made in the University of Saskatchewan Carbon 14 Laboratory (established in 1952 by Drs. Spinks and McCallum and the first of its kind in Canada) date the tenth level of the Mortlach midden at about 1400 B.C. — two hundred years before Priam's Troy was taken and dust closed Helen's eyes. But unlike the Greeks and the Trojans the stone-age people of the great plains left behind them no records, written or oral, of their way of life and thought — only a handful of crude implements relating to domesticity and war, and the dust that was once living flesh, now indistinguishable from the earth that shelters it.

By the year 1691, when the first white man, Henry Kelsey, penetrated inland from York Factory on Hudson Bay as far as the central parklands and plains country, the pattern of plains settlement was fairly clearly defined. The Cree, most widespread of all North American Indian tribes, roamed the barrens, forests, and parklands all the way from the peninsula of Labrador to the

Mackenzie River valley. The North Saskatchewan River formed a traditional but indifferently observed boundary between the Cree and the powerful Assiniboine or Stonies, who hunted over the southern plains and – sometimes in alliance with the Cree – waged intermittent war against the Blackfoot Confederacy (Piegan, Blood, and Blackfoot proper) that ruled the south-western plains as far as the Rockies.

From these wars few economic or territorial gains, in the white man's terms, resulted. Control of the best hunting-grounds was sometimes at stake, but many of the clashes between hostile tribesmen were inspired less by hope of gain than by love of excitement and desire for fame. Indian wars were on the whole less sordid in purpose than those of the white man, and less efficient in execution.

The Woods Cree lived mostly on fish and the small game of forest and parkland. For them life was hard, hunger the gaunt grey wolf skulking always on their trail. The Indians of the plains fared much better. 'The wild ox alone supplies them [the Assiniboine] with everything they are accustomed to want,' Alexander Henry, an independent fur-trader from Montreal, reported in 1775. 'The hide of this animal, when dressed, furnishes soft clothing for the women; and, dressed with the hair on it clothes the men. The flesh feeds them; the sinews afford them bow-strings; and even the paunch . . . provides them with that important utensil, the kettle. The amazing numbers of these animals prevent all fear of want.'

The plains Indians favoured certain campsites, as the Mort-lach midden proves, but they built no permanent villages. They led a nomadic life, simple, innocent, often violent; worshipped a benign Great Spirit; and after death journeyed to that Happy Hunting-Ground whose prospects were so much more in keeping with their needs and desires than the white man's gold-plated heaven.

The first white man to reach the Saskatchewan River, Henry Kelsey, was a Hudson's Bay Company employee who undertook a journey from York Factory on the shore of Hudson Bay in 1691, with no orders or intent to extend the Company empire by building inland posts, but rather to achieve the same end by drawing Indians from the interior into the existing Company orbit. Kelsey did not attempt to navigate the Saskatchewan –

he was a cautious man and the great river runs wild in its lower reaches – but in the company of a band of roving Indians he travelled overland, keeping close to the river valley, possibly as far as the junction of the North Saskatchewan and Battle rivers where Battleford town now stands. Kelsey was in many ways a remarkable man, and not the least remarkable thing about him was his passion for writing doggerel verse. Most explorers have been content to record their discoveries and adventures and apprehensions in sober forthright prose; Kelsey favoured limping iambics:

> *For many times I have often been oppresst*
> *With fears & Cares yt I could not take my rest*
> *Because I was alone & no friend could find*
> *And once yt in my travels I was left behind*
> *Which struck fear & terror into me . . .*

It was, perhaps, Kelsey's preoccupation with a diligent though not always successful search for rhymes that prevented him from describing a single identifiable geographical feature in all the land through which he travelled. However, since he seems never to have strayed far from the river, it can reasonably be assumed that he passed close to the present sites of The Pas, Nipawin, Prince Albert, and Battleford before turning back to York Factory.

No use seems to have been made by the Company of Kelsey's report, nor was any account of his discoveries made available to the government of the day. The journal disappeared from sight for more than two centuries; it came to light in 1926 in Northern Ireland and was first published in 1929. Thus it is that only in our present century has the real truth about the opening of the western prairies been known – that the first penetration was effected not from eastern Canada but directly from England by way of Hudson Bay. Kelsey himself never realized the greatness of his achievement, nor did the company he served. He died old, poor, and forgotten. Today his name is widely honoured throughout Saskatchewan, gracing museums, parks, schools, motels, and cocktail lounges.

There was no follow-up to Kelsey's remarkable journeyings. For more than half a century thereafter the Great Company – stolid, insular, self-assured – was content to wait by the shores of Hudson Bay for the Indians to come from far-off places bringing furs to be traded for trinkets, cloth, knives, guns, and rum. Such a policy could be founded only on absolute freedom from competition, and that freedom vanished with the entry of French traders from Montreal, hot on the heels of the La Vérendryes, into the land which the Company had come to regard as its private preserve. By the mid eighteenth century the Frenchmen had penetrated the plains country to points beyond its centre; their trading-posts ran along a line extending from the Head of the Lakes to the forks of the Saskatchewan; and the Company, in danger of being blocked off entirely from its main sources of trade, stirred clumsily, like an aroused behemoth, into action. Thus began the years of bitter, sometimes murderous, competition, Company men and free traders leap-frogging madly up the Saskatchewan, penetrating deeper and deeper into lands hitherto unexplored, opening up a vast new empire for no other reason than that men wore hats made of beaver fur.

Anthony Henday, a Company man, was the first to reach the Blackfoot country within sight of the Rockies. In 1755 he brought back to York Factory by way of the Saskatchewan River no fewer than seventy-four fur-laden canoes, this in spite of the fact that twice along the way, at Fort à la Corne and The Pas, many of the Indians had succumbed to the smell of French brandy and given their furs to Henday's rivals.

Henry Kelsey and Anthony Henday were Hudson's Bay Company employees; but the most spectacular heroes of western exploration – Alexander Mackenzie, David Thompson, Simon Fraser – were men of the North West Company, a partnership of hitherto independent traders formed in 1779 (re-organized 1784) to present a united front against the Great Company. 'Pedlars' the Company men at first contemptuously called their rivals – with some justification, for the Nor'Westers were not content to wait for the Indians to come to them but carried their trading-goods to tribes in forest, plain, and mountain. They did more – they built posts at a score or more strategic points along the great inland waterways and for a time threatened to strangle the mammoth corporation which until the mid eighteenth century had seemed absolutely invincible.

The Nor'Westers were proud, passionate, and violent men, fiercely individualistic but loyal to one another, and far better equipped by reason of temperament and, in many instances, of blood to win the confidence of the native peoples than were their rivals. The Nor'Westers treated the Indians as companions and equals — unlike the aloof race-conscious employees of the Hudson's Bay Company, or the brutal mountain men of the American frontier who made no distinction between Indians and wild animals except that some wild animals they let live.

'These men were hardy, courageous, shrewd and proud,' W. S. Wallace wrote in his admirable 'Preface' to *Documents Relating to the North-West Company.* 'They spent a good part of their lives travelling incredible distances in birch bark canoes, shooting rapids or navigating inland seas. They were wrecked and drowned. They suffered hunger and starvation. They were robbed and murdered by Indians and sometimes by one another. They fell the victims of smallpox, syphilis, and rum. Yet they conquered half a continent, and they built up a commercial empire the like of which North America, at least, has never seen.'

Courage, pride, curiosity, genius even — these things were not enough to overcome the Great Company. The Nor'Westers were a team of dazzling first-stringers without reserves; the Company had resources in depth. In the end it forced the Nor'Westers to the wall, absorbed them into what was called, to save face, an amalgamation.

Many of the old Nor'Westers accepted service in the Company; others returned to the east and settled down on farms or in trades; and some became wandering Ishmaelites, living out their lives as hunters, trappers, woodsmen — hating to the end the mighty corporation which, so they firmly believed, had made them outcasts.

By the time of the amalgamation (1821) the destruction of the plains Indian was approaching its final stages. The white trader brought to the Indian guns and rum and syphilis and smallpox. He brought him death. The missionary, who bargained for souls as eagerly as the trader did for furs, found himself hopelessly outmatched — sacramental wine could not compete against trader's rum. As early as 1820 three-fifths of the Indians of the Eagle Hills country south of Battleford were dead of smallpox. And in 1834 Maximilian, Prince of Wied, reported that 'The Assiniboine, 9000 in number, are, in the literal sense of the expression, nearly exterminated. They, as well as the Crows and the Blackfeet, endeavoured to flee in all directions, but the disease everywhere pursued them.'

The white man in the Canadian North-west, unlike his counterpart on the American frontier, destroyed the Indian unwittingly. He made him drunk to get his furs, riddled him with disease out of ignorance, and killed him without malice. The Indian came at last to hate the white man, but too late to strike successfully against him. So it is that within a time-span of a few decades the erstwhile lords of the prairies recede into the shadows, where a few handfuls still linger on the fringes of civilization – sad ghosts who are from time to time a trouble to the consciences of those who live in the sun.

Not all the men who came to the Saskatchewan country in the years before the coming of policemen and railways and settlers were traders or missionaries. European gentlemen of substance – and often of title – who had been reared on the romantic tales of Fenimore Cooper and his disciples came to the great plains to hunt buffalo and grizzly bear and see the noble red man in his native haunts. Fenimore Cooper was in fact the first prairie publicity agent, and except for the railroad pamphleteers of a later time by all odds the most successful. 'In boyhood,' Sir William Butler wrote in his *Autobiography,* 'I had read the novels of Fenimore Cooper with an intensity of interest never to be known again in reading.' And he acknowledged that it was the spell of Cooper that drew him first to the great plains.

'Peers on the prairie' one writer has called these wandering blue-bloods with no sacrifice of truth to alliteration. The Earl of Southesk, Maximilian, Prince of Weid, Viscount Milton, Lord Dunmore (who travelled to the prairie hunting-grounds in company with Count Arrigo de Castiglione Maggiore, Chamberlain to the King of Sardinia), and a score more titled Tartarins deliberately went out of their way – so it often seemed to the baffled locals who accompanied them on their mad expeditions – to live as uncomfortably as bad food, inadequate shelter, and thirty-degrees-below-zero temperatures permitted, and afterwards recorded their experiences in books and articles that reflect a high level of literacy and a passionate addiction to the slaughter of bird and beast.

The Earl of Southesk, a high-minded, serious young man who

hunted over the great plains in the years 1859-60, looked upon his journeyings as primarily a means of strengthening both body and mind by submitting them to a variety of ordeals and strenuous exercises. He ate pemmican and bear steaks and skunk with great resolution and no enjoyment, bathed regularly in cold water, and at night, after having recorded the day's activities at length in his journal, pored over the works of Shakespeare and wrote elaborate comments and criticisms thereon. 'Why is it', he asked in his note-book, 'that one is inclined to have more sympathy for Imogene than Desdemona?' This on a night so cold that the Earl's tear-drops, induced by the smoke of the camp fire, froze on the pages of *Othello*.

In his journeyings, during which he touched at most of the principal Hudson's Bay posts, including Forts Garry, Ellice, Carlton, Pitt, Edmonton, and Jasper House, Southesk, like most of his fellows, seems to have gloried in enduring unnecessary hardships, bad food, and worse lodgings. 'This open air life suits me well,' he wrote in his journal, 'though, when one considers it bit by bit it does not seem very charming. Long wearisome riding, indifferent, monotonous eating, no sport to speak of, hard bed upon the ground, wet, no companion of my own class; nevertheless I am happier than I have been for years.'

Why do men climb mountains, cross deserts, freeze in bleak storm-swept cabins, eat indigestible, ill-cooked food, sleep on wretched pallets, deny in the name of sport those comforts their lives are in large measure directed to achieving? Perhaps to satisfy some obscure atavistic instinct; or to recapture, however fleetingly, some of the sensations of a vanished youth, to assert a kind of all but extinguished elemental masculinity; above all, to experience an intimation of immortality born of a Promethean defiance of mighty hostile forces. Says Marlow, Joseph Conrad's storm-battered sailor-narrator:

> I remember my youth and the feeling that will never come back any more – the feeling that I could last forever, outlast the sea, the earth and all men; the deceitful feeling that lures us on to joys, to perils, to love, to vain effort – to death; the triumphant conviction of strength, the heat of life in the handful of dust, the glow in the heart that with every year grows dim, grows small, and expires – and expires too soon, too soon – before life itself.

The heat of life in the handful of dust. It is surely the ultimate incongruity that men should seek the heat of life on the winter-bound ice-cold Saskatchewan plains.

Serious-minded the Earl of Southesk may have been, but few men of his own generation — particularly those who wandered in strange places of the earth — would have questioned his belief that 'intellectual reading in moderation [is] a rest for the body after hard labour; it seems to act as a counter-irritant, drawing off fatigue from the muscles to the brain.' Certain it is that books of wide variety but all of solid worth constituted one of the weightiest items in the baggage not only of wealthy adventure-seekers but of men who worked long hours in the routine jobs of frontier exploration. Typically the British survey party that in 1872-4 helped to survey the 49th parallel from the Lake of the Woods to the Rockies brought with it a library of nearly one thousand volumes carefully chosen by the assistant astronomer, Lieutenant Featherstonehaugh of the Royal Engineers. The books, all of them dog-eared and tattered long before the survey was finished, included a few standard works on field sports, but the majority were the established classics of English and American literature, both poetry and prose.

It is a satisfaction to know that the Earl of Southesk's note-taking and meditations bore fruit in a fine travel book, *Saskatchewan and the Rocky Mountains*, published in 1875, together with a forty-seven-page appendix devoted to critical 'remarks' on the plays of William Shakespeare, and a series of moral reflections under the general heading of 'Patience and God's Providence'.

Of all the travellers who came to the Saskatchewan country in the early days in search of things other than gain, the most engaging personality is Dr. Walter Butler Cheadle, the burly tutor-physician-companion to Viscount Milton, a restless, peevish young man who must often have tested his mentor's patience and good humour to the breaking-point. After an horrendous journey across the plains from Fort Garry the two young men — surely the most incompetent pair of tenderfeet ever let loose in the west — settled down to pass the winter of 1863 in a hut about eighty miles north-west of Fort Carlton, the nearest supply base. They were pestered and threatened by hungry and, worse still, thirsty Indians; they endured semi-starvation and bitter cold;

they were frost-bitten so often and so widely that no parts of the body seem to have escaped unscathed – a point on which Dr. Cheadle is engagingly frank (*froze Johnson* is one of the commonest entries in his journal); they ate a Christmas pudding made of suet and filled with raisins, buckshot, tobacco, and soap – 'as big as my head', Dr. Cheadle noted in the journal. 'Most delicious; not had such a treat since leaving Fort Garry' – and somehow lived to complete, the following summer, a fantastic journey through the mountains to the Pacific coast. On the latter stages of their mad – and mostly blind – wanderings they were accompanied by a frontier eccentric whose personality and behaviour were such as to make him an authentic legend in his own lifetime. Paddy O'Byrne was a bedraggled, besotted, but by no means ill-educated Irishman who wore a tail coat and filthy stand-up collar, read Paley's *Evidences of Christianity* at all times and under all circumstances, devoured enormous quantities of food, and did no work at all. Once, when Cheadle and Milton were building a raft, O'Byrne was persuaded to lay aside the *Evidences* long enough to help Milton carry a heavy log to the river bank. 'After the first few steps,' Cheadle notes, 'O'Byrne began to utter the most awful groans, and cried out continually, "Oh, dear, oh dear, this is most painful – it's cutting my shoulder in two – not so fast my lord. Gently, gently. Steady, my lord, steady – I *must* stop. I'm carrying all the weight myself. I shall drop with exhaustion directly – *triste lignum te caducum!*" and then, with a loud "Oh!" and no further warning, he let his end of the tree down with a run, jarring his unhappy partner most dreadfully.'

In the heyday of Victorianism oddly attired Britishers wandering about in out-of-the-way places of the earth – jungles, deserts, plains – were a not uncommon sight; but Cheadle, Milton, and Paddy O'Byrne constitute a trio unmatched for colour and incompetence in the history of prairie journeyings.

In 1869 the Government of Canada began negotiations with the Hudson's Bay Company for the takeover of the vast territories, then under Company jurisdiction, lying west of Ontario; and for the first time the name Riel was heard in the land. Two years later large numbers of Métis from Red River Valley were travelling westward across the plains in their screeching wooden carts, seeking escape – in the long run impossible to find – from the

incoming white settlers whose dull, land-bound ways were ana-
thema to the nomads of mixed French and Indian blood. A few
of the Métis found their way into the Cypress Hills, but they
mainly established themselves along the South Saskatchewan
River centring on the trading-post of Batoche seventy miles
downstream from the present city of Saskatoon. Here a young
man named Gabriel Dumont, a superb hunter and a prickly
champion of Métis rights, quickly emerged as the leader and
spokesman of his people. Dumont, purged by time of all petty
weaknesses, is now Saskatchewan's favourite folk-hero.

In 1871 Lieutenant William Butler, a young Irishman serving
in the British Army but temporarily in the employ of the Canadian government, made an extraordinary winter journey by
horse, dogsled, and foot from Fort Garry to Rocky Mountain
House and back, a distance of nearly four thousand miles, and
subsequently wrote a report on conditions he found prevailing
among Indians and traders of the Northwest Territories which
is one of the great documents of western Canadian history. One
of Butler's recommendations led to the founding, in 1873, of
that remarkable body of men which has done more to excite the
imagination of the world than any other Canadian institution
– the North West Mounted Police. The famous march of the
rookie policemen from Fort Dufferin in Manitoba across the
southern plains to the foothills of the Rockies was badly organized, ill-conducted, and near disastrous, but it achieved its
objective: the establishment of police posts at strategic points
throughout the Northwest Territories to assure the reign of law
before the coming of the white settlers.

The settlers followed hard on the heels of the police. The
trickle that wound across the prairies in buckboard and wagon
and Red River cart or washed up from below the border on
the fringes of the great wave moving west from New England to
the Pacific widened to a torrent with the building of the Canadian Pacific Railway (the last spike was driven in 1885). The
settlers came singly, in families, in small groups and large,
sponsored by government agencies and land companies and
philanthropists and crooks. Blue-blooded Old Country men intent on creating Little Englands in the middle of the bald-
headed prairie, and, incredibly, as often as not succeeding; hard-
headed thrifty Lowland Scots; hot-blooded Highlanders and
wild, intractable clansmen from the Outer Islands; dour Protes-

tants from Ulster and black-browed Catholics from the rest of Ireland; Spanish-speaking Welshmen from Patagonia; Hungarians whose leader, Count Esterhazy, lent his name to the chief village of the settlement; broad-shouldered labourers, soon to turn farmer, from half the countries of central Europe; industrious Swedes; proud passionate Icelanders bringing with them a love of the arts that time and tribulation have not quenched; persecuted men (meek stubborn Mennonites and strong-willed Doukhobors from Georgian Russia and the Ukraine); Syrian pedlars, Jewish farmers, Americans, Armenians, Chinamen, Dutchmen, rich men, poor men, beggar men, and thieves – a cross-section of the world's people poured into and were swallowed up by that part of the Canadian North-west which in the year 1905 became the province of Saskatchewan.

2. Forever England

It is a safe assumption that the average tourist entering Saskatchewan from the east via the Trans-Canada Highway is a mountains-bound transient, an expatriate returning to visit friends and relatives, or a fisherman whose road will soon turn north towards far-off lakes and rivers. And indeed, the traveller on the Highway between Moosomin and Maple Creek, a stretch of over three hundred miles, will see little to induce him to stay his speed, for the land on either side is characterless, non-committal, neither positively rolling nor absolutely flat, neither forested nor treeless; and the towns that abut gingerly upon the Highway offer little to distract attention from the strip of asphalt unrolling endlessly into the blue distance.

But the curious soul whose appetite for landscape has already been glutted by those obvious scenic attractions in which the rest of Canada abounds (oversized mountains, everlasting forest, and countless inequitably distributed lakes) and whose curiosity impels him to leave the Highway and commit himself to the oil-surfaced or gravelled roads leading into the southern Saskatchewan hinterland will find there things which he has not found elsewhere and which, if he is a sensitive spirit, cannot leave him unmoved: unique memorials of times past (Indian drawings on a soaring rock-face, an English village church in an English village graveyard encompassed round about by prairie, bush, and oil-wells); diminutive bodies of water, in some instances hardly more than ponds, set in Lilliputian forests, the scale of lake and forest in relation to the over-all physical environment so disproportionate from the normal as to communicate the effect of novelty; conversely, pastoral scenes on a scale so immense as to cast the mind back to those early ages of man when the herdsman and his flock dominated all that lay between the eye and the horizon; and above all a landscape which, however varied it may be in its minor components, communicates, like a desert or an ocean, a sense of oneness on a cosmic scale. It is a landscape which, like Hardy's Egdon Heath, 'appeals to a subtler and scarcer instinct . . . than that which responds to the sort of beauty called charming or fair.'

Moose Mountain Provincial Park lies south of the Trans-Canada Highway about forty miles – easily accessible over adequate roads from Moosomin and Whitewood. Lest the tourist on his way to the Park should wear out his eyes and his temper looking for a mass of rock upflung from the plain it must be emphasized that in both Saskatchewan and Manitoba the term 'mountain' is used with peculiar local significance, referring not to a rocky, clearly defined protuberance rising several thousands of feet above sea level and frequently snow-capped, but to a gentle humping of the earth's surface which may extend over an area covering several hundred square miles. Conventional mountains such as those of the Rockies or Himalayas are aloof, Olympian, angular, sexless (no one would ever dream of referring to Everest as 'she'). By contrast Saskatchewan mountains are delightfully feminine; they are softly rounded, companionable, eminently accessible.

Moose Mountain sets the pattern. At its highest point it is only a few hundred feet above the level of the surrounding countryside, and the ascent to the summit through a forest of tall, graceful aspen is so gradual that the traveller is often unaware of any change from ground level until a glimpse through an opening in the trees of a vast expanse of prairie unrolled below persuades him that he must indeed be on an upgrade.

Moose Mountain provides the usual provincial park amenities – playgrounds, campgrounds, parking and picnic areas, assorted harmless wild animals, a golf course cut out of the bush and full of fearful torments for the man who strays a hair's breadth from the straight and narrow, and several small lakes that offer excellent swimming. Their depth sets them apart from most of the lakes scattered over the open prairie, which are often so shallow that the would-be swimmer is able to enjoy the pleasures of a long-distance hike before reaching water deep enough to cover his knees.

Unfortunately, like nearly all Saskatchewan provincial parks, Moose Mountain provides no accommodation worth mentioning for the transient, or indeed for anyone who hasn't made his reservations some months in advance. A clutch of government-operated cabins centring on a chalet, one or two privately run 'resorts', up to date only in their rental charges, and that is all. Most tourists other than campers must as a rule be prepared to make their headquarters at points twenty-five to fifty miles from the park proper, and even then they will find the accommodation provided by small-town hostelries all too often reminiscent of the chamberpot-and-spittoon days. Fortunately, the relaxing of provincial liquor regulations has induced many hotels to improve their general facilities since licences for the sale of liquor in dining-rooms and cocktail lounges are issued only to establishments that meet reasonable standards of cleanliness, comfort, and space. The change in the quality of accommodation and food provided by Saskatchewan hostelries in the past few years has been so emphatically for the better that even the most ardent temperance zealot should be prepared to concede that sometimes out of evil cometh forth good. It is now possible to dine in Saskatchewan, not merely eat.

It must, however, be acknowledged that the general level of public accommodation prevailing throughout the province outside the larger cities is unlikely to prove much of a stimulus to the tourist industry.

Immediately south of the entrance to Moose Mountain Park a sign points east to Cannington Manor. To the outsider the name may mean little; but to the Saskatchewan native it recalls a thousand tales told of a day long past when the Moose Mountain country swarmed with mad dogs of Englishmen who built for themselves great stone houses more appropriate to an English park than the Canadian bush, galloped astride thoroughbred hunters through woodland and pasture in pursuit of fox and coyote and rabbit, played cricket in a local cow-pasture, created within their own ranks a society as rigidly stratified as the one they had lately left; then scattered – almost overnight it seemed – to the four winds, leaving not a rack behind. Cannington Manor is more – or less – than a place; it is a name, a tradition, and, for a few of the very old, a memory.

It is worth while to follow the directive on the signpost.

Cannington Manor lies about twenty miles south-east of Moose Mountain Park. The road is clearly marked all the way as a part of Vacation Trail Number 1 — a route for tourists, signposted by Tourist Bureau men interested in history as well as scenery, which leads the traveller, if he follows it over its full circuit of three hundred miles, into some odd and exciting places. Cannington Manor is odd, not in appearance or location, but in the simple fact of its existence.

Captain Edward Michell Pierce — tweedy, stout, red-faced, a John Bull minus the mutton-chop whiskers — was blessed with a large family, including a gaggle of unmarried daughters, and a substantial income which was not, however, sufficient to maintain him in England according to his aspirations. (In an earlier incarnation the Captain must surely have been a feudal lord.) He looked on the land about Moose Mountain, found it good, and prepared to settle it with Old Country families of good blood and sound imperial sentiments. No matter that the Wood Mountain country was closed to homesteaders — the Captain had friends in high places. A word in the ear of Sir John A. Macdonald himself and the thing was done. In 1882 the community of Cannington Manor was founded in the midst of mixed bush and parkland some forty miles from Moosomin, the nearest settlement and in 1882 the end of steel.

A select band of English colonists came in due season to the land the Captain had spied out for them, and lesser breeds were turned empty away. 'All the land as far as the eye can see,' the Captain said to a man from Ontario on the lookout for a homestead, 'belongs to me and my sons.' (Already he was speaking not merely as the head of a family but as a Founding Father.)

The effects the colonists brought with them included all the appurtenances of civilization as exemplified in the furnishings of an English country home — grand pianos, copper warming-pans, padded commodes, Georgian silver, Wedgwood dinner services, ancestral portraits, steel engravings of the Royal Family and the Stag at Bay, sports equipment (shot-guns, cricket bats, tennis racquets, fishing gear, dogs), manservants and grooms who went homesteading on their own, and a flock of maidservants who promptly married Canadian bachelors and left the young ladies of Cannington Manor to learn from scratch the arts of domesticity. To the credit of the young ladies they did so with-

out a murmur and with fair success; and in due time most of
them, too, married Canadian bachelors.

Captain Pierce's plans extended far beyond provision for his
own family and immediate friends; he invited Old Country lads
of proper social background and strong leanings towards agriculture to serve an apprenticeship at Cannington Manor – fee one
hundred pounds all found. For.their accommodation he provided a large dormitory and for their instruction a sturdy Lowland Scot of sound principles and impeccable agricultural background. Inevitably the Captain's invitation was seized upon by
a number of well-to-do English families as a heaven-sent opportunity to get rid of unwanted younger sons. Few of those thus
summarily shipped off to make good in the colonies ever developed a passionate interest in the arts of husbandry. 'I was glad
when the young gentlemen took to tennis,' their Scots instructor
said, 'so that I could get on with the work.'

Captain Pierce dreamed of a self-sustaining community, a
European manorial village flourishing in a Canadian wilderness,
and towards the fulfilment of the dream he helped to finance
the building of a grist mill, a smithy, a woodworkers' shop (in
which dissenters were permitted to hold Sunday services under
the guidance of an aged Presbyterian minister who read the lessons from the Greek testament), an Anglican church whose
organist and choir-mistress had for twenty-five years occupied
similar roles in, of all places, Constantinople, and a hotel named
the Mitre. In spite of its solidly Old Country-Oxonian name,
the Mitre seems to have been entirely New World in atmosphere. A visitor to Cannington Manor, a relatively unknown but
rapidly rising young British lawyer and M.P. named David Lloyd
George (on a tour of Canada to investigate opportunities for
prospective British emigrants), complained bitterly that the bar-
man-waiter who attended him at dinner punctuated his journeyings to and from the dinner table with near misses and an
occasional bull's-eye on a spittoon at ten feet.

The cultural life of the community, in the main self-sustaining, was from time to time stimulated by visits from Bertram
Tennyson, nephew of the Poet Laureate and a *pro tem.* resident
of Moosomin. Bertram Tennyson played an excellent game of
tennis, and his slim volume of poems and essays, published by
the Moosomin *Spectator* Press, enjoyed wide circulation through-

out south-eastern Saskatchewan. The poems reflect the author's view that life in the Canadian west is a Good Thing – with reservations. To an Old Country friend he complains that

> *The world is fair in this new land, and yet I envy you,*
> *For we have not the primrose pale, and though 'tis just as blue,*
> *The violet in exile here throws out a scentless bloom,*
> *The rose is fair as England's rose, but has not its perfume.*

The most appealing item in the Tennyson collection is a prefatory note to an essay acknowledging the writer's great indebtedness for his subject matter 'to an author whose name I have unfortunately forgotten'.

While Captain Pierce and his fellow enthusiasts were busy building up a self-sustaining community, the young ladies of Cannington Manor, freed from the fear – which would assuredly have haunted them in the Old Country – of being unloved and unwed, were having the time of their lives learning to cook with one hand and fending off or encouraging admirers with the other. Lily Pierce, the Captain's eldest daughter, was wooed for several years by a persistent young Indian brave whose passion burned with such intensity that he even went so far as to offer the Captain a fine rifle in exchange for his daughter. Lily held good blood in high esteem, but the fact that her wooer was the son of a chief doesn't seem to have helped his suit. 'For several years,' Lily reported, 'the Chief's son hovered about at intervals, trying to see me alone. One day he succeeded and in a very insinuating way offered me a pretty bunch of brightly coloured feathers. This I coldly and decidedly refused, as I knew it was "bad medicine", and had I taken it, he would have thought it gave him some hold on me.'

In 1889 the sporting life of the community was quickened by the arrival from England of the three Beckton brothers, Ernest, Billy, and Bertie – wealthy, pleasure-bent, irresponsible English public-school products who had somehow failed to mature mentally beyond adolescence. The Beckton boys – all bachelors – built a stone house large enough to billet a regiment, and a barn long enough (120 feet) to stable the regimental horses. They imported a pack of fox-hounds, organized a hunt club, and every year gave a Hunt Club Ball at which evening dress was *de rigueur*. They bred the best racehorses west of Winnipeg; imported bull-terriers for badger-baiting (who, finding no badger available, dragged down and killed a Beckton cow); played rugby, cricket, and tennis; and followed up every victory or defeat with a carnival of alcohol-inspired high jinks reminiscent of Boat Race Night. By the turn of the century they had squandered most of their money and lost interest in empire-building. They disposed of their livestock, abandoned the great stone house and barn, and fled Cannington Manor to carry the blessing of their quaint folkways into other lands.

The only other settlement in the Saskatchewan country to match Cannington Manor in terms of blood, money, and whoopee was that of the French Counts centring on the village of St. Hubert a few miles north of Moose Mountain and not more than a day's ride from Cannington. The Frenchmen were authentic aristocrats whose dreams far out-soared their capabilities and capital, but while they lasted they outshone even the Cannington Manor crowd in colour and éclat. The Counts ran large herds of cattle and sheep and horses along the Pipestone Valley; they had an eye for natural as well as physical beauty and chose one of the loveliest regions of the North-west to settle in; they imported from the old land, not sports equipment or fox-hounds, but vintage wines and, for their ladies, Paris gowns. They drove to the local race meets – nearly always won by the Beckton colours – in coach and four; they held court once a year in the Whitewood Hotel, and, in contrast to the more exclusive Cannington Manor hosts, invited all the world to share the frolic and the wine; and when they had lost their money (in cheese factories, chicory farms, sugar-beet ranches, and half a dozen other exotic enterprises alike only in their unsuitability to the prairie environment) and gone back to France, they left behind them memories of a most gracious hospitality and a peculiarly Gallic courtesy which invested even such ordinarily sordid matters as unpaid bills with a touch of romance. Thus, when a boarding-house landlady protested to a French Count that one of his compatriots had skipped off without paying his board bill the Count hastened to reassure her: 'My friend has little money, but he will pay you. If you were a man perhaps not so. But you are a lady; he is a gentleman. He will pay you.'

And in due course he did.

Although Cannington Manor survived for less than a quarter of a century – it was doomed to extinction when the railroad bypassed it both north and south – it provided, during the brief period of its existence, an enormous stimulus to local business and put into circulation substantial sums of much-needed capital. All supplies for the settlement had to be freighted by wagon or sleigh from Moosomin or Whitewood over distances of up to fifty miles, and a man owning a team of horses or oxen was sure of steady employment the year round. Carpenters and stone-masons were able to command high wages; and a girl who wanted to earn a dollar or two towards her trousseau could be sure of finding employment as cook or maid in any one of a dozen or more substantial houses.

Captain Pierce lies in the Cannington Manor churchyard beside the little Anglican Church of All Saints which in 1884 he helped to build. The church, built of logs overlaid with board siding, still stands – held upright it would seem, by faith alone. The Captain was an empire-builder whose empire proved all but stillborn; but his dream was not an unworthy one, and there was in the man something of the spirit which in the eighteenth and nineteenth centuries spread the might and the virtues and the shortcomings of England over half the world. Today nothing tangible of his work remains except a few crumbling cement foundations, the little Anglican church, and a tree-shaded churchyard sheltering dust which is, indeed, forever England.

So peaceful is the churchyard of Cannington Manor, so remote from the dust and heat of the arena, that not even the horn of Gabriel seems likely to rouse the huntsmen who sleep in that quiet earth.

3. Trails West

Vacation Trail Number 1 leads from Cannington Manor over Highway 8 into the Souris River country. (Saskatchewan's Vacation Trails form a series of highway routes intended to provide the visitor with the maximum of scenic and historic interest. The Trails are mapped and described in detail on Tourist Information brochures, and marked at regular intervals by distinctive signposts.) Number 1 cuts through pleasant, undistinguished farmland, bypassing far to the east a string of villages whose names – Dumas, Carlyle, Lampman, Wordsworth, Browning – suggest that pioneers with a taste for literature chose an agreeable way to honour their favourite writers. It is pleasant to speculate about the names they might have chosen had radio and television rather than literature been the popular forms of entertainment at the time when they were finding names for their settlements. Instead of Cowper and Hardy and Kipling and Ardath (originally the title of a novel by Marie Corelli) and Robsart (after the heroine of Scott's *Kenilworth*) would we of Saskatchewan be living in towns named Juliette and Sullivan and Goulet and Messer and Berton? Would the twin Battlefords be Wayne and Shuster? And, as my wife has suggested, might not a homesick Scot have christened the Moose and Wood Mountains Ben Cartwright and Ben Casey?

Here in the extreme south-east corner of Saskatchewan literary associations are not limited to the names of villages. The first settler in the lovely and spacious Souris Valley country between Carnduff and the border was a dignified, bearded Englishman named Henry Hutchinson, the son of a Herefordshire vicar, who appears to have found more congenial associations in nature than in the society of his fellow men. An ardent conservationist, he urged that hawks and badgers be protected by law; and on the rare occasions that he went afield he meticulously observed the sportsman's code in which he had been reared. This to the astonishment of his more primitive neighbours who killed for food rather than sport and much preferred to shoot at sitting ducks rather than those on the wing.

'With Henry,' one of the neighbours said, 'anything was safe till it got going.'

Henry Hutchinson himself did not write poetry, but an uncle by marriage did. Henry's aunt, Mary Hutchinson, was the wife of William Wordsworth.

Settlement of the south-east corner began in 1882 immediately following a government survey which threw the land open to homesteaders. Nearly ten years earlier the way had been prepared for the settlement of the North-west by two advance agents of civilization, the one later widely known and honoured, the other almost immediately forgotten. In 1874 the newly formed force of North West Mounted Police made its historic march from Fort Dufferin in Manitoba to the Rockies; two years earlier the British Boundary Survey Commission, working in conjunction with its American counterpart, had begun the monotonous work of mapping the 49th parallel from Lake of the Woods to the Waterton Lakes region of the Rocky Mountains. They completed the job about the time the policemen came to the end of their journey through the wilderness.

Man's passionate interest in the underdog, the lost, the defeated, is no doubt founded on empathy – it is much easier for most of us to identify with ignorant armies on the darkling plain than with those who walk knowledgeably in the sun. Burke and Wills hopelessly lost in the Australian outback, Jack Hornby and his two young companions starving to death stupidly and heroically in the Canadian north, the raw police recruits of 1874 stumbling across the plains and escaping destruction by a hair's breadth – these men are in our eyes infinitely more human and romantic than the members of the Boundary Commission, both British and American, who in the years 1872-4 inched their way along the 49th parallel, endured the dust and cold and heat and labour of the day, survived droughts and blizzards and prairie fires, saved the distracted half-starved Mounties with generous handouts for man and beast, and at all times and in all weathers *knew exactly where they were.* In so knowing they lost their chance of being remembered fondly by posterity. Men who always know exactly where they are in life are bound to be looked upon with suspicion and dislike by those of us who don't – and we are nearly all mankind. So it is that the Mounties, straggling across the plains and in imminent danger at a dozen points of disintegration, take their place in history and folklore alongside Xenophon and the Ten Thousand (another lost bewildered lot), while the superbly competent surveyors pass into oblivion. Except, of course, the company of Seventh Cavalry, forming part of the American Commission escort, which two years later blundered into immortality with Custer at the Little Big Horn.

Recent research into the work of the Boundary Commission has done something to bring back into memory men who should never have been forgotten. *West on the 49th Parallel,* by John Parsons, is a judicious, unemotional account of the work of the survey, which, being based in part on the diaries and journals of the men themselves, does much to bring the hitherto faceless, passionless scientists to life; and a chapter in Wallace Stegner's fine book about his boyhood in southern Saskatchewan, *Wolf Willow,* emphasizes the extraordinary difficulties the surveyors met and conquered without fuss or fanfare.

The British Survey Commission – more efficient and much better equipped than its American counterpart – was made up of four officers, forty-four non-commissioned officers and men of the Royal Engineers (every man a skilled artisan), and forty or more civilians including teamsters, Métis buffalo hunters, doctors, and a geologist. The only dud among the officers was the Chief Commissioner himself, Captain Donald Cameron of the Royal Artillery, whose appointment was popularly viewed as a gift from his father-in-law, Sir Charles Tupper, at the time a member of Sir John A. Macdonald's cabinet. Happily the Commissioner's shortcomings were more than compensated for by the zeal and competence of the officers nominally under his command. In two years they surveyed over a thousand miles of boundary without being embroiled in a single fight with Indians, Fenians, or their American fellow-surveyors, nor did they lose a single man through illness or accident. One of the officers, Lieutenant Rowe, had the bad luck to fall off his horse and fracture his skull, but he was back on the job in no time at all.

Only the Indians were disappointed with the work of the surveyors; they had expected them to build a high wall between Canada and the United States.

It is possible to drive the width of Saskatchewan on roads running only a few miles above the 49th parallel and thus to maintain touch with the trails taken in 1874 by both surveyors and Mounted Police. Since much of the country along the border is sparsely settled and in appearance hardly changed since 1874, it is possible even today – indeed almost unavoidable – to share something of the awe, hatred, and fascination which those earlier journeying men felt for the wild, lonely land they were drawn into by curiosity, circumstances, and the call of duty.

Estevan, a town ten miles north of the U.S. border and easily accessible over excellent roads, provides a convenient jumping-off spot for a journey into the remoter regions of the west. The town – neat, sun-baked, windswept – is in itself nothing remarkable, but it is surrounded by a variety of natural phenomena worth more than a passing glance. Early settlers of the treeless south-east corner of the province drove distances up to a hundred miles to gather coal from the outcroppings along the banks of the Souris River; and the growth of Estevan coincides in part with the large-scale development of the enormous soft-coal resources of the Souris Valley. The coal lies just below the surface of the earth in seams up to ten feet thick; the seams are exposed by huge drag-lines which strip off the overlay of rock and clay, and the coal is then easily scooped up by mechanical shovels.

The most fascinating by-products of open-seam mining are the miniature mountain ranges formed of the clay stripped away to expose the coal seams. Immediately after the stripping the mounds look like great ugly cicatrices scarring the mutilated face of the land, but time and distance work their familiar magic. The older mounds are clothed now with grass and wildflowers, and seen from afar across the flat prairie are easily mistaken for ranges of low hills.

The best-known and most widely publicized geological phenomenon in the Estevan country is La Roche Percée, an isolated sandstone outcropping in the Souris Valley a few miles south of the town. Captain John Palliser examined the Rock in 1857, and his description is still largely accurate: 'The manner in which the sandstones decompose gives rise to curious figures, which the Indians regard with superstitious dread. Hard concretions occur, which resist the action of the atmosphere a much longer time than the softer portions, and they thus become isolated and perched in natural pillars, which are grouped as if they formed the ruins of ancient buildings. One of these pillars standing out from the side of the valley is perforated by a large hole, and is "La Roche Percée" from which the locality derives its name. The Indians never pass this stone without making some offering to the Manito which to their mind it represents, such as rubbing vermilion on it, or depositing beads, tobacco or the like in the crevices. It is also covered with rude designs carved with their knives on the soft surface of the stone.'

Instruments of God and man – wind, rain, pickaxes, jack-knives – continue to play unfortunate tricks with the Rock, breaking down graceful bridge-spans, wearing away the 'rude designs' made by the Indians or overlaying them with the symbols and slogans of a later age and another people.

An easily spotted landmark set beside running water, La Roche Percée drew early travellers like a magnet. Palliser rested in its shadow, the men of the Boundary Survey Commission left their initials on its shoulder, and the force of Mounted Police originals camped at Short Creek near by. 'On our arrival at Roche Percée,' a rookie constable reported, 'the column resembled a routed army corps. For a distance of several miles the road was strewn with broken carts, and horses and oxen overcome with hunger and fatigue.' Today nearly everyone who visits La Roche Percée has himself photographed atop the Rock, poised like an Indian brave scanning the landscape for enemies or buffalo. There is no harm in this, unless an unexpected gust of wind should tumble the unwary poser into a fall of twenty or more feet.

It is one of the fascinating little ironies of life which help to make existence not only tolerable, but at times positively enjoyable, that the rewards of no foresight and little effort often far exceed those of careful planning and meticulous execution. This my wife and I learned when, after spending an exhausting day seeing the routine Estevan sights – temperature just under one hundred degrees – we drove shortly before sunset on the highway north-west towards Weyburn with no other purpose in mind than to escape for a little while from the searing heat still radiating from walls and pavements. In the world around us everything had sunk into a sun-dazed stupor; nothing moved except the oil pumps which are a characteristic feature of the southern Saskatchewan landscape – great praying mantises genuflecting endlessly to the god below. Twenty miles out of town we swung off the highway on to a dubious municipal road running south. Within minutes we were absolutely alone, at the centre of an enormous disc of earth domed by a sky whose western bounds were patterned almost to the zenith by intricately blended bands of colour – a Joseph's coat cut to celestial measurement. From the surface of the disc objects stood up here and there – a house, a herd of cattle (mere insects within the immensity of earth and heaven), a windbreak (man-planted, for no trees grow naturally on the Estevan plains), a windmill, a grain elevator – each object outlined with precision and astonishing clarity against the cloths-of-heaven backdrop. We crossed the valley of the Souris, the river a mere trickle in a bed half a mile wide, and lingered for a long time on the south bank. We saw no one, heard nothing except the songs of innumerable twilight birds and the far-off barking of a dog. 'The true peace of God,' says Conrad, 'begins anywhere a thousand miles from land.' But there are seas of earth as well as of water, and I think Conrad might concede that the spirit whose dwelling is the light of setting suns may be felt as intensely in the middle of the Estevan plains, on a evening such as ours was, as on the farthest reach of ocean.

Let no man be deceived. The Estevan country in most of its moods and aspects is more likely to remind us of Him who made the tiger than of Him who made the lamb. It can be unbelievably cruel – drought-tormented, dust-ridden, wind-battered; it has driven many men and women to despair and some to madness; for here, perhaps more than anywhere else in the west, a man feels himself exposed to the menace of inscrutable and awful powers, with no mountains or hills to hide him from the heavy wrath of God.

Driving west from Estevan on Highway 18 is likely to prove a disconcerting experience for the outlander. No matter how fast he drives, there is no visible evidence to show that he is getting anywhere. He is moving, yes – the machine-gun rattle of gravel against the belly of the car assures him of that – but the great disc of earth moves with him so that he remains a fixed centre

and may well experience – paradoxically, since he is in extravagantly wide-open country – a claustrophobic sensation of being
trapped in time and space. (The sensation is commonest in
winter, when demarcation lines between grey earth and grey sky
completely disappear and a man feels himself fixed forever in
the heart of a boundless void.) But a name, CLEARVIEW, painted
over a farm gateway in a land where nothing intervenes between
the eye and the horizon, is reassuring. Man is here, ponderously
underlining the obvious or indulging himself in the pleasures of
gentle irony. Reassuring too are the diminutive ridges which
begin to appear on either side of the highway – ripples on the
earth's surface whipped up, one is tempted to think, by a wind
that has blown across that surface without intermission since the
dawn of creation.

A short distance past a huddle of frame buildings labelled
Oungre, a sign points to Hoffer, two miles south of the highway.
A five-minute drive along a dirt road over and around a succession of hillocks brings into view first a grain elevator, then a
handful of abandoned tumbledown houses and an immense wall-
safe rooted in cement and standing naked and incongruous in
the midst of a weed patch – all this wreckage centred on a sway-
backed, weather-beaten frame building whose dimensions suggest that it must once have done service as a community hall.

Abandoned settlements in the prairie country, alike in their
ugliness and pathos, are nothing unusual; what makes the deserted Hoffer village different from its fellows is the Star of David
still clearly visible on the gable end of the crumbling old frame
hall.

Persecuted Jews, most of them from Czarist Russia, were
among the earliest of Saskatchewan homesteaders. They came to
the prairies under the sponsorship of the great philanthropist
Baron de Hirsch, a Munich Jew who gave his name to the
Jewish settlement twenty miles east of Estevan. The Jewish
Colonization Society, Hirsch's foundation, was, in the late
nineteenth century, one of the largest charitable trusts in the
world, with a capital, all supplied by Hirsch, of twelve million
pounds. Operations in Canada, directed from the Hirsch Institute in Montreal, were aimed primarily at re-establishing displaced European Jews on the land. Those who came to Canada
and settled in the Hirsch, Oxbow, Oungre, and Hoffer districts
may well have felt that between the pains of religious persecu-

tion and the rigours of the prairie climate there was little to choose. The nineties were hard years on the plains, and of the forty-seven families who in 1892 made up the original Hirsch settlement all except seven had moved out by 1894. Further assistance from the Hirsch Institute and a succession of good crops enabled those still surviving in the southern Saskatchewan settlements to become firmly rooted in the land, and even to endure the dust-bowl years which struck their part of the west the harshest blows of all.

My wife and I explored the abandoned Hoffer village on a beautiful midsummer day. The hall with the Star of David emblazoned on the gable end we found dismal and depressing, as nearly all empty buildings soon to perish are. Shutters banged against rotting window frames, and the wind, forcing itself inside through gaping cracks in the wall-boards, fluttered yellowing copies of *The Judean* that someone, thirty or more years ago, had tossed on the floor. But outside things were different. The fields beyond the village were lush with the promise of a fair harvest; and we knew that the abandoned community did not symbolize the defeat of the people who had once lived there. Rather, the community, like so many established to meet the needs of a pioneer society, had long since ceased to serve any real purpose; it had perished because it had outlived its usefulness.

The Hoffer country even at its greenest is austere, lonely – in winter frightening in its unbroken grey-white immensity. A visit there is a salutary experience for those of us who are conditioned to associate the Jews with an urban society, and makes more readily comprehensible their astonishing achievement in our present century. For the qualities which enabled Jewish settlers to survive the hardships of homestead life on the prairies and to convert empty wastes into richly productive farms are precisely those which, exerted at a later time and in a different place, have helped to make for Jewry a fertile homeland of the deserts of Israel.

A short distance west of Oungre the farmland begins to peter out; a few miles farther on and the prairie breaks into the ragged uplift of the Missouri Coteau.

The Coteau is an escarpment reaching all the way from the South Saskatchewan River near Swift Current to the Missouri basin in North Dakota. It was, presumably, formed during the

Ice Age from the great piles of drift (soil, rock, assorted debris) that had accumulated along the front edge of the Keewatin Ice Cap. When the Cap retreated, or changed direction, the drift was left to form a terminal moraine.

The Missouri Coteau is not, however, a clearly defined geological feature which warns the traveller that he is about to climb to a new prairie level; rather, it merges with the immense bed of the Big Muddy Lake and kindred smaller depressions – all scooped out by the waters of the melting ice-cap – to form a band, in the border country about fifty miles wide, of grotesquely tumbled earth, eroded clay hills, odd isolated buttes, dried-out lake bottoms hedged about by high clay banks. This is wild, desolate, brooding land – beautiful for a fleeting moment in spring when the grass and wild flowers pattern with colour the slopes of the grey old hills; hot and dusty in summer (the dust fanned by furnace blasts that seem to have come hot from hell itself); melancholy in autumn, for there are few trees or shrubs to mask with glowing colours the coming hulk of death; and in winter a vast, snow-shrouded moon-surface from which all traces of life have been wiped clean away.

Municipal roads slice through the Coteau and Big Muddy country only a mile or two above the international border. By midsummer the country has assumed its most characteristic look, that of grey old age; but surprisingly, wild flowers of extraordinary variety and range of colour flourish along the roadside – miniature sunflowers, morning glories, brown-eyed susans, vetches, daisies of assorted colour schemes and sizes, an occasional laggard rose or scarlet tiger lily – and the air is rank with the rich, heavy smell of clover. This is ranch country where most crops are grown for feed, and the valley bottoms and upland slopes and plateaus are dotted with great herds of cattle and, at wide intervals, of sheep. But the ranch houses are few, and those fleetingly visible from a fast-moving automobile – crouched in folds of hills that part for a moment then close quickly like drawn curtains – in their isolation and triviality intensify rather than relieve the sensation of utter loneliness that descends upon the alien spirit with the weight of a physical oppression.

The cattle grazing in the valley bottoms are the white-faced Herefords which I and the ex-farmboys of my generation view with affection and nostalgia; for unlike Holsteins and Jerseys and other milk-producing breeds the Herefords stir no unhappy recollections of bondage to milk pail and cream separator; instead they call back into memory the glorious long winter evenings we spent huddled behind the old Quebec heater or beside the kitchen range reading Owen Wister and Zane Grey and B. M. Bower and dreaming of the day when we would escape the serfdom of farm chores and ride away into the sunset – six-guns slung low on the thigh – over rangelands dotted with white-faces which exacted from us no attentions that could not be dispensed from the back of a horse.

It may be that for natives of the American west, particularly if they come from the upper reaches of the Missouri, the Coteau country possesses no unique attractions; but to Canadians from other provinces who think of southern Saskatchewan as a flat plain covered with wheat-fields and oil wells and gophers the dramatic badlands are likely to prove something of a shocker. The Coteau, incidentally, makes excellent border country; there are no towns close to the line to plunder and no land worth coveting – only grey tumbled earth, clay hills, dried-out lake bottoms, and the immense sky-dome whose rim melts into that of earth in a unity which to the God-seeker symbolizes the eternal spirit which permeates all things – and to the more materially minded explains why so many mystics have come out of desert places.

A physical phenomenon of the Coteau country of some interest to the student of history is a curious cone-shaped hill rising above the bank of a small creek that cuts its way through the badlands a few miles west of Big Beaver. The hill is visible from the municipal road, and easily accessible over a dirt trail leading into a rancher's yard. The hill is not marked on any map that I have seen, but I recognized it instantly as one sketched by Lieutenant Rowe of the Boundary Commission. (The sketch is now in possession of the Public Archives of Canada.) The Lieutenant, being a scientist, did not succumb to the nineteenth-century romantic inclination to make all protuberances, from hillocks to mountains, appear about ten times higher and steeper than they really are. The shape of the hill inspired him to give the stream winding past its base the name of Pyramid Creek.

The Coteau country is surveyors' country. Ghosts of the Royal Engineers have the hills and valleys and lake bottoms and assorted badlands all to themselves; for the Mounted Police in the course of their famous march swung north-west from La Roche Percée and straggled towards the mountains in a line running roughly forty miles above the border. They were, however, wise enough to keep in touch with the surveyors, who from time to time doled them out enough pemmican and oats to keep them and their horses alive until they reached the greener pastures of the Rocky Mountain foothills.

But the great day of the Mounties was close at hand. And it was from two Saskatchewan posts, Fort Walsh and Wood Mountain, that they rode out to become a world-wide legend — which like every legend worthy of the name is rooted fast in truth.

4. The Saga of Wood Mountain

From the border country, a good gravel road, No. 36, leads north to Willow Bunch, home of the Willow Bunch Giant, a gentle eight-foot weakling whose mother, so local legend affirms, wished herself tall enough to reach the berries at the top of a tall saskatoon bush and found her wish fulfilled in her son. But the Giant's own wish for himself, to be a cowboy, he never realized because – again according to local tradition – whenever he rode horseback his feet trailed on the ground. Although living far from traditional centres of exploitation, the Giant was not permitted to spin out his brief thread in peace. He died at the St. Louis Exposition in 1906, aged twenty-one.

Willow Bunch, an attractive well-treed town, most of whose inhabitants are of French descent and speak a curious patois among themselves, is admirably sited against the eastern flank of Wood Mountain. As far back as the 1860s, Indian and Métis hunters wintered in the mountain coulees near by. A trader from Quebec, Jean Louis Legare, built a post close to the winter camps in 1872. A few years later he moved the post to Willow Bunch, where a permanent settlement had grown up.

Wood Mountain is a great land-swell covering an area of some eight hundred square miles and rising at its highest point to about one thousand feet above the level of the surrounding plain. It is easy to understand the attraction of Wood Mountain for the Métis and Indians; the heavily wooded coulees, creeks, and abundant springs make it an authentic oasis in an otherwise treeless and almost waterless land. The Mountain has played a significant role in the development of the Canadian west. Here in 1874 the Mounties established a depot for worn-out horses and ailing men in and around a sod shack originally used by the

Boundary Commission surveyors as a supply base. (It was from their Wood Mountain and Willow Bunch bases that the surveyors sent to the starving policemen and their horses five thousand pounds of pemmican and fifteen thousand pounds of oats.) In 1876 the depot was enlarged and converted into quarters to house a police detachment; and for the next six years two handfuls of policemen, one based at Wood Mountain and one at Fort Walsh in the Cypress Hills nearly two hundred miles west, upheld the white man's law among a dozen or more restless Indian tribes, chased away the whiskey traders, and, working in conjunction with small detachments of their fellows based at points equally remote, made possible the peaceful settlement of the Canadian North-west.

Their job was not an easy one. Indian refugees from the United States appeared in the Northwest Territories in the early 1860s. Driven by starvation and the fear of extermination to deeds of violence and murder, they fled across the border from Minnesota and the Dakotas into a land where the blue-coated American soldiers could not follow – a land in which, however, they had no legal rights, held no reserves, could claim no bounties, were received on sufferance by the Government of Canada and viewed with suspicion and hostility by Canadian tribes long established on the ground. These early refugees at first moved cautiously, kept the peace between themselves and their reluctant neighbours surprisingly well. True, the boundary surveyors came upon – and in the interests of science duly photographed – the bodies of twenty-one Crow warriors who had been surprised by the Piegan while on a horse-stealing raid; but horse-stealing and summary justice for the thieves if caught had always been characteristic features of the Indian way of life, and a score of sun-shrunken bodies lying on the plain betokened no unusual hostile activity.

The major threat to peace in the Canadian North-west came in 1876 when a horde of Sioux warriors, fresh from their triumph over the hated blue-coats at the Battle of the Little Big Horn and fleeing the wrath to come, swarmed into the Cypress Hills country west of Wood Mountain to claim asylum and beg for food. The arrival of the Sioux swelled the number of Indian refugees in the south Saskatchewan country to more than six thousand. With their coming the saga of the North West

Mounted Police, which the extravagant outpourings of romantic novelists and script-writers have distorted but hardly exaggerated, properly begins. The young men who had survived the terrible march west in 1874 were now ready for anything.

In the Cypress Hills Assistant Commissioner Irvine and ten constables rode into a gathering of more than three thousand hungry warriors who, having heard of the annihilation of Custer's army on the Little Big Horn, were restless and eager to kill. The tactics Irvine employed to quell the impulse to revolt were described with elephantine facetiousness by the Toronto *Globe* in a news despatch dated from Fort Macleod:

> While the American papers are teeming with telegrams referring to the movements of General Terry's army of four thousand three hundred men, and of the advance of these troops in three divisions against the Sioux in the Yellowstone region, a similar movement of troops on this side of the line has been successfully made, of which no notice has as yet been taken. On July 18th last Assistant Commissioner Irvine, commanding the North West Mounted Police in this district, advanced upon and completely demoralized a large encampment of Indians at Cypress Hills. The camp numbered over one thousand lodges, of which one hundred lodges were of Sitting Bull's band. Colonel Irvine advanced his troops in a mass of columns, the whole numbering ten men. Having successfully pierced the centre of the camp, he threw among the Indians, at close quarters, hand grenades of a new pattern. . . . These missiles were composed of sea biscuits, tea, sugar and tobacco. The Indians never recovered from the first discharge. On the following day the left wing of the right division, consisting of one man, was dispatched to a mixed camp of Indians numbering one hundred and fifty lodges, with orders to seize a certain number of horses stolen by them from the South Piegans, peacefully if possible, but in the case of resistance, to capture the entire band. The horses were recovered.

At Wood Mountain, Inspector Walsh, a hard-bitten, crusty, and none-too-scrupulous Irish policeman, rode with an escort of twelve men through the ranks of armed warriors including those who had wiped out Custer's cavalry at the Little Big Horn, and meeting with the chiefs in solemn council laid down the laws they were to abide by while living on Canadian soil. The scene, twice repeated, must have been a singularly impressive one – the silent sullen braves, many of them mounted and all of them armed, dangerous men tormented by the frustrations of the dispossessed; the women and children watching impassively from the lodges; the chiefs brave in such regalia as they could muster after long wanderings; and at the centre of things the cluster of policemen in faded scarlet jackets – Walsh, tough-minded, confident, never doubting his power to dominate the chiefs and control their hate-filled sombre warriors.

What were the rules laid down by Walsh and Irvine for the Indians to follow? They were few, simple, and precise. No fighting on Canadian soil; no horse-stealing; no raids or smuggling of ammunition across the border into the United States. The chiefs accepted the terms.

What is more surprising, they kept them. There were, inevitably, incidental horse-stealings, a few fights, an occasional killing; but the fundamental fact is that from 1876 to 1881 two meagre detachments of policemen stationed at Wood Mountain and Fort Walsh preserved an astonishingly high degree of law and order among the greatest concentration of mixed tribes, American and Canadian, ever drawn together by fear and need on the North American continent.

Until 1879 the lot of the Indian refugees was not an unhappy one. Just as the feuding families of the old American Deep South recognized certain gathering-places – landing-stage, courthouse, church – as neutral ground where convention and convenience forbade one to shoot one's enemy, so the Indians of all tribes seem to have accepted Wood Mountain and the Cypress Hills as country where all might find sanctuary and hunt, but to which none could lay permanent and exclusive claim. In the years immediately following the coming of the Sioux there was enough – or nearly enough – food for all; and for Sitting Bull especially, there was something approaching peace of mind as he played with his grandchildren and told them stories of battles not so long ago.

But by 1879 it was clear that the uneasy idyll of Wood Mountain could not endure for ever. Almost overnight the last great buffalo herd was annihilated; and now the gaunt grey wolf skulked among the tepees. The refugee Indians could not expect to be made wards of the Canadian government – not when reserves were waiting for them back home where, so U.S. government spokesmen said, they would all be assured food, shelter, and safety. Most of the refugees accepted the inevitable and in small bands straggled back over the line to the reserves they had fled from several years before. Not surprisingly Sitting Bull, who had much to fear from men burning to avenge the humiliating disaster of the Little Big Horn, refused to go.

It was now, in this desperate time, that Inspector Walsh (who had proved himself capable of throwing an uncooperative Sitting Bull out of a cabin by the scruff of his neck – an episode not to the policeman's credit) revealed in his dealings with his unofficial wards a solicitude bordering on tenderness which helps to explain his immense authority over them. In reference to the hardships endured by the Indians in the grim winter of 1880 he wrote: 'The conduct of these starving and destitute people, their patient endurance, their sympathy, the extent to which they have assisted each other, and their strict observance of all order would reflect credit upon the most civilized community. I am pleased to inform you, as no doubt it will give you pleasure to know, that the greatest good will and consideration was extended to these poor sufferers by the men at Wood Mountain Post. The little that was daily left from their table was carefully preserved, and meted out as far as it would go, to the women and children . . . . I do not think that one ounce of food was wasted at Wood Mountain Post; every man seemed to be interested in saving what little he could, and day after day they divided their rations with these starving people.'

In the spring of 1881 Sitting Bull and twelve hundred of his people made a dramatic march from Wood Mountain to Fort Qu'Appelle, a distance of some two hundred miles, and appealed for the last time for a reservation in Canada. Sitting Bull was given short shrift by Inspector Sam Steele, the big policeman in charge of the Fort Qu'Appelle police detachment, who bluntly stated the Canadian government's point of view – no food and no reservations for alien Indians who had both waiting for them in their own land. On the advice of Edgar Dewdney, the Commissioner for Indian Affairs, Steele gave the Indians rations enough to last them on the journey back to Wood Mountain and sent them on their way.

Sitting Bull returned to Wood Mountain. There it was the lot of Jean Louis Legare, the trader from Quebec who had established a trading-post first in a Wood Mountain coulee and later in Willow Bunch, to be the saviour of the red man. In the weeks when Sitting Bull was reaching the agonizing decision to return to the United States, Legare kept the Sioux alive at his own expense, drawing heavily on the goods – mostly pemmican – which he held in reserve for trade. Legare's disinterested charity earned the highest commendation from Commissioner Irvine, who brought to the notice of the Dominion government 'the good and loyal service rendered by Mr. Louis Legare, the trader, who at times used his personal influence with the Sioux in a manner calculated to further the policy of the Government. His disinterested and honourable course being decidedly marked, particularly when compared with that of other traders and individuals. At the final surrender of the Sioux Mr. Legare must have been put to considerable expense, judging from the amount of food and other aid supplied by him.'

Mr. Legare was indeed put to considerable expense – according to his own estimate to the sum of nearly ten thousand dollars. Of this expenditure he recovered less than half from the United States government.

Sitting Bull, the bitter cry of 'I am thrown away' on his lips, went back to the United States, to be shot down a few years later on the reservation where he had been assured of safety, and with the departure of the great Sioux chief and his warriors the saga of the North West Mounted Police properly and dramatically comes to an end. In a few brief years and without bloodshed the Mounties had tamed the turbulent west, established the rule of law – and now the settlers were clamouring at the gates.

Thenceforth the nature and number of the tasks imposed on the harassed policemen were such as to make conventional law enforcement appear an almost incidental activity. 'In Wood Mountain,' Superintendent Perry reported in 1893, 'our men are found acting as cowboys; rounding up and driving back across the boundary vast herds of American ranch cattle which again and again wandered northward in search of better feed and more water. At Estevan and Gretna they are seen in charge of large herds of quarantined cattle; tending sick milch cows; and at the expiration of the term of quarantine driving them long distances by trail, loading them on trains and conveying them to their destination. In Manitoba they are engaged in enforcing the customs laws, aiding the regular customs officials whose duties they at times perform, and executing the Crown

Timber and Dominion Lands regulations, and in addition to this work of a special nature they are carrying on their regular duties of detecting crime, aiding the administration of justice, acting as prairie fire and game guardians, and maintaining a patrol system which covered weekly some twelve hundred miles.'

Happily, whenever a Mountie *was* called upon to enforce the law under difficult circumstances he usually did so with an efficiency and flair worthy of the finest traditions of the Force, and afterwards reported his achievement in the kind of laconic understatement which is the distinguishing characteristic of early Mounted Police prose. Thus when young Corporal Hogg of the Wood Mountain detachment was called upon to quell a disturbance instigated by an armed badman in a North Portal hotel, he reported the subsequent action in words which in their power to say much in little are not unworthy to stand beside Caesar's famous *veni, vidi, vici* message to the Roman Senate: 'On the 17th inst. I, Corporal Hogg, was called to the hotel to quiet a disturbance. I found the room full of cowboys and one Monoghan, or Cowboy Jack, was carrying a gun, and pointed it at me against sections 105 and 109 of the Criminal Code. We struggled. Finally I got him handcuffed behind and put him inside. His head being in bad shape we had to engage the services of a doctor who dressed his wound and pronounced it nothing serious.'

Louis Legare lived in the Wood Mountain country for nearly half a century, dying at Willow Bunch in 1918. Legare never became a folk hero (perhaps because he never killed anybody), but in recent years there has been a growing awareness of the value of the work he did in helping to maintain the peace in dangerous times. In 1965 a memorial park bearing his name was established a little over a mile out of Willow Bunch in a coulee on Wood Mountain near the site of his first trading-post. The trees — aspen, elm, balsam, maple, willow — grow tall in the coulee and there is running water close at hand. But the chief charm of the Louis Legare Park resides not so much in its natural attractions — which are many — as in its furnishings. Conventional rustic plank appointments are supplemented by old school desks (initials cut fifty years back still showing clearly in their darkened surfaces), ancient extension tables of imitation oak and mahogany salvaged from attics and junk-heaps, and — most original touch of all – old car cushions upholstered in a wide range of covers and so arranged as to look like overstuffed love-seats – a role which many of them may indeed have previously filled. In combination with the extension tables and an occasional sideboard, the overstuffed seats give to the park intended to keep green the memory of a rugged old frontiersman the appearance of an open-air Victorian drawing-room.

Jean Louis Legare would have rejoiced in the spectacle of tired, hungry travellers from the dusty plains stuffing themselves with hot dogs and hamburgers and gaudy-coloured drinks while enjoying a well-cushioned rest in the park which bears his name. His business and his pleasure was to feed the hungry. No man would have approved more enthusiastically the nature and purpose of his memorial.

5. Wood Mountain to Eastend

From Willow Bunch a pleasant run takes us north-west a few miles past the spectacular alkali flats of Willow Bunch Lake to the agreeable little prairie town of Assiniboia. The tourist intent on exploring the Wood Mountain country would do well to make Assiniboia his headquarters, since no other town nearer than Moose Jaw seventy miles farther north offers adequate – or even tolerable – accommodation.

One of the most attractive and exciting spots in the entire Wood Mountain region is the tiny village of St. Victor and its environs, sixteen miles south-east of Assiniboia and reached over unmarked gravel roads. Happily, farmers by the wayside are always willing to provide directions and talk about the crops. The church-dominated village, which might have been transplanted from one of the remoter rural areas of Quebec (it must not be forgotten that the population of this part of Saskatchewan is predominantly French in origin), sits near the mouth of a coulee gashing the side of Wood Mountain. A dirt road winds up the coulee to a well-shaded picnic park overhung by an impressive outcrop of sandstone. The outcrop, which can be reached on foot with some difficulty from the park – and more easily from a point higher up the road if one is dressed for rolling under barbed-wire fences and walking through several acres of spear-grass – is much larger and more impressive than Estevan's far more widely publicized La Roche Percée. Like La Roche Percée the St. Victor outcropping, which regrettably bears no colourful and easily remembered name, has been eroded into grotesque shapes – hobgoblin torsos, surrealist faces, and giant toadstools – which to the Freudian eye are unmistakable phallic symbols no doubt fashioned by Mother Nature herself in one of her more lascivious moods.

But the prime interest of the outcropping lies in the Indian petroglyphs which adorn the sandstone surfaces – more extensive and more clearly visible than those on La Roche Percée. (A *petroglyph* is a carving *in* a rock surface; a *petrograph* a painting or inscription *on* a rock surface. Both are often conveniently lumped together under the general term *pictograph*.) A hoofprint, a hand, a face, a mouth containing teeth (this last of particular interest to the archeologist since nearly all petroglyph mouths are toothless) – all these and many things besides are distinguishable in the St. Victor outcropping to those of keen eye and uninhibited imagination. It is generally agreed that most of the St. Victor petroglyphs are religious symbols, although precisely what they symbolize is not clear. Unfortunately they are in grave danger of being obliterated, not only by weathering but by the symbols of a later time – initials, political slogans, and the inevitable four-letter word to which archeologists of the future will no doubt attribute religious significance.

Even if one is not much interested in petroglyphs the St. Victor outcropping is well worth a visit. The view from the top of the great rock is one of the most spectacular in Saskatchewan, embracing as it does an enormous sweep of plain diversified by eroded escarpments, alkali flats, salt lakes (dead seas coffined within drab grey walls), here and there on the horizon's edge a grain elevator shimmering in the heat-haze, and out beyond the escarpments and the alkali flats the farmlands, in spring and summer great squares and rectangles of green and black, in autumn gold and black – God's chessboard laid out on so vast a scale that at last the geometric designs and colours cease to have individual existence; they blend and blur and become indistinguishable from the sky itself.

The village of St. Victor presents a charming post-card appearance, set against a backdrop of mountain (prairie variety) with half Saskatchewan for a front yard. St. Victor boasts certain amenities which make it well worth a visit for its own sake – a Jubilee swimming-pool large enough to accommodate the entire population of the village simultaneously, a postage-stamp golf course adhering to the mountainside, and an unusually high proportion, even for a French-speaking community, of remarkably handsome girls.

The municipal roads leading from Assiniboia to Wood Mountain village, like so many of the Saskatchewan secondary roads, carry no signs to assist the stranger on his way. The view of most municipal authorities seems to be that municipal roads are used only by local residents who don't need signs to tell them where they are going. The road from Assiniboia to Wood Mountain is marked on the official road-maps of the province; unfortunately, many of those that branch off from it are not. If, however, the traveller chooses wisely at intersections, and is at all times careful to distinguish between the main road and its branches, he will come at last, after a passage of thirty miles or so through a silent, sunburnt land, to the village of Wood Mountain.

The village comes as a distinct shock, even to the visitor already familiar with the kind of prairie community huddled around a grain elevator or two which has long since ceased to serve any vital purpose and survives only because it lacks strength to die. Wood Mountain stands sun-bleached and wizened in the middle of an empty flatland. It has no past to excite the imagination and no future to cast a warm colouring of hope over the drab present. It has, however, one claim to distinction – a Romanian Orthodox cemetery. Settlements of central Europeans crop up in odd places in the Canadian west – but for a settlement of Romanians Wood Mountain seems the oddest place of all.

Happily, history, romance, and even beauty are close at hand. Four miles south of the village the road, which for the last mile or two climbs steadily among low buttes, leads us up past a vast open-air arena dedicated to the peculiarly western form of entertainment, the rodeo, and thence to the entrance a few hundred yards farther on of the Wood Mountain Historic Park.

Here is sacred ground. Here the Mounted Police established a post in 1876, and from their primitive barracks rode out to administer the law and exercise the authority of the great Queen across the water over thousands of restless Indian braves who knew that their sun was almost set and felt an entirely comprehensible urge to kill their destroyers, the white men, before they themselves perished from the earth.

Of the original post nothing remains except shallow depressions which are the nearly filled-in cellars over which several of the buildings stood. The post was abandoned as late as 1918; and it has taken less than half a century of time and weather to wipe out all traces of what was once the centre of an authoritarian power exercised over an area of twenty thousand square miles.

Today a log hut, recently built, houses a few relics of the kind usually found in small museums devoted to exhibits of western culture – pioneer tools and utensils, old guns, arrow-heads, articles of clothing, yellowing letters, and faded daguerreotypes. Areas once occupied by the post buildings – barracks, guard-room, stables, cook-house, mess – have been neatly railed off and labelled; but what is usually impressed upon the observer's mind is an awareness of how completely the past in any tangible form has been erased from the Saskatchewan country and, indeed, the whole of the west. Such is the penalty for building in wood instead of stone and for the hour instead of eternity. Here in Saskatchewan visible evidences of the past seldom amount to more than a handful of artifacts, a crumbling chimney, an almost-obliterated cellar, and – very occasionally – parallel depressions in an untilled prairie meadow made by the wheels of pioneer cart or wagon. And that is all. Wind, weather, and plough have done their work with devastating thoroughness. In Saskatchewan the past is a written record, an old man's story, an Historic Sites Board marker, a cluster of headstones.

There is some talk of rebuilding the Wood Mountain post in its original form, as has already been done with Fort Walsh and Fort Macleod and is currently being done with Fort Carlton. I have never been entirely satisfied about the wisdom of such attempts to reconstruct visual images of the past. Most reconstructions that I have visited are so sanitary, so admirably organized and supervised, so obviously intended to attract the kind of visitors the originals never knew, that whatever life resides in them seems to have little to do with a time gone by. Perhaps if we can find no authentic ruins to preserve or restore, an Historic Sites marker beside a hole in the ground is the next best thing. It may not stimulate the imagination but at least it leaves it free.

The curator of the Wood Mountain Historic Park is a gentle, soft-spoken native of Quebec who farmed in the Willow Bunch country before assuming his present post. He is a man passionately interested in Wood Mountain lore, and full of fascinating scraps of information about the people who once lived in and around the post: the English nobleman who married a local Cree girl and after siring six children abandoned her and went back to England; the Edinburgh University-educated Scot who lived in a shack in the bush near by, read the Bible in Gaelic, and like so many recluses of his kind went queer in the head; the

two Mounties, one of whom married an Indian girl, who lie
buried on the summit of a lonely butte overlooking the post,
guardians even in death of a region they could never forsake in
life. All these and a dozen more. The curator has, too, his peculiar
treasures which he showed to my wife and me with immense
pride, and an eagerness which made the revelation of them less
a personal favour than a sharing of cherished secrets: clusters of
flowers rarely found on the prairie; springs of clear water bub-
bling out of hidden places; a tree of unusual size from around
which the curator had laboriously cleared away all underbrush;
several shallow depressions in a patch of ground deep in the
woods, as yet untouched by the excavator's spade, which may
be ancient graves – all these delights reached over a path twisting hither and yon through the woods on a course dictated by no
other consideration than the whim of the man who first trod it
out.

The curator is an ideal man for the post he occupies – without
professional training but alert, curious, concerned. A fortunate
man, too, to have found comparatively late in life, when his
family (which includes a nurse, a priest, an engineer, and a
doctor) are scattered, an occupation which has given him renewed
zest for living.

The collector's keen eye and enthusiasm never desert him. 'I
found this,' he said, showing us a faded picture of Louis Riel
and his Council of the North-west, 'in a magazine in my neighbour's privy. Of course I saved it.'

The Wood Mountain Historic Park is playing an important
role in preserving the traditions and folklore of a region whose
significance in the early history of the North-west is scarcely
known to the average Canadian. It is time, surely, that steps
were taken to convert the entire Wood Mountain area into a
provincial or, better still, a national park. The Mountain is an
impressive example of the prairie grasslands country at its handsomest and best; it harbours some of the most interesting and
unusual Indian remains in Canada; it is ideally suited to the
building of extensive camp-grounds at little cost; and the takeover of the land would involve little dislocation of population.
The fact that such a park would be, in general appearance and
major points of interest, totally unlike any other in Canada
should attract many visitors within its bounds.

The road west from Wood Mountain leads through desolate windswept countryside and desolate windswept villages, the monotony of the journey being relieved by an occasional tremendous vista – a southern Saskatchewan specialty – opening out below an imperceptibly achieved height of land. A few miles beyond Manota the road swings sharply south and west to Val Marie, a town buried in the wide valley of the Frenchman Creek. Val Marie is the centre of an irrigation project harking back to the depressed thirties; but Saskatchewan farmers do not take kindly to irrigation. Their indifference and at times downright hostility, combined with the widespread rains and heavy crops of recent years, have discouraged expansion of the irrigated area beyond a few thousand acres.

Last summer my wife and I were driving towards Val Marie on a blistering hot afternoon over a dust-shrouded dirt road when we were flagged down by a husky farmer who had emerged from a truck at the roadside. He explained that he wanted to leave his truck – one of three monsters he owned – for his hired man, and could he hitch a ride with us to town? We were happy to oblige. He scrambled into the back seat, and we had time to exchange a few desultory remarks about the weather before his curiosity overcame him.

'None of my business I know,' he said, 'but would you folks mind telling me what the hell you're doing, driving a road like this?'

After we had relieved his mind he told us something about the Val Marie country. 'All of us farmers live right in town now,' he explained. 'Only two farm-houses around here still occupied and they're fifteen miles apart. Folks just won't live in the wilderness any more.'

It was easy, driving through the treeless, waterless, empty plain above the valley, to sympathize with the folks who chose to live in the village rather than in a countryside which in a dry season must look like the land God might well have given to Cain. Especially since, as our passenger was at pains to point out, Val Marie has everything. Hotel, movie-house, dance-hall, curling-rink, and three churches.

And he added, saving the best for the last, 'We even got mixed drinking.'

He told us that he farmed 3,500 acres – and from 2,000 acres of wheat expected a return of at least forty bushels to the acre. This in what was once considered one of the driest and most irreclaimable parts of the Palliser desert.

Val Marie is celebrated, in a modest sort of way, not as the centre of an irrigation project, but as the jumping-off place for a community unique in Canada and rare in North America. Roughly ten miles south of town (in one sense the adverb is precise), in a settlement reached over wandering trails which should not be attempted without a guide (since this is rural Saskatchewan there are, naturally, no signposts anywhere), five hundred or more prairie dogs occupy the most northerly colony of its kind on the continent.

Unless one is a patient man – I, unfortunately, am not – a visit to Prairie Dog Town is likely to prove both exhausting and frustrating. Prairie dogs are bashful creatures; it is possible, so I am told, to spend hours in the settlement without sighting a single resident, and a click of a camera shutter is likely to send the whole colony below ground for the rest of the day. Prairie dogs are rodents of sombre hue and portly physique; they communicate with one another by barking, need no water to survive (this helps to explain their presence in Saskatchewan), live far underground in an extraordinary complex of tunnels, hibernate in the winter, and dislike being stared at in summer. The dedicated nature-lover or connoisseur of the off-beat can hardly afford to miss Prairie Dog Town; but for my own part I am content to study the behavioural patterns of the prairie dog's distant and ubiquitous cousin, the common gopher. This I did with some thoroughness during my homestead boyhood, when the municipal authorities paid a bounty of ten cents a dozen for gopher tails.

Rodeos provide one of the most popular forms of community entertainment in the south Saskatchewan country during the summer months, and there is no better way to catch something of the flavour of life in the ranchlands than to attend one. The modest grandstand is usually rickety and weatherbeaten, the roof made of poplar branches laid across poles; and no matter where you sit or stand the wind is sure to fill your eyes and mouth with arena dust. But the discomfort is a small price to pay for the experience of watching authentic cowboys at what they call play. They are not slick professional entertainers and neither are the broncos they ride or the steers they dog, but there is a feeling of authenticity and intimacy about the small-town rodeo altogether absent from the big-city stampede. The lads who ride – or fall off – at the local rodeo have come in from the local range; and the brilliantly attired cowgirls, splendid horsewomen all of them, who provide background and colour, are the sisters and sweethearts of the brave boys in the arena. In due season some of them will marry and settle down on the home range; others will go away to become school-teachers and nurses and stenographers, and they too will marry and settle down, perhaps in far-off places, and mature – or wither – into conventional suburban housewives, with this difference between them and their neighbours, that they will always have a keener eye for a horse than an automobile.

It is, however, the old men who lend the most effective touch of authenticity to the local rodeo, for they have taken on the appearance and colour of the land they have ridden over all their lives. Faces which at the huge professional stampedes are lost in the crowds stand out clearly here – seamed and cracked like the earth's surface, brown fading into grey to harmonize with the grey old hills. Grey faces under grey stetsons – except at funerals where in some fashion-conscious rangeland communities black stetsons are worn by relatives and friends of the deceased.

In the evening following the rodeo there is sure to be a dance in the local hall, sometimes with a name band from the nearest big town in attendance, more often with local talent. There will be some attempt at square dancing, but among young people reared on television the modern dances are more popular. Indeed, square dancing now belongs properly to those folk activities so enthusiastically participated in by everyone except the folk.

It is unwise to stay in town overnight when the rodeo is in progress. My wife and I did so – once. When we staggered bleary-eyed and wretched into the hotel corridor to grope our way downstairs to breakfast we found a party in the room across from ours in full swing – door wide open to ward off claustrophobia from men accustomed to lots of elbow room, or perhaps to allow the empties to spill out into the corridor. Whether the party was just getting under way or carrying on from the night before there was no way of telling.

From Val Marie several routes, all of them more or less devious, lead to the Cypress Hills. Travellers who have not yet had their fill of windswept empty plain seamed with dry creek beds should follow the gravel roads running south and west through Climax and Croydon, then north past the imaginatively named Old Man On His Back Plateau to Eastend. Others, eager to find some kind of shelter from the terrors of infinite space, would do well to take the faster route north on Highway No. 4 to Cadillac, and thence to Eastend via Shaunavon, a town at the centre of a large area once predominantly rangeland but gradually being surrendered by the raisers of beef to growers of wheat. But Shaunavon is still in spirit a cow-town. The lobby of the principal hotel is decorated with ornately designed riding-gear; and the immensely wide and wind-blasted main street makes the man accustomed to riding the open range feel right at home.

Shaunavon's principal exports are commonly assumed to be beef and wheat, but it has contributed much to the cultural as well as the economic life of the nation. It is the birthplace of that most gifted of Canadian actresses, Frances Hyland.

Whatever road the traveller takes on his way to the Cypress Hills he shouldn't miss Eastend.

Prairie towns have for long been looked upon with scorn and horror by inmates of eastern haunts of ancient peace who, lulled by the murmur of doves amid the immemorial elms, drowse away their lives amid Arcadian scenes where never wind blows loudly. Rupert Brooke, the lad from the town where the clock stands forever fixed at ten to three, was clearly shaken by what he saw from his coach window when he crossed the prairies in 1913: 'Each village . . . seems to be exactly like the next. . . . They seemed to be emptied of their folk this Sabbath morn; though whether the inhabitants were at work, or in church or had shot themselves from depression induced by the weather it was impossible to tell. These little towns do not look to the passer-by comfortable as homes. Partly, there is the difficulty of distinguishing your village from the others. It would be as bad as being married to a Jap. And then towns should be on hills or in valleys, however small. A town dumped down, apparently by chance, on a flat expanse, wears the same air of discomfort as a man trying to make his bed on a level unyielding surface such as a lawn or pavement. He feels hopelessly incidental to the superficies of the earth. He is aware that the human race has thighbones.'

Until comparatively recently the view that the prairie small town was devoid of either physical comfort or aesthetic charm had a good deal of validity. Thirty or forty years ago there was little about it to praise. Its components, as Rupert Brooke's observations suggest, seldom showed much variation: a row of false-fronted frame buildings facing a wide and dusty main street edged with wooden sidewalks; gaunt two-storey frame houses and dispirited weatherbeaten shacks surrounded by ragged caragana hedges or open to the street; empty lots overgrown with pigweed; grain elevators standing tall, stark, and uncompromising against a brassy sky; tin signs creaking monotonously in the wind; dust whorls dancing queer devil's jigs across the baseball diamond; a combined poolroom-barber shop the centre of the town's Saturday-night life; a Chinese restaurant permeated with the odours not of the exotic orient but of rancid grease; and on the corner next the station, the Palace (or Ritz or Queen's) Hotel, kept alive by the grace of its beer-parlour, a frowsty, joyless den whose drab uncongeniality drove customers in self-defence to drink themselves stupid.

There are still many such towns in the west – grey, shrunken hamlets which, paradoxically, have been destroyed by increased prosperity and improved transportation. Fast cars and good roads bring shoppers to the larger towns – village stores cannot compete against readily accessible big-town supermarkets; schools and medical services are centralized in the larger towns; and the villages, existing now in the shadow of bustling communities which half a century ago were too far away to offer serious competition, no longer serve any useful purpose. Except, perhaps, to provide a residential centre for retired farmers, widowers and bachelors mostly, who cannot bear to separate themselves from the community of which they have for so long been a part. Greyfaced, white-haired men, shrunken like the village itself, and like it – and Charles II – an unconscionable long time a-dying.

But the larger towns, which have been able to draw in recent years on the resources of a constantly expanding and increasingly prosperous rural area, are a far cry indeed from what they were thirty or forty years ago. They represent the new west, and except at certain superficial points bear little resemblance to the generally stark and comfortless settlements of the early years of the century. Those false fronts built across gable ends to create the illusion of size – the most blatant symbols of bluff in the entire history of architecture – are nearly all gone now, the frame buildings they fronted having been replaced by more substantial structures of brick and cement. The streets are paved, water-mains a matter of course rather than wonder, and – most significant change of all – in the residential areas trees grow tall, and lawns, almost unheard of forty years ago, luxuriate. These towns are still young but they are no longer raw; even the beer-parlour has changed its nature and gone heterosexual.

Thus far no claims can be made for a distinctive prairie architecture. The two-storey frame white house with green trim has given way to the multi-coloured ranch-type bungalow which hugs the ground, a style no doubt better adapted to a wind-blown environment, less spirited but more harmonious, symbolic of acquiescence rather than defiance.

Eastend is not a typical prairie town. Its attractions are distinctive, not commonplace; they derive in large measure from two sources – physical environment and a highly individualistic citizenry.

The most western-looking (in the movie sense of the term) of Saskatchewan towns, Eastend sits comfortably under great black poplars that look like cottonwoods, in the deep valley of the Frenchman Creek. The Frenchman flows out of Cypress Lake thirty miles west; the walls of the valley that confine it are high and eroded – most spectacularly at Eastend and at Ravenscrag fifteen miles upstream. Viewed from a distance the landscape around Eastend looks infinitely old – so grey and wrinkled and pitted that even the field of forty-bushels-per-acre wheat alongside the road and the oil pumps working in the field can hardly persuade us that all life has not long since been drained from this part of the earth.

Eastend itself is young (incorporated 1914) but its immediate surroundings strengthen the impression of age which the great valley of the Frenchman creates. Near-by Chimney Coulee owes its name to the crumbling stone chimneys marking the sites of cabins built more than a century ago by Métis hunters; and Isaac Cowie, a well-known Hudson's Bay Company trader, built a Company post in the coulee in 1871. The post was destroyed the following year by marauding Blackfoot.

Other relics of the past take us back not decades and centuries in time but aeons. The valley of the Frenchman and its tributary coulees are the happy hunting-grounds of palaeontologists, the resurrection men who bring the past to life by digging up and reassembling its bones. The admirable exhibit of dinosaur bones which occupies the basement of the Eastend school is not, however, the work of a professional palaeontologist but of a local amateur antiquarian, Corky Jones.

Corky Jones came to the Eastend country from England in 1898, many years before the town of Eastend came into being. For several years he rode the range as a cowboy, and took part in the huge round-ups of the 76 and Circle Diamond spreads – the latter American-owned – in the flats of the Frenchman Creek near the present site of the town. The American cattle, he recalls, were mostly Texas longhorns 'that could run like deer. When driven their joints would crack, their hoofs click and horns knock, making quite a clatter.' The Canadian cowboys rode unarmed, the Americans carried six-guns. Most of the American cowboys came from Texas – and there are still some old-timers around Eastend who insist that the wind blows across their part of southern Saskatchewan with a Texas drawl.

Corky Jones was not content to herd cows all his life. He is a man largely self-educated, whose curiosity and passion for knowledge led him first to wide reading and then to intensive searching in his own community for evidences of past life. He is an old man now; he has lived nearly all his adult life far away from the great centres of learning, but his years have been rich and full. He is a prime example of what a man whose only equipment is intellectual curiosity can make of his life.

Surprisingly, Eastend has so far made no attempt to capitalize on its most unusual attraction – it doesn't invite tourists to dig for dinosaurs.

6. Old-Timer

The term 'old-timer' may seem vague to the uninitiated; but in most communities where it is in current use its meaning is in fact precise. The old-timer is the man who has been on the scene from the beginning, or very nearly the beginning, of the life of the community. A man may live to be a hundred or more in Toronto or Montreal but this means nothing, for the life of the city reaches much further back than a century; but if he lives to be a hundred in Estevan or Maple Creek or Whiskey Gap he can count on being stuffed and put in a museum.

In the Canadian west the old-timer is a venerable and venerated figure who is listened to with respect if not with interest and all too often urged to write down his reminiscences. Nine times out of ten the reminiscences turn out to be a series of factual statements about crop and weather conditions from the turn of the century on, which may be of some value and interest to agricultural historians or meteorologists but hardly make exciting reading for the common man. Happily, there are some old-timers who do not assume that remembrance of things past is in itself a guarantee of stimulating writing and conversation. They are men wise enough not to confuse literature with nostalgia, and to know that the literal truth is never good enough for art. They are knowledgeable about the past but they live in the present and do not fear the future.

Such a man is my friend Billy Bock of Eastend, an authentic old-timer who has, no doubt, committed in the course of a long life his fair share of sinful deeds, but never that of boring his auditors.

I first met Billy Bock at Fort Qu'Appelle where for several summers I conducted a course in creative writing for the Saskatchewan Arts Board. Billy, then a puckish white-haired gentleman of seventy-four, had joined the class in the hope, so he told me, of picking up a few hints on how to string words together 'from the mouth of a horse that was in the racket', a statement which in its blend of humility and optimism I found a little disturbing. At our first class meeting I was further disconcerted to find Billy sitting directly in front of me, well in advance of the rest of the students. 'I'm a mite deaf Skipper,' he explained. 'Hope you don't mind me sitting right under the muzzle of the gun?'

He listened with passionate interest to the few feeble volleys I discharged, then hurried off presumably to cash in on whatever tips he thought he had picked up straight from the horse's mouth. But whatever illusions he may have laboured under that opening day about the ability of himself and the class, under my guidance, to produce a round of masterpieces died an early death. A night or two after our first meeting, when I was marking class assignments in a stiflingly hot dormitory compartment full of dead fish-flies and live mosquitoes, I heard Billy's voice vibrating in the farthest reaches of the made-over army hut that housed us – 'Ain't it a shame the poor old Skipper's got to spend a night like this reading all that b.s. we shovelled on to him?'

It was then I realized that Billy had the makings of a first-rate literary critic.

Billy's prose I found characterized by a cavalier disregard of orthodox punctuation, and a phraseology which like a lightning-bolt always illuminated and frequently devastated the object which lay in its path. I still recall with much pleasure his description of a lady whose appearance was not to his taste: 'She had a figure like a busted couch, a voice like the noise produced when a man files a bucksaw, and her face was a plastic surgeon's dream of raw material.'

Billy Bock has been many things in his time – Klondike miner, lumberman, farm labourer, barber, homesteader, Prairie Farm Rehabilitation supervisor, and even Member of Parliament (elected by acclamation for the constituency of Maple Creek in 1927), but it is as a ballad singer that he has won modest fame. Deservedly so, for he is one of the few authentic balladeers singing and composing in a time when the folk-song has been degraded to the point where its original form and significance have been almost completely lost sight of. Billy neither laments nor protests; he tells a story in verse, and in the manner of the ballad singer of old time founds his story on a local incident rich in drama and conflict. Thus the great Eastend flood of 1952, when the Frenchman Creek ran wild and forced the evacuation of the town, had hardly begun to subside before Billy – who had played a major role in the conduct of the evacuation – was celebrating its fury:

> *'Twas the fifteenth of April, and the night was cold,*
> *The lightning was flashing and the thunder rolled.*
> *You could tell by the roar and the spray in the sky,*
> *That the Frenchman River was a-running high. . . .*

> *I met Corky Jones on the Chimney Coulee Trail,*
> *He'd been out putting salt on a dinosaur's tail.*
> *He was humped in the saddle, all covered with mud,*
> *And he said, 'Boys, get ready for a big-time flood.'*

> *The gates in the dam were all opened wide,*
> *She came over the top and around each side.*
> *She kept on rising and she rose some more,*
> *'Twas a mile and a half from shore to shore. . . .*

> *The women and the children they were all afloat,*
> *We gathered five hundred of them up by boat.*
> *We tallied them out and we never lost one,*
> *And herded them over into Shaunavon. . . .*

A year or two later the outbreak of the bitter Eastend Civil War, fought over the issue of water- and sewer-pipe installation, prompted Billy to burst forth once again into song:

> *Eastend was once a happy town where harmony and love*
> *Was busting out at all the seams, and in the trees above*
> *The doves of peace were nesting, there were no signs of strife,*
> *For each man loved his neighbour (and sometimes his*
>   *neighbour's wife).*

> *But a sudden change has come about, storm clouds are in the sky,*
> *Nobody stops to kiss a body, coming through the rye,*
> *Housewives no longer spill the beans across the garden gate,*
> *And each man eyes his neighbour with malice and with hate.*

The concluding stanza of the ballad briskly summarizes the happy outcome of the campaign to modernize the town:

> *But when the votes were counted, slop-pailers met defeat,*
> *And draglines started tearing up our quiet village street.*
> *Now, once more peace and harmony replace the grapes of wrath,*
> *So when next you visit Eastend just stop in and have a bath.*

Perhaps the best of Billy's ballads is one he composed when he was nearly eighty – founded on a story once widely circulated throughout the Saskatchewan-Montana country, but long since forgotten. What gives the ballad a peculiar significance is the degree to which it indirectly communicates a geographical and historical fact – that in the days of the great cattle-spreads the international boundary line had no effective existence; cattlemen looked on the area extending from Swift Current south to the Missouri as a unit – as in fact it was. Slippers, the hero of the ballad, is unaware, it would seem, that he moves back and forth over a boundary line theoretically separating two countries.

The genesis of his ballad Billy explains this way: 'I got to know Slippers pretty well when he was breaking broncs for the Z-X ranch in 1909. (This spread had its headquarters where our town of Eastend is now located.) We used to wonder how he ever got his nickname, and only a few knew what his real name was. He was rather quiet, generally, but under the influence of artificial inspiration in a poker game he promised to reveal the secret of how he was re-christened. He kept his promise, for later when I got him oiled up he told me the story.'

This is Slippers' story, as retold by Billy:

> *I met a lonely cowhand, he was way past his prime,*
> *His stetson hat was faded, and caked with sweat and grime.*
> *His hair was streaked with silver, and I fancied that a tear*
> *Was stealing down his furrowed cheek and dropping in his beer.*
>
> *I sat down there beside him and ordered drinks for two.*
> *I said, 'Tell me the reason why you look so doggone blue?'*
> *Said he, 'You'd hardly understand why I should feel so low,*
> *But I've been behind the eight-ball since thirty years ago.*
>
> *'I used to be top cowhand, I rode the Texas range*
> *From the Panhandle to Lethbridge where it seldom ever rains*
> *And when I hit the Cypress Hills, they used to call me Tex*
> *So I bedded down at Eastend and rode for Z Bar X.*

'I liked to ride the short grass range and watch the dogies grow,
They rustled through the winters when Chinooks took off the
    snow.
This Frenchman River Valley was a range beyond compare,
And when that last round-up is called I hope they plant me there.

'I rode down south to Havre 'bout thirty years ago
To catch up with my gambling – I was well heeled with dough.
I met a black-jack dealer there and sure stuck out my neck –
He busted me by dealing from the bottom of the deck.

'I staggered to a honky-tonk and met the madam there,
All dressed in silk and satin, though most of her was bare.
I told her I was busted and I had no place to stay,
If she'd put me up till morning I'd pay her back some day.

'She grinned and looked me over in a calculating way,
She saw my fifty-dollar boots and said, "All right, O.K.
I have always been a sucker for you cow-punchin' galoots,
You can stick around till morning, but you'll have to leave your
    boots."

'When I awoke next morning my hat and boots were gone,
I was lying in an alley just back of Madam's lawn.
I headed for the livery barn way down on River Street,
When I noticed I was wearing Madam's slippers on my feet.

'I got my horse and saddle, and without my boots and hat
I headed down the valley through the old Milk River flat,
And then struck north to Willow Creek, fed up with hootch and
    sex,
And two days later landed at the welcome Z Bar X.

'I told of my adventures when the punchers asked "How come?"
I said 'twas booze and poker that had put me on the bum.
They smelled the scented slippers still clinging to my feet,
And make remarks that I would be reluctant to repeat.

'The bunkhouse rocked with laughter as I told my dismal tale,
They promptly named me Slippers, and after, without fail,
When brandin' steers or bustin' broncs, no matter where I go,
That name stuck like a sand burr from here to Mexico.

'I've rode for Circle Diamond, T Down, and Turkey Track,
And cracked my slats at rodeos from here to hell and back,

So now you know the reason why I seldom shout and cheer –
It's cause those buzzards changed my name –
LET'S HAVE ANOTHER BEER!'

Since then the Frenchman River flats have undergone a change,
With farmers growing wheat and oats where once was open
    range,
While warm Chinooks in winter still melt the ice and snow,
While down in Manitoba it's forty-two below.

Old Slippers left us years ago, the best of us must die,
No doubt he's bustin' broncos at the round-ups in the sky;
And although his bones are resting down beside the river's
    bend,
I recall the tale he told me in the bar-room at Eastend.

Billy Bock filed claim on a homestead in the Eastend country in 1910. He drove his bride from Gull Lake to the homestead by democrat in mid-January thirty-degrees-below-zero weather over rock-hard open prairie, and spent his wedding night in a crowded stopping-house where privacy was assured the guests by means of strips of rag carpet hung between straw mattresses laid on the floor and spaced about eight feet apart. 'The acoustics of the place,' Billy recalls, 'were excellent.'

The early years on the homestead were difficult (Eastend is situated in one of the drier parts of the dry south-west), but Billy remembers them as a time not of tribulation but of co-operation, when every man was ready to lend a hand to his neighbour in time of need; a time, too, of improvisation, when fractured parts of farm machinery and model-T Fords were held together by barbed wire – and curling-stones were made of pickle pails and chamber-pots filled with cement.

Retired farmers are among the unhappiest and most restless of men, particularly if they move, as they so often do, to a large town or city, or to some far-off spot – down east or the coast – where the physical environment, however attractive to the eye, is alien to the spirit. Billy Bock has been wise enough to move no farther from his farm than to a pleasant back street in his home town. And peace of mind is his because he has carried with him into retirement an avocation which has been a joy to him all the days of his life. 'Often when I have been tempted to blow off some emotional pressure by going on a bender with the boys,' he says, 'or prospecting for romance with the fair sex, I have followed the habit of retiring quietly before I got to the fighting or love-making· stage, and spending the rest of the night just writing stuff.'

Writing stuff – Billy is a contributor to several weekly newspapers – has not been his sole pleasure in retirement. A few years ago he began to experiment in making pottery from Eastend clay; and today his pot shop, as he insists on calling his studio, is a popular point of call with souvenir-hunting Eastend visitors.

Billy Bock has expressed the hope that 'I may have my boots off when Gabriel pipes me from the stage with his celestial horn.' It is unlikely that his wish will be fulfilled. No matter when the horn sounds it will cut Billy off in mid career – foaming in full body (like the Frenchman Creek in flood) rather than 'miserably straggling to an end in sandy deltas'. And this, says Robert Louis Stevenson, at whatever age death overtake a man, is to die young.

7. Hills of Refuge

There are places on earth which cast a permanent and in a sense inexplicable spell over individuals whose association with those places may be intermittent and fleeting. Conversely there are places which, so sentimentalists avow, should powerfully attract us by reason of long and intimate association, but which in fact do nothing of the kind. In my own experience a pilgrimage to the place of my birth excites no emotion in me except possibly a faint repulsion; and a visit to the homestead where I spent what are alleged to be the most formative years of my life (and which I vowed passionately I would some day go back to and live on forever) starts no ghosts walking. The modest plot of land I now call home has now the strongest claim on my affections, but the region which excites the most powerful emotions and promotes the most extravagant dreams has never been a part of my daily life. It is not likely, however, that the attraction which the Cypress Hills exert upon me derives from unfamiliarity; I am satisfied that had I grown up among those Hills they would be dearer to me than any other part of earth.

They are kindly sheltering hills – slopes thick with poplar and lodge-pole pine and furrowed deep by densely wooded coulees which afford protection to man and beast against winter's cold and summer's heat. There are trails in these hills of a kind rare in Saskatchewan; winding up through meadow and forest and across lofty uplands they avoid the monotony which in the north woods and on the open prairie is inescapable and often oppressive. True, coast dwellers and down-easterners are likely to be contemptuous of such water attractions as the region has to offer. Cypress Lake, lying among bare brown hills twelve miles south of the provincial park, covers an area of some thirty square miles; it is rich in bird life and harbours some pickerel, but it is beyond question smelly, and visitors accustomed to lakes hedged about by substantial vegetation are likely to be appalled by its starkness. Cypress Lake is a body of water all right, but one naked and unadorned. The provincial park proper encloses a diminutive pond which a New Zealand friend of mine, accustomed to using the Pacific Ocean as a paddling-pool, unkindly describes as a stagnant prairie slough held in place by a ten-foot dike; and a few sluggish creeks wander here and there through the hills. Tourist information booklets affirm that the creeks are full of trout; and men whose probity is – I think – beyond question tell me they have caught their legal limit within an hour of making the first cast.

In most Saskatchewan 'mountain' regions the uprising above the level of the surrounding plain forms a more or less unified and coherent mass, but the Cypress Hills are an exception. They are formed of a grouping of buttes, plateaus, benches, and ridges which cover an area of just over one thousand square miles and rise to a height of slightly under five thousand feet – the highest point of land in Canada between Labrador and the Rockies. The region is immensely rich in herbage as well as trees, for it receives, on the average, four inches more rainfall per annum than the surrounding plains, and it lies within the Chinook belt. These are the factors that help to make the Cypress Hills the best ranching country in Saskatchewan.

The flora and fauna of the Hills are both indigenous and exotic. All the common prairie flowers are here, and some less common, including a wild delphinium which in early summer turns the green hill-sides into a blue and purple blaze; in addition – and this explains the lure of the region for botanists, zoologists, and entomologists – the Hills abound in specimens of animal and vegetable life normally found four to six hundred miles farther south. No explanation is entirely satisfactory to account for the existence in the Hills of some fifty species of flora and fauna not to be found elsewhere in Canada – including the subtropical Yucca grass, several varieties of cactus, and such extravagantly un-Canadian creatures as horned toads, hog-nosed vipers, kangaroo rats, scorpions, and relatives thereof known as solpegids. (Even the lodge-pole pine doesn't grow naturally elsewhere for several hundred miles.) The commonest explanation of these phenomena, and fortunately the one easiest for the lay mind to grasp, is that in the pre-Ice Age the plains country enjoyed a climate fostering the growth of semitropical forms of life; and that at least a few of these flora and fauna survived high up in the Hills at a time when the rest of the prairie was submerged beneath the ice-cap. Most of the exotic plants and animals are to be found today not in the Hills proper but on their arid southern slopes and in the valley of the Frenchman Creek; and it is assumed that having survived the Ice Age at a high altitude they have crept down by degrees, following the retreat of the ice-cap, to drier, hotter areas.

Familiar forms of wild animal life also flourish in the Hills. Fine herds of antelope – a glorious sight on the skyline of a far-off ridge or hill – roam the south-west corner of Saskatchewan, all the way from the border north into the country of the Great Sandhills – an eerie dishevelled land lying between Maple Creek and the South Saskatchewan River where trails peter out in a wilderness of shifting dunes and sagebrush. In the hunting season, so a game warden assured me, it is possible to stand on a high point at the edge of the Cypress Hills Provincial Park and see herds of antelope streaming across the plains towards the Park, seeking refuge from the guns of those whose pleasure it is to destroy, in the name of sport, one of the most harmless and beautiful of earth's creatures.

French fur-traders, mistaking the fine stands of lodge-pole pine for cypress, gave the Hills their name. First official notice of the Hills was taken by Captain John Palliser in 1859, who found them 'a perfect oasis in the desert we have travelled' – the desert being the western part of what was later called the Palliser Triangle, a semi-arid area which Palliser mistakenly considered unfit for cultivation. (The base of the Palliser Triangle extends roughly from Emerson, Manitoba, to the foothills of the Rockies, with its apex fixed about two hundred miles north on the Alberta-Saskatchewan boundary.) Oddly enough the Hills do not appear to have been permanently occupied at any time by any Indian tribe or combination of tribes – this in spite of excellent pasture, a wide variety of game, and an abundance of food and water. The Hills seem at times to have constituted a buffer between the tribes that swirled restlessly about its base, at other times a Debateable Ground where war parties sought to exterminate one another. The Assiniboine had, perhaps, the strongest claim to possession of the Hills; they wintered in Medicine Lodge, the great coulee at the western end, and according to Commissioner Irvine of the North West Mounted Police 'always looked on the Cypress Hills as their home'. But their hold was at best a tenuous one; and until the arrival of the Police no Indian or white man could count himself safe within the region.

Métis hunters built winter camps in Chimney Coulee at the eastern end of the Hills, and Isaac Cowie operated a Hudson's Bay Company Post near by. There too came the independent fur-traders with their rotten whiskey, but neither Cowie nor they stayed any length of time. Cowie in fact abandoned his post after a single year; he was hardly out of sight before Blackfoot raiders swooped down on the post, killed nine Assiniboine whom they caught grubbing about in the debris, and burned the post to the ground. A well-known trader named Abel Farwell then built a post in the vicinity for the T.C. Power Company trading out of Fort Benton, Montana; but he, too, moved out following the most tragic episode in the blood-stained history of the Cypress Hills, and one directly responsible for the immediate formation of the North West Mounted Police.

To attempt to reconstruct a scene of violence from the evidence of the participants is frequently to invite confusion. Two thousand fighting men survived the Battle of the Little Big Horn, and many of them were subsequently interviewed, yet to this day there is no real agreement about what happened to Custer. Similarly, nearly every white man who played a part in the Cypress Hills massacre later told his story, but no two stories agree in detail and in some the discrepancies are wide indeed. But the broad outlines of the tragedy appear clear enough.

In the late spring of 1873 a party of wolfers were robbed of their horses near Fort Benton, Montana. Thirteen of the wolfers, including several French and Anglo-Canadians, rode north into the Cypress Hills, acting on the unwarranted assumption that a band of Assiniboine under Chief Little Soldier, then camped near Abel Farwell's post, were responsible for the theft. It was at this point that a subsidiary actor, whose role was none the less to be a significant one, makes his appearance. George Hammond, an unsavoury loafer, had for some time been hanging around Farwell's post helping Farwell sell whiskey to the Indians. Hammond was a good friend of John Evans, the leader of the wolfers. A few days prior to the arrival of the wolfers at Farwell's post, an Indian belonging to Little Soldier's band had stolen Hammond's horse. Hammond got the horse back, but at the time of the wolfers' arrival his feelings towards the Indians were definitely hostile.

The wolfers did not find their horses nor did they find any evidence to connect Little Soldier's band with the theft. (The horses were, in fact, never recovered.) All might have been well had not the wolfers got drunk on Abel Farwell's whiskey, and had not an Indian stolen George Hammond's horse for a second time.

Mad with rage and whiskey, Hammond snatched up a rifle and at once started for Little Soldier's camp. Farwell, the trader, who was naturally anxious for the sake of his business to preserve the peace, went with Hammond to act as intermediary and interpreter. Between Hammond and Little Soldier – the chief too was drunk – a furious argument quickly developed. Farwell, who knew little of the Assiniboine tongue, almost at once lost the thread of things – and with it all chance of successfully playing the role of peacemaker.

So far the course of events is fairly clear; but what happened to bring about the firing of the first shot no one can say. The wolfers had come up to lend their support to Hammond, and both sides were spoiling for a fight – the Indians because they hated the white men who had systematically corrupted them with bad whiskey, the wolfers because they still honestly believed that the Indians had stolen their property. (It should be remembered that these wolfers belonged to a frontier society which punished horse-stealing – whatever the colour of the offender – with summary lynching.) But the exchange, the word, the gesture that precipitated the catastrophe cannot be known.

Someone fired. The wolfers retreated, took cover behind a cutbank. The term 'massacre' is entirely appropriate to describe the action that followed. The wolfers were crack shots, armed with repeating Henry rifles. The Indians carried ancient muzzleloaders, ineffective except at close range. Three times, with almost suicidal bravery, the Indians charged. From behind cover of the cutbank the wolfers shot into the oncoming mob with their repeating rifles and did not miss. When the slaughter was ended, one wolfer lay dead, and thirty Indians. Probably twice that many Indians were wounded. According to Abel Farwell the wolfers celebrated their victory by getting drunk all over again, then raided the Indian camp, now deserted by all except women and children, and enjoyed an orgy of looting and rape. But Farwell, as various stories attributed to him suggest, had a pulp-magazine mind.

The wolfers sobered up, more or less, and gave their dead companion a hero's send-off by burying him under the floor of a near-by trading-post owned by one Moses Solomon, and then setting fire to the post. When the funeral pyre was well alight they rode off west to look for their horses among the Blood Indians.

As soon as news of the massacre, inevitably exaggerated in transmission, reached eastern Canada there was an immediate public outcry for vengeance upon the perpetrators. A good deal of the indignation felt by easterners stemmed not so much from pro-Indian as anti-American sentiment; the wolfers had in effect 'invaded' Canada – this at a time when the Fenian scare had not entirely subsided – and the invasion rather than the actual killing of Indians was their essential and unpardonable crime. On the American side of the line, public opinion, distorted by violent anti-British and anti-Indian sentiment, was all on the side of the wolfers; and attempts to extradite the offenders from Fort Benton the following year precipitated a series of anti-British demonstrations led by a prominent Fenian agitator, 'Colonel' J. J. Donnelly.

The extradition proceedings failed, in part because of Abel Farwell's hopelessly muddled and inconsistent testimony. The wolfers were accordingly discharged, and Colonel Macleod of the Mounted Police, who had come to Fort Benton to press the proceedings on behalf of the Canadian government, was himself arrested on a charge of having falsely and maliciously accused innocent men of criminal acts. He was released in time to escape the wild celebrations touched off all through Montana by news of the dropping of the extradition proceedings. In Benton the wolfers were honoured with a torchlight parade supplemented by an indoor reception in a hall decorated with murals showing the British lion in full flight with the American eagle twisting his tail. Colonel Donnelly, who was in excellent voice, gave an hour-long report on the English oppression of Ireland.

Three of the wolfers were later arrested in Canada and tried in Winnipeg on a charge of murder. Public hostility towards the accused men was intense but the presiding judge, Chief Justice Wood, without hesitation acquitted them. Abel Farwell's testimony was again at times muddled, at others clearly perjured: and three Indians summonsed to appear as witnesses for the prosecution actually testified for the defence.

Whether the wolfers were in fact guilty of perpetrating an act of senseless violence or whether, as most Americans believed, they were simply run-of-the-mill frontiersmen who, when on an entirely legitimate errand defended themselves heroically against a murderous attack, is in the light of history of small importance. What is important is that Canadian public opinion made it clear that conditions which were accepted as commonplaces of American frontier life, including the corruption and frequently wholesale slaughter of Indians, would not be tolerated in the Canadian west.

Happily the action taken to ensure the reign of law on the prairies was swift and decisive. Three months after the Cypress Hills massacre the Canadian Parliament approved the establishment of the North West Mounted Police.

The exact locale of the massacre is a matter of dispute among local antiquarians, but those of us who derive a melancholy pleasure from contemplating scenes of man's inhumanity to man will doubtless derive some satisfaction from seeking out the Historic Sites Board sign which marks the spot where Abel Farwell's trading-post stood. From that post George Hammond, full of righteous wrath and rot-gut whiskey, went forth to the fatal interview with Chief Little Soldier.

Cypress Hills Provincial Park lies high up in the hills, fifty-odd miles north-west of Eastend and twenty-five miles south of the Trans-Canada Highway. The twin ponds named, with neither imagination nor irony, Loch Lomond and Loch Leven (Loch Lomond has no water in it) are rimmed by private cottages. The public amenities, including cabins and a swimming-pool, are huddled at one end of Loch Leven, and, as is true of such amenities in most Saskatchewan provincial parks, suffer grievously from lack of elbow room. Happily, the campsites – which reach deep into the pine woods and spread along the slope of a valley flooded by beavers and filled with dead ghostly trees – are ample and admirably provided with the orthodox campsite conveniences. It is only the tourist who travels without camping equipment and seeks a roof over his head for a night or a week who is almost sure to be turned empty away. Unless of course he has made his reservations far in advance.

The trails for walking and riding are numerous and all of them delightful; and for golfers there is a sporting nine-hole course laid out on top of the world – a course to delight the eye and banish dull care until one tees off and lands in the buffalo grass bordering the appallingly narrow fairways. Buffalo grass is thick and long and tough; playing out of it a work, not of art, but of excavation, the appropriate implement a shovel. Here too the visitor from other lands or parts of Canada encounters for the first time another characteristic feature of the smaller prairie golf courses besides buffalo grass – the sand green. The sand green is quite literally what the name implies, except of course that it isn't green. A circular excavation a few inches deep and, in the eye of an imprecise golfer like myself, about the diameter of a dinner plate is made in the prairie sod and filled in with sand. The cup is placed in or near the centre of the sand circle. The green is small and hard to find, but when he reaches it the veriest duffer can be reasonably sure of being down in not more than two putts. Particularly if he has studied the art of dragging the green.

Dragging the green, an operation intended to remove all imperfections in the sand surface created by the feet of golfers who have just holed out, is done with a coconut doormat attached to a broom handle. (There is a doormat at every green.) In addition to levelling off bumps and filling hollows the skilful dragger is able, through pressures applied at the right points, to draw an almost imperceptible groove in the sand extending from his ball to the cup. He will be further aided in sinking his putt by the slope of the green, which, since dragging is done *away* from the cup, tends nearly always to be downhill towards the centre. On some sand greens the downhill slope is so pronounced that balls occasionally roll from the edge of the green into the cup of their own accord.

Golf on a sand-greens course – and this is particularly true of Cypress Hills – partakes of the nature of target practice. The man who shoots straight and true down a narrow fairway towards a distant circular target centred by a bull's-eye cup is reasonably sure of a par or better; but the man who strays ever so little off the straight line and lands in the rough will probably never get out. I myself, being a strong hitter with a confused sense of direction, have spent most of my golfing life in assorted roughs, but there is none other in my experience of resistant power comparable to Cypress Hills buffalo grass. It is not only thick and tough and long and tangled – it is also elastic. It is, in fact, the only rough I know of from which a club, when brought down with sickening violence in the general vicinity of the ball, actually rebounds.

Fort Walsh, built by the Mounties in 1875, can be reached from the provincial park by the loveliest road in Saskatchewan – in actual fact a trail winding for ten or twelve miles through pleasant pastoral countryside, then across a magnificent valley floor where great herds of whitefaces graze in lush green fields, thence through a rancher's yard, up a steep valley wall, across a plateau, and down into a second narrow valley – that of the Battle Creek. Here, close to the creek, stands Fort Walsh. Of the original post nothing survives except a pair of cannons, astride which small boys delight to have their pictures taken. A good deal of building has been carried out in recent years, but since the Fort has been in constant use as a horse-training centre it is happily free from the combined museum-and-good-housekeeping look which characterizes most reconstructions.

From 1875 to 1883 the young men of Fort Walsh, working in close co-operation with their fellows at Wood Mountain, maintained control over the seemingly countless refugee bands that roamed the Hills, and in the evil times following the annihilation of the buffalo helped to keep them alive by sacrificing a generous share of their own none too plentiful rations. They terrorized whiskey-traders and horse-thieves, tracked down an occasional murderer, and rode hundreds of miles each week on patrol. To avoid boredom they made pets of wild animals and birds (of these Constable Hardy's Canada goose, which paraded with the men and did sentry duty all night, was the best-known and – to late returnees hoping to slip past the sentry-box unnoticed – the most obnoxious); they staged theatricals in the mess-hall; played cricket, football, and tennis; danced in one or another of the two dance-halls operating in the Métis settlement just outside the Fort limits; made love to such complaisant damsels, mostly Indian and Métis, as came within their purview (the long arm of the law was not extended to embrace malefactors only) – and sometimes married them. And when the term of their service was up many of the young men either enlisted for a second term or settled somewhere among the Hills, which had cast over them a spell that no recollections of clear streams and green pastures in far-off places could ever break.

Some of the policemen died at Fort Walsh – mostly of typhoid. Two drowned in the creek flowing past the Fort. Only one met a violent death. Constable Marmaduke Graeburn was ambushed and shot, presumably by a disgruntled Indian. The little grave-yard on the valley slope overlooking Fort Walsh harbours their dust; and few of them, one suspects, would have preferred another burial place. Heroes belong to that part of earth which their deeds have made memorable.

The spell of the Cypress Hills depends on a variety of elements. They are hills of refuge even today – a sure and cool retreat from the burning plains; they surprise and comfort, and they reassure. And here, perhaps more readily than anywhere else in Saskatchewan with the exception of Batoche, it is possible to establish contact with the past, to share vicariously actions of a bygone day which, although trivial in immediate scope and action, were as far-reaching in their consequences as deeds cast in the epic scale, and reflect just as truly a grandeur of the human spirit. The horn of Roland never sounded in the valley of the Frenchman Creek, but Roland and Oliver, under different and more prosaic names, rode the Hills. Unfortunately their deeds have been for the most part celebrated by indifferent prose-writers rather than great poets.

The Cypress Hills stretch away westward into Alberta to end as abruptly as they rise. For the traveller who is satisfied merely to come out *some*where there are marvellous twisting trails to follow on both the Saskatchewan and Alberta sides of the line, and unexpected beauty spots to explore that lie far from the main roads. But however he makes his way out of the Hills he should be sure to visit Maple Creek.

Maple Creek lies twenty miles north of the Cypress Hills. It is the last town in Saskatchewan near the Trans-Canada Highway and one of the pleasantest in the west. Spacious old red-brick houses which might have been lifted out of any one of a hundred Ontario villages dream away their declining years, not under feathery elms but under great false cottonwoods (black poplar).

The cottonwood is no doubt an annoyance to housewives, for in the springtime it litters yards and porches with white fluff; but to the western-fiction or movie fan it is a tree as sacred as the laurel was to the ancients – though for different reasons. Old-time lynching parties invariably hanged rustlers and badmen from a convenient cottonwood; and beneath cottonwood boughs the hero and heroine of the traditional Western held hands and – in the more risqué sequences – exchanged a chaste kiss or two before riding off together in the moonlight.

There are modern ranch houses too in Maple Creek, and bungalows, and even a few shacks; but the red-brick houses set the tone and pace of life – a pace belonging to a more spacious and leisured age than ours. The frenetic booster spirit finds no place here; Maple Creek does not, thank God, proclaim itself the capital of anything nor the gateway to anywhere; nor does it claim for itself those alleged western virtues – friendliness, hospitality, forthrightness, and the like – which, if they actually do exist in the west in greater abundance than elsewhere, should none the less be left to outsiders to extol.

Part of the charm of the town derives from its contradictions and contrasts: red-brick houses under cottonwoods; a cowboy – the real thing, not the drugstore variety – in high-heeled boots and blue-jeans strolling down the main street arm-in-arm with a girl wearing a dress bought not out of a mail-order catalogue but a big-city boutique; sombreroed, bewhiskered old-timers riding brand-new convertibles; adjoining show-windows featuring saddles and Hondas; and a stock-car-racing handbill side by side in the same window with a black-bordered card announcing the death of a village ancient and urging friends to 'please accept this intimation as your invitation to attend the obsequies.'

Maple Creek might with some justice call itself the cow capital of Saskatchewan for it is surrounded by some of the finest ranching country in the west, and the Cypress Hills rise almost at its back door. But instead of wasting their spare time thinking up banal slogans to advertise the town the citizens of Maple Creek wisely spend it gardening. (The great danger inherent in booster-ism is that the boosters may, through repetition, come to believe their own propaganda, to hold that quantity does in fact equal quality, and that figures, whether of bust measurements or factory output, alone are certain good.) The gardens of Maple Creek, next to the red-brick houses, are the greatest attraction the town

has to offer. Like the houses they surround, the gardens are mar-
vellously reminiscent of a bygone day. The flowers are mostly of
the kind we denominate old-fashioned; mignonette is a favourite,
and hollyhocks grow madly everywhere – roof-high and a foot in
diameter. Although I have never been able to grow them, I have
always had a feeling for hollyhocks – they evoke so wonderfully
the atmosphere of an early Victorian world populated by elderly
tea-drinking Trollopian clergymen, and young ladies strolling
sedately under parasols, and anxious doting mothers fluttering on
the sidelines, and old ladies puttering about among the roses in
sunbonnets and gauntlets, and underlings who know their place
and are content to keep it without fussing. And if instead of an
elderly lady in sunbonnet and gauntlets there should appear in
the garden – and this happens often in Maple Creek – a brown
young thing in shorts and halter, I do not complain.

A man might do worse than retire to Maple Creek and grow
hollyhocks.

8. Queen of the Plains

No cities with the possible exception of Sodom and Gomorrah have ever been founded in less congenial physical surroundings than Regina, the Queen City of Saskatchewan. On every side the plains unroll without a wrinkle to the horizon; no trees grow anywhere except those planted by man and assiduously tended thereafter; the soil on which the city is built is a gumbo clay that, when wet, adheres to whatever it touches with the tenacity of molasses, so that the man who walks abroad in it in wet weather soon finds himself carrying an acre or two of soil on each foot. (It has been estimated that before the city streets were paved more rubbers were lost in Regina per annum than in all the rest of Canada – this in spite of a scanty average rainfall and ground frozen solid about six months of the year.) In dry weather the gumbo, rich and heavy though it may be as soils go, rises effortlessly into the skies. Regina's dust-storms in number and density can easily match those of any other part of the west.

The natural water supplies of Regina's earth are as scanty as those cast down by heaven. Regina was built on a sluggish stream originally called by the white man Pile o' Bones – later for obvious aesthetic reasons re-christened officially by its Indian name, Wascana, which means much the same thing but sounds better. Pile o' Bones Creek was so called because of the alleged existence somewhere along its banks of an enormous pile of buffalo bones. The precise location of the pile is not known, and accounts of its size and significance vary widely. The obvious explanation of its existence is that it was an accumulation of buffalo bones beside a favourite camping-ground of Indian and Métis hunters. Year after year the hunters pitched their tents beside the running waters of the creek, rode out to slaughter the buffalo, and returned with their kill to the camp where the women made pemmican and jerky of the buffalo flesh, tanned the hides, and added the bones to the pile that had accumulated for years on the outskirts of the camp. A Saskatchewan pioneer, Dr. A. E. Porter, writing sixty years after the event, says he saw the pile in 1878 when 'it was 30 or 40 feet high . . . and covered two or more acres of ground.' According to Dr. Porter the pile marked the site where a peace pact had been agreed upon among several Indian tribes, hence it had acquired in Indian lore a semi-religious significance.

Time possibly magnified for Dr. Porter the size of the pile; reliable observers reported in 1883 no more than two or three cartloads at the spot. Three years later the last bone had disappeared from the banks of the Wascana (to be made into fertilizer in Minneapolis), and there was nothing to mark the site of the original pile.

The choice of a creek-crossing in the midst of desolate, featureless prairie – one of the bleakest spots in the whole west (with the beautiful well-watered Qu'Appelle Valley lying only a few miles north) – as the site of the new capital of the Northwest Territories has always been a puzzle to geographers and historians. In favour of the site was the fact that it occupied a position central to the southern plains region; that it was on the line surveyed for the C.P.R.; and that building a city on the flat was cheaper and easier than building it in a valley or on a hill-side. But the possibility of certain influential individuals who had large holdings in prairie real estate being able to direct the pattern of development cannot be entirely discounted. The role played in the selection of the Regina site by Edgar Dewdney, one-time Commissioner of Indian Affairs and in the crucial year 1882 Lieutenant-Governor of the Northwest Territories, is at best ambiguous. Dewdney – who sported the finest set of Dundreary whiskers west of Ontario – always had a keen eye for the main chance. He owned 480 acres of land immediately adjacent to the spot pin-pointed as the site of the new capital of the Northwest Territories, and he was one of Sir John A. Macdonald's favourite subordinates.

Opposition to the impending official choice of Regina as capital of the Territories was vociferous and embittered. An editorial comment in the Manitoba *Free Press* (which naturally advocated Winnipeg as the logical choice) is typical:

> That Pile of Bones lacks every one of the essentials for a city, or even a modest market town – wood, water, drainage facilities, a surrounding agricultural country – is a fact which no amount of booming will remove. . . . At the present moment the Creek is not more than 12 inches deep. . . . Every stick of wood for fire or building purposes will have to be brought in by railroad or dragged a distance of from 15 to 20 miles. . . . It may be trumpeted and boomed without end [but] having no solid basis, it will topple to pieces like a house of sand.

The following year (1883) Regina found its voice and advocate in Nicholas Flood Davin, editor of the newly founded Regina *Leader* and one of the most personable and forceful of western editors. These old-time editors were an impressive lot who gave real significance to the hackneyed and often meaningless phrase 'power of the press'. Davin, Patrick Gammon Laurie of the old Battleford *Herald*, Frank Oliver of the Edmonton *Bulletin*, a little later John Dafoe of the *Winnipeg Free Press*, were giants in the land – literate, individualistic, pugnacious, subservient to no one. Of them all Nicholas Flood Davin was the most colourful and, with the exception of John Dafoe, the most talented. Davin was a tall, handsome Limerick Irishman. He had the gift of the gab, he believed passionately in Canadian nationhood within the British Empire at a time when Goldwin Smith was blandly proclaiming the inevitability and desirability of annexation to the United States, and he trumpeted his views first in the *Leader* and later in the House of Commons to which he was elected as Conservative member for West Assiniboia in 1887. (The Northwest Territories had been granted representation in the Dominion Parliament a year earlier.)

Davin was inevitably the champion of Regina as capital of the Northwest Territories against the bitter slurs of every other settlement west of Ontario, but his defence, it must be admitted, consisted mainly of heaping scorn and obloquy on his opponents rather than answering their criticisms – a practice which he carried over into his political life. 'Arch-hypocrite' and 'political Pharisee' were a few of the milder epithets he applied to his Liberal opponent in the election of 1887; his opponent's supporters he described as 'whiskey-inspired ribald hucksters of calumny' and 'malignant spirits of a baffled and disorganized faction'.

Davin, as was far commoner among public men one hundred years ago than now, wrote verses which he did not hesitate to publish and in which he obviously took great pride. Most of his odes, elegies, and sonnets are feeble imitations, liberally sprinkled with stale classical tags, of existing models; but occasionally he was goaded into replying to attacks on his beloved town of Regina in stanzas worthy of a minor-league Pope – as when a versifier in the Winnipeg *Times* forecast the fate of Regina in a poem headed *Pile of Bones* which began:

> *'What mounds are these, carefully ploughed around?*
> *Some hunter's grave or Indian burial ground?'*
> *'Not so my friend – some twenty years gone by,*
> *A town sprang up right here where you and I*
> *Now stand, which first as Pile of Bones was known –'*

To which Davin replied:

> *A pleasant city on a boundless plain,*
> *Around rich land where peace and plenty reign;*
> *A legal camp, the province wisdom's home,*
> *A rich cathedral, learning's splendid dome;*
> *A teeming mart, wide streets, broad squares, bright flowers,*
> *A marble figure whence a fountain showers –*
> *What city's this? A gentle princess, famed*
> *For happy genius, it Regina named.*

> *Its youth – though born beneath a happy star –*
> *Was stormy, and each cur, from near and far,*
> *Barked at the town; each ribald loudly talked;*
> *Hirelings – projectors whose vile plans were balked.*
> *They lied; they swore; loud was the ceaseless bray;*
> *Reginans smiled – Regina held her way,*
> *The while traducers perished one by one,*
> *And fate o'ertook each guilty mother's son.*
> *Failing to bleed the tenderfoot they bled*
> *Themselves, or like their sires by hempen thread*
> *Expired; and Winnipeg the city where*
> *They lived and died, soon perished like a pear*
> *That had the yellows . . .*

In the *Leader* Davin once reported that 'a man in St. Louis who had been drunk for 20 years died within a few hours of sobering up. What a terrible lesson to those who are thinking of sobering up.' Davin himself took the lesson to heart. None the less he died in 1901 by his own hand, aged only fifty-nine.

For Regina the years of infancy were even harder than for most early prairie settlements. A poor water supply, inadequate sanitation, acres of mud whenever a shower fell and drought and dust the rest of the time, poor crops, economic stagnation – such were the afflictions Regina was called upon to endure in the closing years of the century. But from the beginning the town boasted a stable element – a civil service. Let all else perish, but the work of government must go on. It is probable too that many of the first settlers in the new town were defiantly determined to prove the critics of Regina wrong; to demonstrate, at whatever cost, that a huddle of frame buildings standing naked on a naked plain could in time be nurtured and shaped into a fair city. With this end in view – and to provide themselves with a water supply – they dammed Wascana Creek and so created a lake which today forms the central part of one of the most unusual and attractive park developments in western Canada and has called down on the heads of its makers the blessing of all who have come after them.

The tide of fortune turned with the birth of a new century. Rains fell, crops grew tall and heavy, and settlers poured in from east and west and south to claim the rich lands of the vast expanse of prairie now known as the Regina plains. Regina itself boomed as a distribution centre – and always it had that hard core of government employees that was the city's real assurance of permanence to fall back on if need be. In 1911 the Legislative Building was completed – domed Government Gothic no better or worse architecturally than a hundred like it scattered all over the North American continent, but deriving an added dignity from the amplitude of its setting in a reclaimed cow pasture on the south side of Wascana Lake. Today the one-time cow pasture is a delightfully landscaped park. The floral displays around the Legislative Building are, in their variety and jungle-like luxuriance, another obvious manifestation of that defiant spirit which challenged the view that Regina could grow nothing but cactus and sage-brush – both of them stunted.

The province of Saskatchewan was created in 1905 with Regina as its capital. Thereafter for nearly forty years the Liberal party, except for one brief interval, ruled the legislature. But the election in 1944 of the first socialist government in Canada, the Co-operative Commonwealth Federation, came as no surprise to those familiar with the temperament and mentality of the Saskatchewan voter. If radical political experiments were to be made anywhere in Canada Saskatchewan was the obvious place for them.

Since 1944 the head-on collisions between socialist and private-enterprise philosophies have made the Saskatchewan political front the hottest in the west, the gladiatorial combats in the legislative arena easily surpassing in verbal ferocity anything that Saskatchewan's sister provinces have so far been able to come up with.

Regina was the focal point of national interest for the first time in November 1885, when Louis Riel was hanged there for treason; for the second time in June 1912, when a cyclone – a rarity in Saskatchewan – ripped through the city, killing twenty-eight people and injuring two hundred; and for the third time in the mid-depression year of 1935 when the Dominion government made the city the point *not* to be passed by several thousand strikers from the labour camps of British Columbia who were on their way to Ottawa to appeal for more government relief. An ill-advised attempt on the part of the R.C.M.P. to arrest the leaders of the striking workers precipitated a riot, with the stones, bricks, and clubs of the strikers matched against the tear-gas and occasional gunfire – shots fired high – of the police. One man was killed, hundreds were injured, enormous damage was done to property – and nothing was resolved. The Regina riot, and that precipitated a little earlier in Estevan when police broke up a parade of striking miners (three miners were cut down by gunfire), are a part of Saskatchewan history which most of us would like to blot out of memory.

Regina's growth – impressive since the end of the Second World War – has precipitated a decline in the fortunes of a sister city which once dreamed of being the dominant industrial and distribution centre of southern Saskatchewan. Moose Jaw, forty miles west of Regina, huddles in a setting of tangled ravines and creeks, unable to escape – even in bright sunlight – the long shadows cast by the Queen City of the Plains; doomed, it would seem, to be no more than a subsidiary distribution centre for Regina. Moose Jaw enjoyed a brief gaudy hour in the twenties when it was in some ways the most vital and colourful city in the west – although the ways were hardly a guarantee of future growth. The town, located at the end of what was called the Soo line running from Minneapolis, provided, so it was alleged, a hideout for Roaring Twenties gangsters who had made Chicago and other cities convenient to the Soo line too hot to hold them. In the same purple period Moose Jaw enjoyed its share of the bootleg-whiskey trade when fortunes were made – and a few people killed – running booze across the line into the parched Dakotas. The gaudiest hour of all came towards the end of the decade when the Ku Klux Klan, which at one time claimed a membership of forty thousand in Saskatchewan, moved up from the States and made Moose Jaw its headquarters. Since there were few Negroes in Saskatchewan the Klan directed its hate against Roman Catholics. 'Know what those bastards did?' I heard an old-timer declare. 'They took some tough old pros off of River Street, dressed them up to look like nuns and turned them loose in the hotels to make pick-ups!'

The end of the twenties marked the end of Moose Jaw's boom days. In recent years industries have moved out, the population has diminished. Artificial government-provided stimulants will no doubt keep the town alive; but the elementary truth appears to be that there is no place in southern Saskatchewan where two full-blown cities can survive and flourish only forty miles apart.

The issuing in 1919 to a Regina resident, R. J. Groome, of the first Canadian commercial flying licence was historically appropriate, for it was near Regina, in the village of Balgonie fifteen miles east, that experiments carried out by the local blacksmith led to the first airplane flight in Canada made with a Canada-built engine. William Wallace Gibson was a Scot whose father pioneered in the Wolseley district with Chief Piapot's Indians for neighbours; and it was on the homestead that young Willie first showed a penchant for soaring aloft – the Indians honouring him for his high-jumping exploits with the name of Jumping Deer. Here, too, his enthusiastic experiments in flying resulted in the first tragedy in Canadian air-transport history: a basket containing nine gophers which he sent aloft attached to a seven-foot kite broke away from the kite and crashed, killing all the passengers aboard. (Willie, uncannily anticipating modern techniques, conducted a thorough inquiry into the cause of the crash and discovered that one of the passengers had chewed through the string attaching the basket to the kite.)

Years later in his Balgonie smithy Gibson experimented with small model planes that actually flew, and worked on an engine which he was confident would some day carry him aloft. In 1910, the year following the first British Empire flight, made by McCurdy in Cape Breton, Gibson, then living in Victoria, flew a plane equipped with his own engine, and thus triumphantly vindicated the experiments he had begun several years before in a Saskatchewan village.

From the air Regina looks like a cardboard cut-out set up in the middle of a multicoloured cosmic-scaled billiard table. Nearly everything that Regina is, with the exception of the gumbo soil on which it stands, is man-created; and the full measure of the achievement of its citizens cannot properly be understood unless this fact is borne constantly in mind. In one respect only did the original city-fathers – many of whom must have held substantial interests in real estate – plan badly. In order to make available as much land as possible for sale they laid out meanly narrow streets in what was to be the business section, and in the residential areas pushed houses close together on meanly narrow lots. So it is that modern downtown Regina is denied the elegance which is the concomitant of spaciousness; the main business section is pinched, characterless – without a single street of the amplitude befitting the dignity of a capital city.

The public buildings of Regina are in several instances impressive, the pride of them all being the Saskatchewan Power Corporation Building, a splendid example of imaginative office-block construction. For elegance of design the S.P.C. Building can hardly be surpassed anywhere in Canada; in the delicately curved flawlessly balanced front, architecture flows into poetry. Near by stands the Hotel Saskatchewan – stolid, dignified, massive, by contrast with its elegant neighbour a bit dowdy and old-fashioned, but already acquiring something of the attraction of a period piece. I find in railroad hotels certain charms not shared by more up-to-date hostelries – not the least of these being their seeming durability. They are among the few structures in western Canadian cities which look as if they had been built to last for at least a century.

North of the Legislative Building, near the intersection of Albert Street and College Avenue, stands in spacious grounds the Saskatchewan Museum of Natural History, architecturally uninspired but so furnished as to provide for him who troubles to look inside a painless and fascinating tour of the chief regions of Saskatchewan. The habitat display cases are designed with taste and an eye for accuracy; they are three-dimensional, thus creating for the observer the illusion of being actually present on the scene displayed. In an hour or two at the Museum it is possible for the visitor to form a distinct impression of terrains as varied as those of the Cypress Hills, the Qu'Appelle Valley, Lac La Ronge, Meadow Lake, and a dozen more, and of the birds and beasts that inhabit them. It is probably true to say that an hour so spent would provide the tourist ignorant of Saskatchewan with more basic information about the province than he is ever likely to get from the conventional advertising literature available at every tourist information booth.

The R.C.M.P. Barracks, an elaborate police-training establishment on the western fringe of the city, dating from 1882, draws many visitors, some of whom are disappointed to find that recruits are now trained to handle high-powered auto cruisers rather than mettlesome horses. But the attractions of the Barracks are still numerous. They include any number of highly photogenic young men in red coats scattered about among the buildings, and a museum, established in 1933, which features an elaborate display of weapons employed in the commission of notorious crimes. A piece of the rope by which Louis Riel was hanged no doubt has some fringe-appeal for necrophiliacs.

Most visitors find the Police chapel, the only one of its kind in Canada, the most moving reminder of the great days of the Force. The walls are lined with plaques memorializing the names of men who, in life and in their manner of leaving it, created and maintained a noble tradition of devotion to duty.

What gives Regina distinction, what may in fact make her in time one of the fairest cities of Canada, is the Wascana Park development, which surrounds and includes the artificial lake created as long ago as 1883 by damming Wascana Creek. The waters of the lake are turgid, and sometimes give off vile odours, but they compensate for such aesthetic offences by providing an area of marshland embracing nearly four hundred acres. The Wascana marsh forms one of the finest bird sanctuaries in Canada, and certainly the most impressive to be found within city limits. Crowfoot, cattails, plantains abound in the waters of the marsh; and among them the traditional marsh-dwellers — red-winged and yellow-headed blackbirds, coots and terns and grebes and muskrats and frogs and all manner of aquatic insects and the curious little fairy shrimp that swims always on its back — rear their young in comparative security and provide splendid entertainment for Regina citizens and nature lovers from all over America. There are some Canada geese here too — handsomest of all our birds with the exception of the all too rare whooping crane. Open water near the power-house invites many birds to remain in the marsh all year round — a satisfactory enough arrangement so long as the word is not spread through Saskatchewan that since warm water and free grub are available in Wascana Park no birds need go south for the winter.

The new University of Saskatchewan, Regina Campus, occupies a substantial part of the Wascana development, and, more specifically, of what is called the Wascana Centre project, an ambitious plan 'to provide facilities for government services, University development and cultural and recreational activity in the heart of the city of Regina'. The University, which started in a modest way as a Methodist college in 1911, has been accorded independent degree-granting status although still a part of the provincial university system. The campus is raw, naked, untreed; but the buildings thus far completed and those still in the planning stage seem likely to compose a highly imaginative, aesthetically pleasing harmony (the work of a Japanese architect, Minoru Yamasaki) which will be a far cry from traditional muddled College Gothic.

Regina is not an exciting city to visit or live in. Nearly one-third of her citizens are employees of municipal, or provincial, or federal governments, and civil servants have never been noted for colour — 'a common greyness silvers everything.' Reginans, it seems, are not much interested in projecting an image that will attract attention to themselves, and for this they deserve all praise. (In passing, let me protest the modern usage of the word 'image', which is an absolute falsification of its original meaning. Image once meant 'likeness'; today it means a false front or mask which hides the real man with all his weaknesses and warts. Nine times out of ten the modern image, so called, bears little or no resemblance to the person or thing it is alleged to stand for; it is the P.R. or ad man's conception, not of what actually exists, but of what it is expedient that the public should believe exists.) Among the more obvious examples of contemporary image-worship are the efforts of certain western communities – which shall be nameless but, I hope, readily identifiable – to appear what they are not; to create for – not of – themselves images that will associate them in the public mind with a time and a spirit other than and alien to their own.

Reginans – and this is surely a sign of maturity and witness of grace – are content to live with and be themselves.

The Parklands

9. The Great Valley

Since we have taken everything else from the Indians it is no doubt fitting that we should appropriate their legends too and adapt them to suit our own peculiar tastes. Whenever I read a so-called Indian legend in popular form I am reconfirmed in my conviction that somewhere, some time, a committee of high-principled Victorian females (presidents of missionary societies, wives and sisters of curates, dowager aunts, and the like) had sat in judgement on all stories emanating from the wigwams of the red man, sifting, sorting, re-arranging, bowdlerizing – with the single aim in view of making the stories fit for young ladies of good family and impeccable morals to read.

Consider, for instance, the legend which purports to explain how the Qu'Appelle Valley got its name. 'The river is so named by the superstitious natives,' Daniel Harmon wrote in 1804, 'who imagine that a spirit is constantly going up and down it; they say that they often hear a voice distinctly which resembles the cry of a human being.' Harmon's account offers no hint of the nature or significance of the cry, but we can, I think, be fairly sure that the spirit said to be wandering up and down the valley was that of an Indian warrior killed in battle and seeking to retrieve his scalp before setting off for the Happy Hunting-Grounds. But what is the version of the legend most widely circulated today – indeed the *only* version?

An Indian brave, young, handsome, kind-hearted, and poetic, was paddling his canoe across one of the Valley lakes to visit his beautiful young bride-to-be when he heard someone calling his name. Startled, he shouted back in French – he was a bicultural-ist – 'Qu'appelle? Qu'appelle?', thereby unwittingly christening the valley and the river flowing through it. When he landed on the opposite shore of the lake, he found his beloved dead of unknown causes, but at least he had the satisfaction of learning that it was she who had called his name. Pauline Johnson, whose peculiar talent was for translating alleged Indian talk into the pure Victorianese of Mrs. Felicia Hemans and Adelaide Anne (*Lost Chord*) Procter, explains:

> *A storm of wrecking sorrow beat and broke*
> *About my heart, and life shut out its light,*
> *Till through my anguish someone gently spoke*
> *And said, 'Twice did she call for thee last night.'*
> *I started up – and bending o'er my dead,*
> *Asked when did her sweet lips in silence close.*
> *'She called thy name – then passed away,' they said,*
> *'Just on the hour whereat the moon arose.'*

The Indian swain still wanders about the Valley, a forlorn ghost who appears to derive a certain masochistic pleasure from listening to the legend Miss Johnson has created for him:

> *The paleface loves the haunted lakes they say,*
> *And journeys far to watch their beauty spread*
> *Before his vision; but to me the day,*
> *The night, the hour, the seasons are all dead.*
> *I listen heartsick, while the hunters tell*
> *Why white men named the valley the Qu'Appelle.*

Perhaps, though, it is as well that a tender little love story should thus be associated with the Valley. True, in the old days it was many times the scene of violence and death, for the Indians loved the Valley and fought fiercely with one another for possession. But in its stillness, its serenity, its detachment from the winds and stresses of life on the uplands, the Valley seems at odds with deeds of blood. It is the kind of place that appeals strongly to romantic souls – and particularly to honeymooners, who in shedding a tear for the poor Indian brave forever deprived of his sweetheart feel an intensification of their own happiness, never so acute, so Keats assures us, as when tinctured with melancholy.

The Qu'Appelle Valley is a gouge in the earth's surface made by the waters of a melting ice-cap fifty thousand years ago. It extends for nearly three hundred miles from a point near the town of Elbow to a junction with the valley of the Assiniboine just inside the Manitoba border. No single geographical feature separates precisely the Saskatchewan plains country from the parklands, but the Qu'Appelle Valley comes as close as any to doing so. South of the Valley the land is mostly flat and open; north it tends to roll and the bush is in places heavy. But such geographical generalizations are subject to numerous exceptions, and in trying to construct a bird's-eye view of Saskatchewan it is best to regard the old Palliser Triangle as defining the boundaries of the true plains country.

As do so many Saskatchewan valleys, the Qu'Appelle shocks the eye and excites the imagination by its sheer unexpectedness. No matter what direction you approach it from, there is no preparation for the spectacle of a depression in the earth's surface between two and three hundred feet deep, up to two miles wide and running east and west as far as the eye can see. By comparison with its majestic bed the Qu'Appelle River is an absurdity – no more than a sluggish little creek which in the manner of nearly all western clay-bound streams meanders waywardly hither and yon over the valley floor, its opaque waters slow-moving, at many points reed-fringed and rich in the kind of bird and insect life that flourishes in marshy places.

There are in Canada many chains of lakes strung together by meandering rivers, but nowhere except in the Qu'Appelle Valley is the chain compressed between nearly three hundred miles of high banks arranged at many points in fluted folds which create, particularly towards sunset, stunning effects of alternating light and shadow. In winter the patterns resemble formal geometric designs – dark lines of heavily treed gullies standing out against a background of white, with here and there, as if to provide relief from these geometric severities, curlicue cattle trails and footpaths following the line of least resistance up and down the valley slopes.

The Qu'Appelle Lakes, when viewed from almost any high point along the banks, usually appear a rich, dazzling sky-blue. The first of any size in the chain, Buffalo Pound near Moose Jaw, supplies the cities of Regina and Moose Jaw with much of their water. Buffalo Pound is an isolated lake flanked by stark bare hills; and in spite of the development of a provincial park and a ski resort along its shores it preserves a kind of bleak virginal austerity hardly shared by its sisters down the Valley – particularly the closely allied group commonly called the Fishing Lakes: Pasqua, Echo, Mission, and Katepwe. The Fishing Lakes are rimmed by substantial summer settlements, most of the cottages owned by Regina citizens who have long used the Qu'Appelle Valley as a backyard playground and week-end shelter from plains dust and wind. There are two rather cramped provincial parks on the Fishing Lakes and two towns, Lebret and Fort Qu'Appelle. Two more lakes lie farther down the Valley, Crooked and Round – the latter as yet hardly developed but perhaps the loveliest of all.

The finest view of the Fishing Lakes is to be obtained from the Fort Qu'Appelle graveyard in the rim of the Valley high above the town. The Valley lies open to the eye for many miles both east and west, and the chain pattern of lakes-linked-by-river is laid out with exquisite clarity of detail on the Valley floor far below. The town of Qu'Appelle is itself without distinction; but when seen from a point sufficiently far removed to hide its most obvious blemishes it acquires a curious kind of ethereal charm not commonly associated with western towns.

The most notable occupant of the Fort Qu'Appelle graveyard is Captain John French, a one-time Irish policeman who in the Riel Rebellion commanded a detachment of irregular volunteers raised mostly in the Valley. He was killed in the last hour of the fighting at Batoche. Oddly enough, the only other Saskatchewan graveyard I have seen whose beauty can rival that of Fort Qu'Appelle is the Métis burying-ground at Batoche, where lie the bones of the Métis killed fighting against French and his fellows.

Daniel Harmon, a North West Company trader, and fortunately a most conscientious if stiff-jointed journalist, haphazardly explored a small part of the upper Qu'Appelle Valley in 1804. An uncomfortable experience – for Harmon was short of supplies, plagued by bad weather and drunken Indians, and curiously enough, for he was a veteran of the wilderness, terrified of being eaten by unidentified wild animals – 'The last night was so unpleasant to me that I could not even sleep, arising in part from the constant fear I was in of being torn to pieces by wild beasts.' In spite of his apprehensions Harmon's over-all impression of the Valley and the country to the north was highly favourable. 'Here we have arrived,' he wrote in his journal while camped beside one of the Fishing Lakes near the end of March 1804, 'and I am happy in reaching a place where I can take a little repose after so long and fatiguing a journey. Yet it has been, in many respects, both pleasant and profitable. The country which I have travelled over was beautifully situated, and overspread with buffaloes and other kinds of animals, as well as many other delightful objects, which in succession presented themselves to our view.'

In 1857 the Hudson's Bay Company established a post on a site, not yet positively determined, a few miles south of the Valley, and in 1864 in the Valley itself. An Anglican catechist named Charles Pratt, part Indian, part English, had preceded the Company by a few years, and a mission house of sorts already stood in the Valley. Charles Pratt was a missionary whose extraordinary mental convolutions are probably without parallel in the history of Christian thought. He was convinced from his Old Testament studies that the Indians were the Ten Lost Tribes; it followed, therefore, that before being converted to Christianity they should first be restored to the faith of their forefathers – Judaism. There is nothing to show that the Star of David was ever emblazoned on the Qu'Appelle Valley mission house, but it seems likely that the Indians were a sadly confused lot. By comparison with Pratt's teachings those of the Catholic missionaries who came a few years after Pratt must have seemed childishly simple.

Certain it is that the priests made a good deal more headway than had the poor catechist. On a spot overlooking the Valley, now marked by a minuscule chapel and reached by the Stations of the Cross up an impossibly steep bank, Father – later Archbishop – Taché is said to have planted a cross, thus symbolically annexing the Valley to the Church's spiritual empire. In 1884 an Indian Industrial School was established on the shores of Mission Lake with Fathers Hugonard and Lebret (who gave his name to the settlement that sprang up around the school) in charge.

I have swum in the Fishing Lakes and emerged a bright semipermanent blue (the algae which at times pollute the water appear to possess some of the qualities of a dye); I have fished in them many times and caught nothing but snags; I have driven innumerable golf balls into a rough second only to that of the

Cypress Hills course in its resistant power to ferocious bludgeoning; but I go back to the Valley again and again, and always with the assurance that sooner or later in the Valley's keeping I will achieve a serenity of spirit that will triumph over an endless succession of snagged hooks and a golf score in three figures.

It is of course a dangerous place, a sort of lotus land which people who have lived in it for any length of time never want to leave – not even those who have created for themselves reputations extending far beyond the Valley walls. Here in 1915 a Scottish artist of more than common talent settled on the outskirts of Fort Qu'Appelle and for nearly fifty years painted Valley scenes that eventually won him a modest national reputation. James Henderson might have been a better painter had he not allowed the Valley to claim him so completely that he hardly ever left it. He lived out of the world in a spot far removed from art galleries and schools and movements and coteries, content to employ to the end of his life the vaguely impressionistic techniques he had acquired as a young man. And content, it would seem, to sacrifice a larger reputation for peace of mind. Most of Henderson's pictures now hang in local galleries, public libraries, and private collections, but two of his best Valley scenes have found a place in the National Gallery in Ottawa.

Here, too, there lived in retirement for more than twenty years an ex-Dean of Arts and distinguished classical scholar who played golf regularly on the local course until approaching ninety years of age, and met once or twice a week with the local vicar – so legend affirms – to discuss the progress of the Peloponnesian war in the classic Greek of Pericles. The story is no doubt apocryphal – but it is the sort of thing that *could* happen in the Valley.

And here lives Stanley Harrison, Saskatchewan's answer to Australia's Adam Lindsay Gordon – as passionate a horse lover as Gordon and just as good a poet. A volume of poetry published by the Thoroughbred Press of Lexington, Kentucky, with illustrations by the author, hardly invites eager inspection; but the pleasing truth is that Stanley Harrison's *Gentlemen, the Horse* is not only a well-made book but a collection of verses on a level considerably higher than that achieved by most of our prairie bards. Mr. Harrison's love of horses is at times neatly supported by the kind of reference with which a solid Old Country classical education has amply provided him, as in his salute to Chiron, the mythical Centaur, through whom, according to Harrison 'the ancient Greeks predicted the noble alliance between man and horse in the long struggle through the landscape of history –

> *Are we not all, like thou of fabled song,*
> *Half god, half beast, each with its secret goal?'*

Happily, Harrison's view of the horse is not entirely sentimental, nor does he fall into the common error of attributing to him human emotions or responses:

> *I loved them all who were more brave than wise,*
> *More spirited than kind, and mean as hell*
> *Among themselves. . . .*
> *Some few have shown me true affection – few*
> *Indeed, but many bore me gifts of joy*
> *On dancing feet, unconscious of the gift,*
> *And all uncaring, like a branch that bends*
> *To eager hands that pluck the luscious fruit.*

Only when he writes of his splendid horse killed in the First World War does he allow sentiment – in this instance perhaps acceptable – to cloud his normally clear-eyed view of man and beast:

> *Somewhere in God's own space,*
> *There must be some sweet-pastured place*
> *Where creeks sing on and tall trees grow,*
> *Some Paradise where horses go;*
> *For by the love that guides my pen*
> *I know great horses live again.*

The love that guides Stanley Harrison's pen is not confined to horses; it is extended to nearly all created things. Next to horses he loves birds best. (The only creatures he really hates are the hunters who shoot them.) He himself has hunted birds with binoculars and camera and reported his findings to the appropriate interested organizations; he once established a bird hospital (in a chicken coop), known to all the youngsters of the Valley, and there he repaired broken wings, sheltered orphan fledglings, and fed the indigent and starving. He has been, in fact, much too busy with his hospital and similar interesting non-profit projects ever to achieve any great material success for himself. But, like James Henderson, he has lived a happy life. There are deeds as well as thoughts that savour of content.

The plastic arts, too, have their exponents in the Valley. In the Fort Qu'Appelle Pottery and Handcraft Centre, Folmer Hansen, a silent Dane who worked for a time in the Deichmann Pottery in New Brunswick, and David Ross, an amiable, fair-haired, intermittently bearded Canadian giant, shape, from Saskatchewan clay, pottery of exquisite design and glaze. Their shop is one of the chief tourist attractions of the Valley and deservedly so, since they practise their craft under public scrutiny with superb skill and great good humour.

Of all the arts the potter's, I think, must be the most completely satisfying. It shapes useful things, beautiful things, and at the same time satisfies – legitimately, in the name of art – the yearning that is in all of us, but sternly repressed since childhood's mud-pie days, to get our hands into lovely muck.

In ancient days, so geologists tell us, the waters of what is now the South Saskatchewan River flowed east down the Qu'Appelle Valley. When the waters formed from the melted ice-cap of the Ice Age had receded below a certain point, a height of land showed itself near what is called the Elbow of the South Saskatchewan, effectively cutting off the flow that had hitherto spilled into the Valley and forcing it to turn north along its present route. The Valley was thus left to be watered by the modest stream called the Qu'Appelle River (whose headwaters are on the east side of the Elbow height of land) and smaller streams draining into the huge depression from the plains, bringing with them deposits of silt which formed large stretches of rich flatlands along the Valley bottom. Occasionally, according to the tales of Indians and early traders, the ancient water route reasserted itself on a modest scale. A creek flowing into the Saskatchewan from the height of land near the Elbow was said to reverse its direction when the South Saskatchewan rose to an unusually high level and actually to flow backwards into the Qu'Appelle Valley. The Indians, so the story went, gave to the reversing stream the appropriate name of River-That-Turns.

Into the Valley in 1858 came Henry Yule Hind, an opinionated, highly skilled young professor of geology from the University of Toronto, at the head of an expedition sent out from the university to investigate the possibility of creating a waterway through the Qu'Appelle Valley that would link the Saskatchewan and Assiniboine rivers. Hind's report was favourable to the creation of such a waterway. He found no evidence to support the story of the River-That-Turns, but he established that the height of land between the Qu'Appelle and Saskatchewan rivers was only eighty feet higher than the normal summer level of the Saskatchewan. Hence he was prepared to recommend that 'a dam of eighty-five feet high and six hundred to eight hundred yards long . . . across the deep narrow valley of the South Branch . . . would send its waters down the Qu'Appelle Valley, thence down the Assiniboine past Fort Garry, thus establishing a splendid and probably uninterrupted navigation for steamers of large size for a distance of six hundred miles.'

Hind's plan, which if carried out would in fact have created a waterway reaching from Fort Garry to the Rockies, looked fine on paper; but, partly on the advice of S. J. Dawson, a government surveyor and explorer whose word carried a good deal of weight with those in high places, the plan was rejected by the government. Dawson feared that raising the level of the water in the Qu'Appelle Valley might result in frequent and serious damage to the already flood-prone Assiniboine and Red River basins.

No doubt if Hind were alive today he would feel himself vindicated, for the plan he proposed more than one hundred years ago, has, with certain elaborations, recently been put into execution – although not for the purpose of creating a steamboat waterway from Manitoba to the Rockies.

The South Saskatchewan River Dam (officially named the Gardiner Dam after a prominent Saskatchewan politician) represents the fulfilment of a project first seriously talked about in the dry years of the thirties. Built at a point on the river fifteen miles north of the town of Elbow and seventy miles south-east of Saskatoon, the earth-fill dam is the largest of its kind in Canada – two hundred feet high and more than three miles long. The country through which one drives to the Dam, from any direction, is uniformly bleak, treeless, and in appearance arid – ideally suited, it would seem, to irrigation, indeed crying out for it. But appearances are misleading; most of the farmers in the vicinity of the Dam are bitterly hostile to irrigation. Over the past few years the rainfall in the district has been generous, crop yields have been high. In the common mind irrigation is associated not with vast spreads of golden wheat but with market gardens and sugar-beets and the kind of field labour that your true wheat farmer looks upon with loathing and contempt. In actual fact it seems now that irrigation will be little more than a by-product of the Dam, whose major functions will be to provide hydro-electric power, facilitate control of water resources, and create a huge recreation area in the hitherto desolate central plains area of Saskatchewan. Behind the Dam a lake is building up, which at its fullest extent will cover an area one hundred and forty miles long and ten miles wide. In a few years the lake will be fringed with thousands of cottages and a score or more of provincial parks.

In addition to creating the great central lake, the Dam will divert water from the Saskatchewan into the bed of the River-That-Turns and so over the height of land and into the Qu'Appelle Valley, thus fulfilling, almost to the letter, William Yule Hind's plan drafted over one hundred years ago. A second dam built near the headwaters of the Qu'Appelle River will control the flow of water into the Valley and avert any possibility of the flooding that Dawson and his colleagues feared might affect the Manitoba river-basins. The water level of the Valley lakes is to be raised for recreational rather than commercial purposes; and it is anticipated that the higher level and increased movement will help rid the lakes of the algae infestations that intermittently plague them with unpleasant consequences for man and fish and beast.

Assuming the success of the diversion in improving the quality of the Valley waters, it is not absurd to assume that, within a decade or less, a double-branched recreation area will extend all the way from the great Dam between Outlook and Elbow up-river one hundred and fifty miles to the Crossing north of Swift Current; and, in its second branch, from the South Saskatchewan near Elbow along the full length of the Qu'Appelle Valley to the Manitoba border.

It is fair to say that if anyone, as recently as twenty-five years ago, had forecast a day — which now seems imminent — when central Saskatchewan would swarm with tourists come to enjoy the water sports, he would have been pronounced mad on the spot.

Fort Qu'Appelle was built in the Valley in 1864, and for a brief hour played an important role in the fur trade as chief distributing centre for the southern Saskatchewan district. Its primary function was to gather, process, and distribute food – in particular, pemmican. Métis, Indian, and free white hunters brought to the Fort buffalo meat and hides, which they traded for the usual Company goods. Company employees (mostly Métis and Indians) dried the meat and afterwards packed the strips into bundles, or, more often, beat the dried meat almost to a powder, stuffed it into canvas or buffalo-hide bags, and poured buffalo tallow over it. The mixture, called pemmican, was extraordinarily nutritious, as evidenced by the daily ration of food issued to the Fort employees: twelve pounds of buffalo meat per person, or six pounds of dried meat or *three pounds of pemmican*. The dried meat and pemmican intended for distribution were done up in 'pieces' of about ninety pounds' weight, and then carried from Fort Qu'Appelle by Red River cart or occasionally dog-teams to posts scattered over an area covering thousands of square miles.

Around the Fort mushroomed the inevitable settlement of Indians and mixed bloods; and here in 1874 the Cree and Salteaux, in the presence of numerous Dominion government dignitaries, signed a treaty (No. 4 of a series of ten signed by the Indians of the Northwest Territories) whereby they surrendered to the white man title to the land that they and their forebears had occupied for centuries, in return for a reserve or two and treaty money of five dollars a year per head. A detachment of militia from Fort Garry was on hand to lend colour to the proceedings and to impress upon the Indians the power of the Great White Queen to take by force for her subjects whatever lands could not be acquired by peaceful means.

In the town of Fort Qu'Appelle a cairn marks the spot where the treaty was signed.

In 1877 a Mounted Police post was established across the river from the Hudson's Bay fort. (The cellars of the post are still clearly visible on the golf course.) To the police post in 1881 came Sitting Bull with his starving band to make a last fruitless appeal before Inspector Sam Steele for permanent sanctuary in the Canadian west. 'There was something solemn and imperious about him,' Father Hugonard said. 'A certain reserve and dignity.' The good Father was not, however, above profiting from Sitting Bull's distress; he traded the great chief a few bags of flour for five horses and a dozen watches which the Sioux had taken from American cavalrymen killed at the Little Big Horn.

Many trails led out of the Valley in the days of the fur trade. One, followed by Isaac Cowie, who had come to the Fort as a Hudson's Bay Company apprentice in 1867, led him up the Valley to a point close to where Last Mountain Lake drains into the Qu'Appelle, and thence across the high uplands to the newly established Last Mountain post – a subsidiary of Qu'Appelle. Here, as long as the buffalo herds lasted, Cowie did a flourishing trade, although his sojourn (1869-71) was made uncomfortable, at times precarious, by the almost constant presence in the neighbourhood of a band of Indians called Young Dogs. The Young Dogs (who should, Cowie coyly suggested, have properly been called the Young of Lady Dogs) were cross-breeds – mixed Cree and Assiniboine, whose common habits, social, domestic, and sexual, so revolted the pure-blooded, highly moral tribesmen of the plains that the Young Dogs were turned into wandering Ishmaelites. (These habits included casual murder, kidnapping, wife-beating, incest, and sodomy.) Even the Great Manito regarded the Young Dogs with gravest disapproval. In the year 1866 a band of Young Dogs set up their tepees a mile or so away from a Cree camp which they had been forbidden by the Cree to share. One afternoon a violent storm broke over the Young Dog tepees – and a rain, not of water but of liquid fire, descended on the evil ones. When the storm had passed there remained in the Young Dog camp only charred bodies and tepees that disintegrated at the touch of a finger.

No doubt the scientist sees in the incident no more than an exaggerated account of the effects of a lightning bolt; but Charles Pratt, the catechist, would surely have found in the tragedy strong support for his theory that the Indians were the Lost Tribes of Israel. An angry Jehovah had clearly inflicted the same fate on the Young Dog camp as he had on those other evil settlements of the plain – Sodom and Gomorrah. And for the same reasons.

There was even a salt lake near the scene of the tragedy.

Last Mountain Lake, so named from Last Mountain, a modest

pimple erupting from the plain to a height of nearly one hundred feet and clearly visible on a good day from a distance of several miles, is a narrow sixty-mile-long body of water which provides convenient beach accommodation for Regina citizens, and for commercial fishermen an abundant supply of the queer hump-backed buffalo fish, in demand in certain parts of the United States. The buffalo fish was imported as a stock fish in mistake for black bass, and has in large measure displaced all other species in the lake. It is, unfortunately, looked upon with the utmost disfavour by sportsmen and gourmets.

The best way to reach Last Mountain Lake is by Highway No. 20, which branches off Highway No. 11 on the outskirts of the pretty Valley town of Lumsden and leads on north to Saskatchewan Beach and beyond. All signs of the old Hudson's Bay post have long since disappeared; but in its approximate vicinity the Department of Natural Resources has created a delightful provincial park – Rowan's Ravine.

Last Mountain Lake is chiefly notable not as a fishing- or swimming-resort or historic site but as a wild-fowl sanctuary. All the islands in the lake and twelve or more miles of northern shoreline were, as early as 1887, set apart as breeding-grounds and protected stop-over points for migratory birds. Here, from early September on, the multitudes of wild fowl winging south to their winter habitats pause for a while, safe beyond reach of sudden death by buckshot. The birds come in mostly at twilight, dropping down from far northern skies or from near-by grain-fields where they have risked shotgun fire in order to fill their crops. With the coming of daylight they take off again, some back to the grain-fields, others – swinging high and far out of danger – to resume their flight down the birdways which they follow as precisely as an airplane follows its radio beam. Here in the course of a season are to be seen ducks of a dozen species, sandhill cranes as numerous as Milton's angels under the nether scope of hell, whistler swans and cormorants and spotless white pelicans and – noblest of all the migratory tribes – Canada geese in numbers to exceed even the sandhill cranes. 'The most magnificent bird spectacle I ever witnessed,' reported the Assistant Director of the U.S. Fish and Wildlife Service – a man who has been around – after a visit to the Last Mountain Sanctuary in the fall of 1959.

The Sanctuary can most conveniently be reached by driving west from Govan off No. 20 Highway for about ten miles.

But of all the trails leading out of the Valley the best-known in the fur-trading days was the one linking the Valley with the famous Carlton Trail – the chief overland route from Manitoba to the far reaches of the North-west. The Carlton Trail began at Fort Ellice near the junction of the Qu'Appelle and Assiniboine rivers and pursued a course north-west through Humboldt, Fort Carlton, Fort Pitt, and Edmonton. Never much more than a cart track, the Qu'Appelle Trail, from its junction with the Carlton Trail near Punnichy, wandered north-east to its terminus at Fort Pelly, two hundred miles out of Fort Qu'Appelle. Pelly, located on a branch of the Swan River about twenty miles north of the present town of Kamsack, was in its heyday the most important Hudson's Bay post west of Fort Garry, but its fortunes declined rapidly with the takeover of the Hudson Bay's dominion by the government of Canada.

It is possible today to follow the approximate route of the old Qu'Appelle Trail by driving north from the town of Fort Qu'Appelle on Highway No. 35 about forty miles to Leross thence east a few miles on No. 15 to the site of the old Touchwood Hills trading-post a few yards off the highway between Lestock and Punnichy. Touchwood Hills, originally a subsidiary of Fort Pelly, eventually did a roaring business on its own and became an important stopping-place for travellers on the Carlton Trail, which the Qu'Appelle Trail here intersected. In 1883 a telegraph station was established near by, part of the system linking Qu'Appelle with the main line near Humboldt. Nothing remains now to mark the site of the old post except a few foundation fragments, but the surrounding area has been made into one of the pleasantest picnic parks in central Saskatchewan. The countryside is rolling, lush-meadowed, heavily wooded; and it is easy to understand the enthusiasm with which, in the old days, travellers crossing the arid plains greeted the first sight of the far-off green Touchwood Hills.

From the Touchwood post the traveller may follow any one of several routes to Fort Pelly (on Highway 49 fifteen miles from the Manitoba border) and Fort Livingstone a few miles above Pelly. Fort Livingstone was the original headquarters of the North West Mounted Police, built with great difficulty on a site far removed from any source of supplies. It was assumed that the transcontinental railway would pass close by, since the original railway survey, later abandoned in favour of the southern route, followed the old Hudson's Bay Company trail from Fort Garry across the Lake Manitoba Narrows and on to Swan River, Humboldt, Battleford, and Edmonton. Livingstone was a remote, uncomfortable spot, difficult to get into or out of, and plagued by garter-snakes, which swarmed out of a rocky hill-side and turned up in the most unexpected places, including more than one pair of policeman's boots. In 1875 police headquarters were moved to Fort Walsh, and, except for a brief period when the Honourable David Laird, Governor of the Northwest Territories, took up residence in the police quarters preliminary to a move to the new government building in Battleford, Fort Livingstone was thereafter relinquished to the snakes.

The road to Last Mountain, the road to Touchwood and Pelly and Livingstone are but two of the many that lead in all directions out of the Qu'Appelle. But for some of us their chief attraction is not that they take us to fascinating places where the Historic Sites marker is the most obvious feature of the landscape, but that, if we simply reverse our direction of travelling, they lead us back into the great Valley which it is impossible to know and not to love.

10. Melting-Pot

Most clichés survive in our common talk because we are too lazy to find fresh turns of phrase to replace them with – a few because they express a common truth in terms that can hardly be improved upon. Of these useful and justifiable clichés 'melting-pot' is surely one. Nothing can represent more concretely what has happened to ethnic groups living side by side in the Canadian west than the image of originally disparate elements thrown together and reduced over a period of time by contiguity and the operation of powerful environmental forces to a substance of comparatively uniform appearance and texture. Inevitably such a process involves loss as well as gain, particularly of distinctive ethnic arts and crafts which seem unlikely to be practised with much enthusiasm or success beyond the time of the present generation.

Nowhere can the process of reduction be observed more obviously and conveniently than in the eastern part of Saskatchewan lying between Whitewood and Moosomin on the south and Yorkton and Kamsack on the north – an area about one hundred miles long by forty or fifty wide. The countryside itself, except for the occasional glimpses it provides of the Qu'Appelle Valley, is frankly dull – flat, fairly heavily wooded, and in many places surprisingly raw-looking; but the communities of the area tell a story of settlement that is repeated many times throughout the west but rarely in so complicated a form.

The names of the towns in the area constitute in themselves a précis of the story; within a radius of twenty miles we find Dubuc, Bangor, Stockholm, Esterhazy, Langenburg, Thingvalla, Churchbridge – in origin French, Welsh, Swedish, Hungarian, German, Icelandic, British – intermingled with American and

111

eastern Canadian settlements whose centres bear no distinguishing ethnic labels.

Some settlers arrived in this part of Saskatchewan as early as
the 1870s, making their way from Manitoba by ox train and Red
River cart; but the vast majority came after 1884, spilling out
over the prairie from the colonist cars, which, until just before
the end of the First World War, were a characteristic feature of
nearly all passenger trains running west. They came sometimes
on their own, but often in groups sponsored by land companies
who, for a fee, undertook to locate a man on a homestead, or by
British and European government and philanthropic agencies
bent on solving unemployment or integration problems by re-
locating the problems in far-off places. And certainly no other
part of the Canadian west ever assembled within its boundaries,
in less than two decades, a greater variety of cultures than did
eastern Saskatchewan, or a more representative assortment of
bewildered Britishers and Europeans whom the hunger for land
and freedom or the influence of the philanthropist had summarily torn away from all familiar things.

The town of Saltcoats, originally British to the core, was in the
eighties and nineties the centre of an all-nations society speaking
a babel of tongues, clinging to a dozen cultures — a society supervised more or less benevolently by representatives of the Department of Immigration, clergymen of a wide variety of denomina-
tions, and members of the North West Mounted Police. In her
golden age of youth and hope Saltcoats, now a conventional
prairie small town, was one of the liveliest communities in the
west. The village was served by a weekly train running from
Winnipeg over the old Manitoba and Northwestern Railway,
and in turn, until overshadowed by Yorkton forty miles to the
north, served as distributing centre for a wide area. Unlike Cannington Manor, Saltcoats never ran to a Hunt (most of the citizens, even those of good Old Country middle-class stock, were for
a long time desperately poor); but the near-by lake provided
nautical and aquatic entertainment at small expense, and nearly
everybody had had the foresight to include cricket bats and tennis rackets among his settlers' essential effects. (On more than
one occasion cricketers were summoned from their Saturday
afternoon play by the police to fight near-by prairie fires, with
disastrous consequences for the players' white flannels.) In winter

a barn-like town hall provided accommodation for an ambitious program of amateur theatricals, mostly farces, whose names, 'Freezing a Mother-in-Law', 'Box and Cox', and the like, are preserved in advertisements still to be read in the yellowed pages of the Saltcoats *Siftings* and its successor, the *Herald*. At Christmas the players usually risked a pantomime, 'Ali Baba' or 'Robinson Crusoe' – costumes of the gorgeous east made from dyed flour-sacks, and for Robinson Crusoe from local rabbit-skins. Occasionally outside entertainers, including that ubiquitous elocutionist Pauline Johnson, came to town, but they seldom measured up – so everyone agreed – to the standards established by the local talent. More serious cultural activities included public debates, literary readings (mostly from the works of Tennyson and Browning), and sacred concerts in which such nineteenth-century religious hits as 'Jerusalem' and 'The Lost Chord' figured prominently.

A few miles north of Saltcoats, one's ear was likely to be assailed by a very different kind of music from that heard in the Saltcoats town hall. No tremulous warblings at eve, no *basso profundo* subsiding into the cradle of the deep, no schoolgirl duo coyly whispering hope in dubious harmony, but rather that eeriest and – to an outlander – most unnerving of all alleged musical sounds, the wail of the bagpipes played by a Scot homesick for his native heather. For here on the fringes of the Saltcoats community were settled in 1889, at the expense of the British government, a colony of Hebrideans who for long had endured semi-starvation among the beauties of their native islands with no hope of better things to come.

The Hebrideans were frankly misfits; they were fishermen accustomed to handling boats, not livestock. According to one observer who could hardly believe his eyes and ears, 'they ordered their oxen to starboard or port, and called the land the shore.' The Hebrideans spoke only Gaelic, played the bagpipes with passionate abandon, fought fiercely among themselves but closed ranks and fists against outlanders who sought to direct them into ways they did not choose to follow. Somehow the older generation managed to survive their allotted span. The men of the younger generation – English-speaking, adjusted to the soil, but still bonny fighters – nearly all died in the First World War. So it is that in eastern Saskatchewan the Hebridean strain is not easily marked now; the bagpipes are silent, and the dying fall of the Gaelic no longer strikes pleasingly if incomprehensibly on the ear. The survival of a minority group depends to a significant extent on numbers; and a mere handful of Gaels could hardly hope to preserve their identity beyond two generations.

Ten miles south of Saltcoats a colony unique even in the multi-racial settlement story of the North American continent established roots in the prairie soil. There, in the late nineties, one Evan Jenkins, a bubbly energetic little Welshman, came hot-foot to spy out the land on behalf of a group of his countrymen – living not in Wales but in Patagonia, less than a thousand miles from the southern tip of South America. A party of Welsh families, assisted in their move by an imperial government only too happy to dispose thus of a social and economic problem, had emigrated from Wales to Patagonia in the 1860s and settled in the valley of the Chibouk River which flows out of the Andes and empties into the Atlantic eight hundred miles south of Buenos Aires. There for thirty years the Welshmen survived but hardly prospered. They irrigated the valley and grew good crops, but floods were a common catastrophe. To add to a growing sense of dissatisfaction, many of the colonists felt uneasy about living under a foreign flag. Evan Jenkins reported favourably on the Saskatchewan country; and in 1902 four hundred Patagonian Welshmen – the second generation speaking Welsh and Spanish but no English – arrived in the Saltcoats district and were settled on land centring on a tiny village appropriately named Bangor. The Patagonian Welshmen, unlike their Celtic cousins the Hebrideans, created no great stir among their neighbours. They were law-abiding folk, quiet except when through their choral society they praised the Lord and their homeland or celebrated a victory of their invincible soccer football team. Like so many loyal British communities the Welshmen suffered fearful losses in the First World War. The descendants of those who survived now play baseball and hockey instead of football, and speak neither Spanish nor Welsh – though no doubt some of them are at the present time busy learning French.

A few miles south-east of Saltcoats the community of Churchbridge was founded in 1887 by an Anglican Church society whose agent, resident in England, urged the colonists – so the story goes – to buy oxen instead of horses on the grounds that the oxen, in addition to serving admirably as beasts of burden, would provide their owners with an abundant supply of milk

1   Hill and plain meet near Swift Current to create a landscape that reduces man and his machine to insignificance.

2   Holiday riders in the Qu'Appelle Valley – a region that provides horses and trails to accommodate every taste and aptitude.

3 Indian and white mothers share a common interest on the shore of McIntosh Lake, fifty miles north of Lac La Ronge.

4 The Nistowiak Falls, on the Churchill River system near the northern boundary of Lac La Ronge Provincial Park.

5   Antelope, swiftest and most graceful of
Saskatchewan's wild animals, run far and free through
the Cypress Hills and north to the Saskatchewan River.

6   The Cypress Hills, Palliser's 'perfect oasis in the
desert we have travelled' — still a cool and tranquil
refuge from the dust and heat of the great plains.

7   Amisk (or Beaver) Lake, a few miles south-west of
Flin Flon — beautiful at all times of year, most
beautiful in autumn.

8 Wild cactus grows in the Cypress Hills and north to the Saskatchewan River — country that nurtures both desert growths and magnificent stands of grain.

9 The South Saskatchewan River winds for 200 miles through eerie, eroded badlands from the Alberta-Saskatchewan border to the newly created Diefenbaker Lake.

10   Grey Owl – the Englishman Archie
Belaney, who looked and thought like an
Indian chief – with a pet beaver at his home
on Lake Ajawaan in Prince Albert National
Park.

11   The face of grief is universal – Ukrainian
women attending a funeral in Krydor, near
Saskatoon. The traditional costume still worn
by the elderly is now discarded.

12   The Fishing Lakes, Qu'Appelle Valley. A sketch from Henry Yule
Hind's *Narrative of the Canadian Red River Expedition of 1857.*

13   The Stations of the Cross leading up from the mission village of Lebret to
a minuscule chapel built on the spot where Father (later Archbishop) Taché
is said to have erected a cross in 1860.

14 The Western Development Museum, Saskatoon. A democrat, the station-wagon of horse-drawn vehicles, is exhibited against an authentic fifty-year-old stage backdrop.

15   Lieut. Arthur Howard of the U.S. Army behind his Gatling gun which
the Canadian government allowed him to test on the Métis in 1885.

16   Big Bear's Cree Indians camped by a slough on the plains near the North Saskatchewan, 1883. In the spring of 1885, his warriors killed nine unarmed white men at Frog Lake.

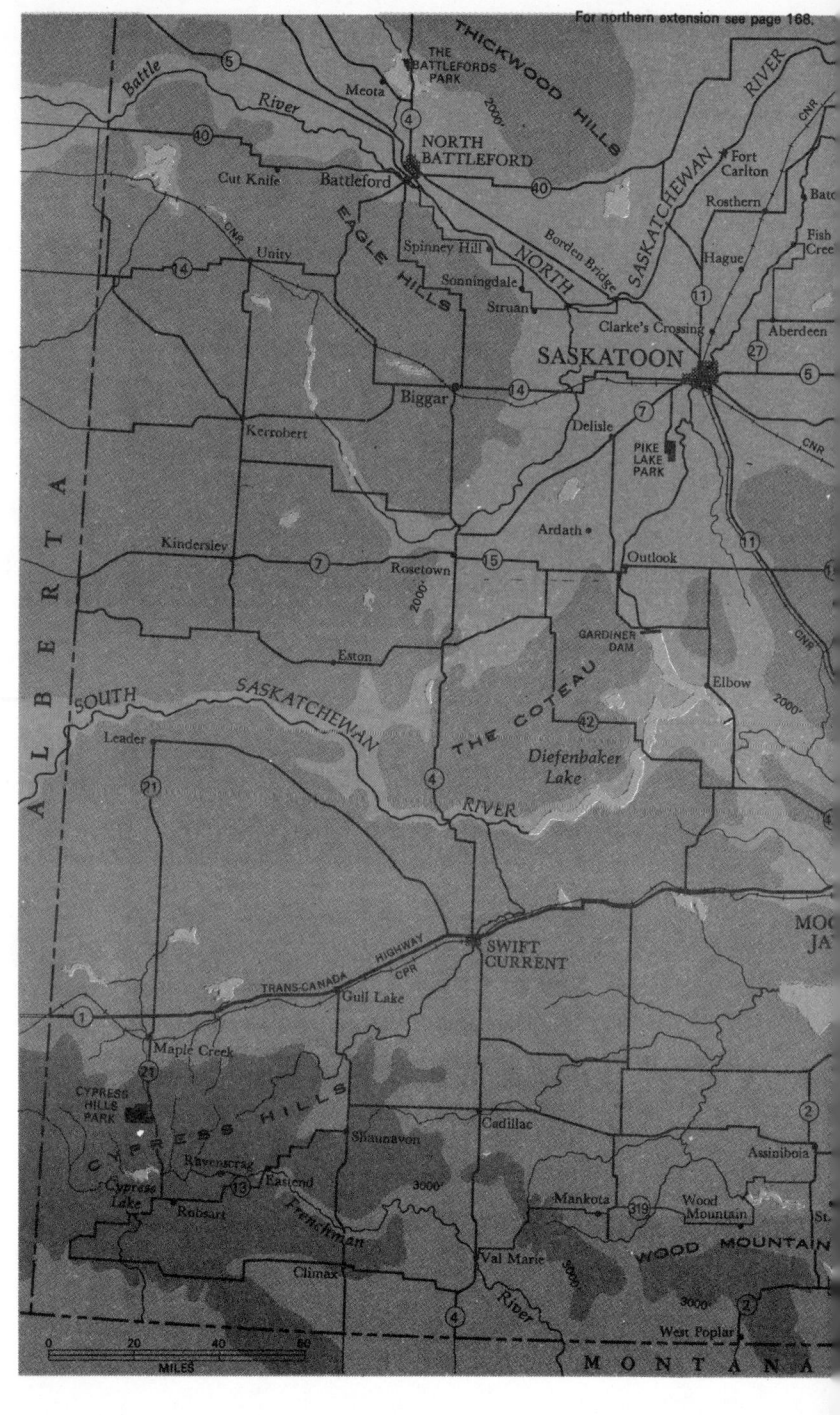

For northern extension see page 168.

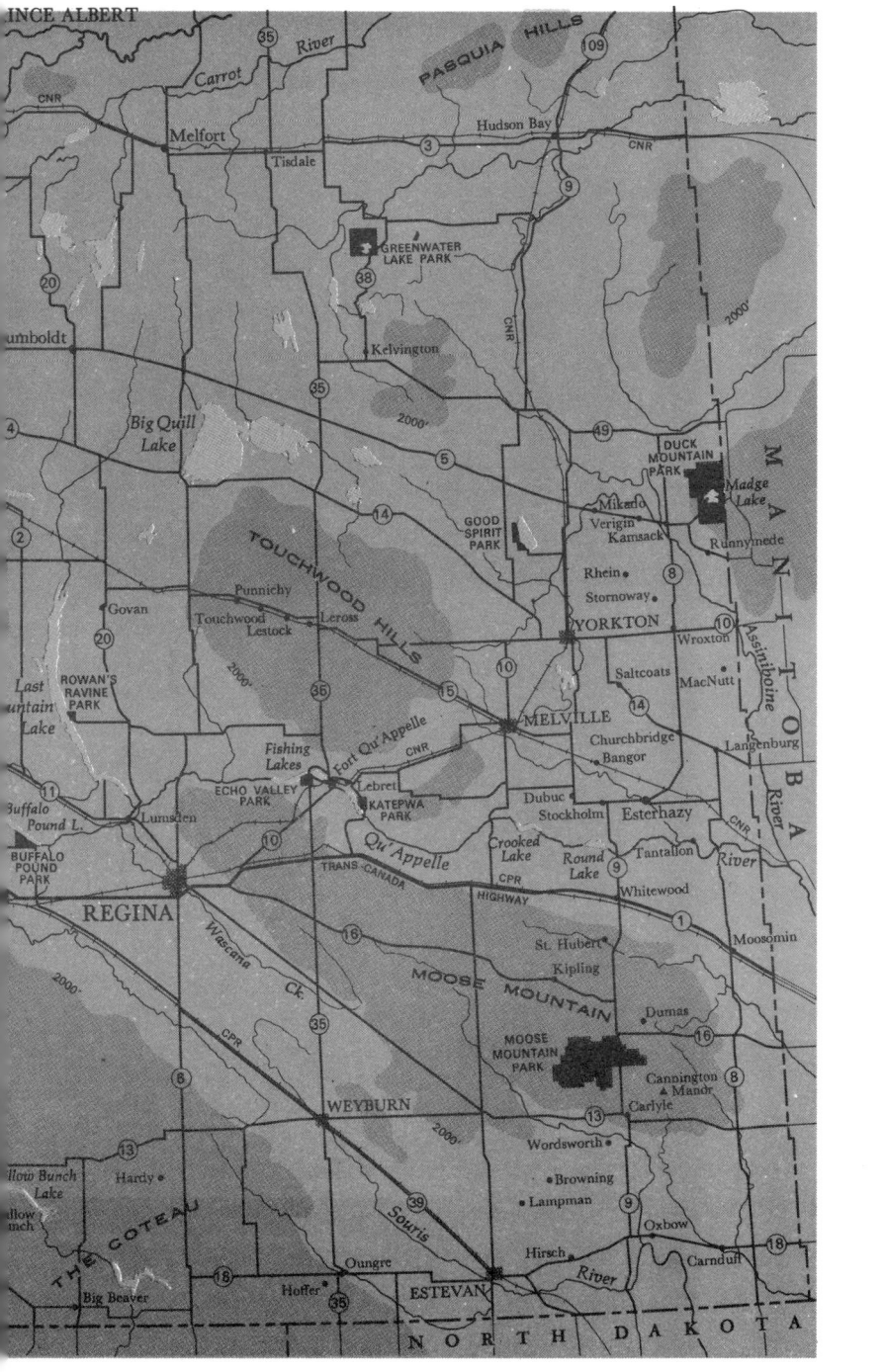

17 The original Fort Walsh in the Cypress Hills, headquarters from 1875 to 1883 of the Mounties, who controlled restless Indian refugee bands, including Sitting Bull's Sioux.

Frosst

This is for
David Watson
The doctor's son

entrophen*

(acetylsalicylic acid tablets, USP)
enteric-coated with POLYMER 37*

*Trademark

18 The Governor General's Body Guard garrisoned the telegraph station at
Humboldt during the Riel Rebellion. The man on horseback is probably
a Mountie on patrol.

19 A typical pioneer sod home on the great plains, *circa* 1890 – perhaps a
little roomier than most. The newly planted windbreak to the left is evidence
that these pioneers were determined to stay.

20   Métis scouts attached to the British section of the International
Boundary Commission, 1872-4. These superb hunters kept the commission
men lavishly supplied with fresh buffalo meat.

21 The Rev. Moses Barr (right) leaving Saskatoon for the Promised Land, which he never reached.

22 Old-time cowboys (*circa* 1914) of the Turkey Track Ranch south of Swift Current, enjoying a leisure hour in the old-time way.

23 A supply train accompanying Middleton's Northwest Field Force during the Rebellion of 1885, with militiamen acting as escorts.

24 Bachelor Hall at Cannington Manor – built by the Beckton brothers in the days when Cannington Manor was a Little England in the midst of a prairie wilderness. The house still stands.

25 The Saskatchewan Power Corporation Building in Regina – a superb
example of imaginative office structure design.

26 Ali Baba's treasure cave, Saskatchewan version. The interior of the huge
storage building for potash at Esterhazy.

27 The mighty Gardiner Dam, with Diefenbaker Lake forming behind it
and arid plains country reaching into the far distance.

28   Saskatoon's famous bridges, reflected in the water of the South
Saskatchewan River. The Bessborough Hotel, also reflected in the water,
dominates the west bank.

29 Oil refinery on the north-east outskirts of Regina, projected against a typical prairie sunset.

and butter. The Churchbridge colony made little impact; most of the settlers, in the opinion of one critical observer, were too old and set in their ways to make good in a new land: 'I did not fancy the colonists here were quite the sort of people to make good and successful colonists,' he wrote (this in 1889). 'They appeared to be drawn from the well-to-do class in England rather than the yeoman farmer or agricultural classes, and were generally too far advanced in years to make a fresh start in life.'

Straight north of Churchbridge a group of Icelanders – superbly adaptable, self-reliant, and highly intelligent pioneers – founded a colony bearing to Anglo-Saxon ears a strange, haunting name – Thingvalla. South of Churchbridge along the rugged slopes of the Qu'Appelle Valley, Finnish farmers grew excellent stands of wheat and raised tobacco (no longer a cultivated crop in Saskatchewan) which they cured and pressed by primitive but apparently effective techniques. 'My Finnish neighbour put the leaves together and allowed them to heat or ferment,' an interested Canadian observer reported. 'He had a section of log about eight inches through and sixteen long. Through this he bored holes with a two-inch auger. In these holes he rammed the tobacco and left it there for quite a while. Then he split the log with his axe and out fell big rolls of dry tobacco.'

In the opinion of a veteran land-company agent, the Finn was in terms of general adaptability and efficiency the best of all prairie settlers. 'For hardiness, industry, resourcefulness and all round competency in meeting pioneer conditions and cleaning up a rough country,' he reported, 'I put the Lutheran Finn easily first.'

Langenburg, the next town on the line south-east of Churchbridge, is German in origin (Catholics north of the town, Lutherans south) and still preserves something of a Teutonic flavour in family names, traditional dishes, and the like; but the melting process has been tolerably effective here, and the old, hard outlines of a distinct ethnic group have long since become blurred and softened. The same is equally true of the community of Stockholm, a one-time Swedish settlement a few miles south-west of Langenburg, and perhaps less true of the old Hungarian settlement of Esterhazy – so named after the philanthropic Hungarian nobleman under whose aegis the colony was founded. Most of the Hungarian colonists had already had some farming experience in the United States before removing to Canada, where they were, however, shortly joined by emigrants coming direct from the old land. They, like their neighbours, were within a generation or two partially absorbed into the mass.

Today Esterhazy figures prominently in the industrial life of Saskatchewan as the centre of an immense potash development. To drive over a highway within striking distance of Esterhazy at a time when shifts are changing at the mines is, for strangers, apt to be a bewildering experience; the last thing a motorist driving through rural Saskatchewan expects to be caught in is a traffic jam. While conceding the benefits of industry to the general populace, many Esterhazy citizens have been frankly unhappy over the disruption of a relatively placid and comfortable semi-rural life by the intrusion of a giant industry. In particular, what they regard as the takeover of their town by company interests has been a source of irritation and at times downright anger. Between high-powered efficiency experts and devotees of an unhurried agrarian way of life characterized by freedom from industrial turmoil and tension, there is inevitably little sympathy and no affection.

Signs on the outskirts of the town inform us that Esterhazy is the 'Potash Capital of Canada'. Two hundred miles to the north-west similar signs (also radio and TV slogans, car stickers, pennants, hatbands, ash trays, cushion covers) proclaim Saskatoon the 'Potash Capital of the World'.

One thing is certain – there is a lot of potash in Saskatchewan.

North of Saltcoats, settlers from Central Europe, the first of Clifford Sifton's 'peasant in a sheepskin coat with a stout wife and half a dozen children' moved into burnt-over bush country to make for themselves new lives away from the hardships and petty persecutions they had endured in their native lands. Galicians and Bukovinians – hostile to one another although coming from the same vast territory, part Russian, part Polish, known as the Ukraine – were admirably adapted by physique and temperament to the task of wresting a living from rough, raw land, but a good deal less so to adjusting to alien ways and speech and laws. They spoke no English – one large party arrived in Saltcoats in the charge of an interpreter carrying a whip – brought with them very little money, and were for a long time bitterly resentful of government efforts to persuade them to send their children to school.

Not all central Europeans took immediately to farming. Many, including a large number of Romanians, were brought out by the C.P.R. to work as labourers on the numerous branch lines proliferating throughout the north-west towards the close of the century. But the land-hunger was in them all; and the railway workers, as soon as they had earned a modest stake, laid down their pickaxes and shovels and hurried off to look for homesteads in the as-yet-unclaimed spaces of the prairies. In eastern Saskatchewan the Romanians concentrated around what is now the village of MacNutt, twenty-five miles east of Saltcoats; but the fact that so many of them worked on the railroad accounts for their distribution as far west as Assiniboia and Wood Mountain.

The oldest Romanian Orthodox congregation in North America was founded in Regina as early as 1902.

It is easy to understand the rush to acquire homesteads in the Canadian west. To men hitherto confined to tiny land-plots or acres not their own, or huddled in city slums, the acquiring of 160 acres of land in return for no more than a trifling registration fee, with the assurance of more acres available for purchase once they had proved up their homestead claims (i.e., cultivated thirty acres of land and lived in a 'habitable' house on the homestead for at least six months of each of three years), must have been a reality outmatching the most extravagant of dreams. And for a few the reality continued over the years to surpass the dream.

For a very few. For most, the struggle, not to achieve wealth or additional land but quite simply to survive, was for a long time all-demanding. Life on the homestead in winter – the nearest settlement frequently twenty or thirty or even fifty miles away, to be reached only after infinite toil over drifted trails or no trails at all – was a grim endurance test which, on the women at least, often left permanent scars. Settlers from Great Britain tended at first to build houses of logs – often poplar – that warped and shrank so that, outside or in, the bitter cold was impossible to escape except in the immediate vicinity of stove or heater. The central Europeans fared rather better than the Britishers. Many of them were reared on the great steppes of Russia and knew well how to combat cold. Like many of the settlers from eastern Canada the Europeans were content to begin their new life with sod shacks – but sod shacks with a difference. The conventional

North American sod shack is exactly what its name implies – no more or less than a hut built of sods cut out of the prairie and laid on top of one another to form the walls, and on poles to form the roof. Such a primitive dwelling the Russian or Hungarian was capable of transforming into a remarkably comfortable home. An English homesteader, accustomed to the rude shelters fashioned by himself and his bachelor compatriots, reported almost with awe on the superiority of the homes of two of his central European neighbours:

> My Russian friend was the leader of the settlement, and a superior man. His living house was comfortable enough, but the sleeping house was a dream when one considered it was built of nothing but mud. The walls were putty-coloured with a fine wash of clay and were quite smooth and shiny. There was a neat painted cornice running around the rooms, consisting of flowers and figures. They were home made and the paint or dye was home made from vegetables and ochres in the vicinity. . . . And the bed! I slept between two of the softest, cleanest, most billowy and restful feather beds I have ever struck.
>
> I remember another beautiful bit of mud architecture. This time the artist was a Hungarian. The floor of the good room was made of poles plastered over. That floor gave under one's feet as if it were rubber; yet it was shiny and solid, and without the slightest indication of a crack in its surface. But these results were not produced by any haphazard methods. These folk have been sheltered by the mud of Mother Earth for untold generations long before America was dreamed of. They prepare this mud according to formula. Occasionally one might catch a woman not too extravagantly clad treading mud in a barrel.

For the first few years the homesteader normally conducted all transactions on credit – he paid what he could when he got his crop off in the fall – and shared his animals and his machinery with his neighbours. Oxen were at first the almost universal draft animals, particularly with central Europeans, who were more familiar with the ox's ways than was the Britisher or American. Long after the time when the ox had given way to the horse or tractor, many of the early settlers still spoke of the massive Biblical beast with affection. The ox was strong, patient, enduring, dependable. He pursued the course he had set out for himself with an inflexibility of will born of the knowledge that he was always right. He never got lost in the roughest blizzard; he knew precisely how to hold back a heavy load on a down-hill grade; he never panicked, never kicked over the traces, never bolted; and he always accepted the idiosyncracies – sometimes downright imbecilities – of his frequently green driver with benignant tolerance. He kept himself in excellent condition on modest rations and was hardly ever ill. By contrast the horse was delicate, skittish, unpredictable – and much more demanding of attention and food. But he was faster than the ox. Much faster. The ox's pace – unhurrying, unvarying, uncompromising – was too slow for the twentieth century. So he has passed into history – but not before making a notable contribution to the opening of the Canadian west.

Bachelor homes were common on the prairies in the early days – sod or log shacks sheltering young men who had come away from office jobs and shopkeepers' hours and paternal acres they could never inherit to lead free lives and, they hoped, to acquire vast estates and matching bank-accounts. For many of them life was intolerably lonesome (one young man in order to pass the long winter hours regularly conducted debates with himself in which he argued both affirmative and negative sides of the question put to the house; another preached himself sermons three times a week although there is no evidence to suggest that he was particularly devout). The prairie west of seventy or eighty years ago was thus fair hunting-ground indeed for the single woman, who, in almost any given rural community, might have her choice among three or four or half a dozen eager suitors, regardless of handicaps, physical or mental, which might have scratched her from the matrimonial stakes in a community providing any sort of competition. Old Country families of substantial income and good social standing made a practice of getting rid of unwanted younger sons by shipping them off to one or another of the colonies and paying them a handsome allowance to stay there. It is regrettable that upper- and middle-class mores forbade them to get rid of unmarried daughters the same way. Had they been able to do so, many a girl condemned to wither into genteel, impoverished spinsterhood might have found herself mistress of a section or more of land and mother of a brood uniting the Anglo-Saxon blood strain with that of any one of half a dozen others – all more or less exotic. If the unmarried daughter had relatives living in the colonies, she could of course be sent to visit with them for an indefinite period – nearly always with satisfactory results; but for an unmarried girl to go on her own, and particularly to the raw, uncouth Canadian west, was unthinkable.

The bachelor farmer contemplating matrimony, who already had a woman in his sights and was ready for the kill, was, so many a veracious old-timer will tell you, frequently to be observed circulating among his pigs and cattle – and particularly his milk cows – clad in a toga-like garment made of flour-sacks or even draped in an old horse-blanket, the purpose of the masquerade being to condition the animals to accept with equanimity a creature clad in garments other than those to which they had become accustomed.

It need hardly be said that most marriages in a pioneer community were arranged and legally consummated with business-like purposefulness and despatch, involving, as the decisive step, a journey undertaken by the principals – possibly by ox-team – to the nearest person authorized to perform the marriage ceremony. There were, however, occasions when the marriage was surrounded by an aura of high romance, as when young Harry Carey of the Sumner colony south of Saltcoats wooed and won the devastatingly beautiful red-haired Louise Teitelbaum of Esterhazy, while both communities looked on in a state compounded of breathless excitement and dewy-eyed rapture.

The Rev. T. A. Teitelbaum, son of an exiled Hungarian patriot and an English mother, was an Anglican priest who ministered to a huge parish based on Esterhazy and Saltcoats and extending northwards as far as his clergyman's zeal might take him – even to the High Arctic if he felt disposed to go there. One summer he was joined in the vicarage by his exotic red-headed sister Louise, who promptly fell in love with the west and all things in it – including westerners, cows, horses, gophers, sunsets, and a young Englishman named Harry Carey, like herself a visitor from the Old Country. But Harry's parents were of good middle-class English stock and income. No doubt Louise Teitelbaum's connection, through her brother, with the Established Church told heavily in her favour; but it could not be overlooked that she was half Hungarian and everyone knew that Hungarians were much the same as gypsies and just as unstable. Harry's parents therefore forbade the reading of the banns.

It would be pleasant to be able to record at this point that young Harry, in defiance of family edicts and middle-class convention, simply snatched up the fair Louise and rode off with her into the sunset. Regrettably, the truth is much more prosaic. Young Harry was no Lochinvar; he shared the practical outlook of his class. To the disappointment of the sentimentally disposed of the community – and, one suspects, to Louise in her secret heart – he began the long journey back to England in the hope of being able to persuade his parents to relent.

He had been gone from Sumner only a few days when a letter arrived for him in the weekly mail. It was from his parents, and possibly contained news of the gravest import. The local post-mistress accordingly summoned a meeting which was attended by whatever leading citizens happened to be available. The Church, represented by Mr. Teitelbaum, gave its blessing to the proposal that the letter be opened – and word spread through the community like a prairie fire that Harry's parents, who by now had had time to investigate thoroughly Louise's antecedents, had withdrawn their opposition to the marriage and sent their blessings instead. Whereupon the Rev. Mr. Teitelbaum, who no doubt loved his sister dearly but must have found living with her anything but conducive to priestly meditation, hitched up his team of fast horses and drove thirty miles to the nearest tele-graph station. His telegram caught Harry just as he was about to board his ship, and brought him back by the next train.

The wedding was, inevitably, a community affair, ending with a feast from which no one was turned empty away, and a dance-till-dawn in the Sumner town hall.

Those early years were years of confidence, of hope. How, after all, could a man possessing fifty to one hundred times as much land as he could possibly have aspired to back home fail to be-come an even greater landholder, run fine herds of cattle on the inexhaustible free range, provide hitherto unimaginable house-hold comforts for his family? He quickly learned that failure came more easily than success – and oftener. Frost, hail, drought, grasshoppers, low prices for produce were never mentioned in land-company or government advertising literature; nor was com-pound interest, which for many a purchaser doubled or tripled the price of land he bought before he cleared the title – or lost the land back to the original vendor. And yet, over the long haul the outcome of the struggle between the settler and the forces – natural, social, economic – working against him was inevitable. Sooner or later the land was cleared; drought and grasshoppers were, up to a point, controlled by scientific farming methods, hail losses covered by insurance, prices above subsistence level established through co-operatives and increased world demand. All these things were to come, but for the pioneer settlers who first came to grips with the terrifying immensity of a world such as the Canadian prairies – a harsh raw world which left them naked to the at best indifferent and at worst savagely hostile forces of nature – those early years must have provided as great a share of heartbreak as of exaltation.

To this new world of rich, uncultivated, and almost uninhabited land stretching to far horizons came not only those seeking economic security or a chance to make their own place in the social scale but men and women who above all else sought that freedom, denied them in their homelands, to live and worship according to the dictates of conscience. Of the persecuted from the Old World the first to come into Saskatchewan were the Mennonites who spilled across the border from still earlier settlements in Manitoba. The term Mennonite is one that frequently causes confusion, since it is used to refer to both a church and an ethnic group, although a member of the ethnic group is not necessarily a member of the church. Most of the original Mennonites who settled in the Canadian west came from Russia. They were evangelical, fundamentalist, pacifist, hence in their own country inevitably in conflict with temporal and spiritual authority. The first large Mennonite community in Saskatchewan was established at Herbert, about seventy-five miles west of Moose Jaw. The towns of Rosthern and Hague, farther north, are today centres of flourishing Mennonite communities. The Mennonites have on the whole made excellent citizens. Fear on the part of certain groups among them that their liberties were being infringed upon by government has led on two occasions to migrations south – to Mexico and Paraguay – but the vast majority of Mennonites have remained in Saskatchewan to build up splendid local communities, which in their encouragement of temperance and cleanliness in all things set an example that others might do well to follow.

Of all the groups who fled Europe seeking refuge from persecution the Doukhobors have attracted the most attention to themselves. They came to Saskatchewan in 1899 to the number of eight thousand, under the sponsorship of Leo Tolstoy, who, although not himself a member of the sect, was in his later years a firm believer in most of the principles it upheld. Like the Mennonites the Doukhobors were fundamentalist, evangelical, pacifist, temperate – but in all things, including temperance, they were extreme. They were vegetarians who carried their abhorrence of animal food to the point of rejecting butter and grease; and the more extreme among them refused to work with tools or machinery made of metal on the grounds that the shaping of metals defiled the original works of God. They shared with Rousseau a belief – which they did not, however, derive from that notable sceptic – in the natural goodness of man; hence it follows that there is no need of an intercessor, either church or priest, between man and his God.

Doukhobor determination to render everything to God and nothing to Caesar inevitably brought them into conflict with governments wherever they lived. In Canada their pacifist views have always been respected, at least in law; their reluctance to educate their children and pay taxes has not.

In the nearly seventy years of settlement the Doukhobors have tended to split into three distinct groups, representing right, centre, and a rapidly growing left. Those at the centre adhere as far as possible to the old ways but avoid direct conflict with government; they pay their taxes, send their children to school, but otherwise live as much as possible to themselves and out of the world. The left is represented by an increasing number who have rejected wholly or in part the old ways and to the horror of their elders no longer seem much concerned about preserving an ethnic or religious identity. The extreme right is represented by the group which is really the only one known to the rest of Canada – the Sons of Freedom, who, as those of the left and centre have grown more lax in the observance of the old ways have become correspondingly more rigid, more fanatic.

The Sons of Freedom are now concentrated mainly in British Columbia, but there was a time when they gave the Saskatchewan authorities a good deal of trouble. Most of the Doukhobors who came out under Tolstoy's sponsorship and with Quaker assistance were located on land around Yorkton (originally settled by Englishmen from Yorkshire) and Kamsack – impressively rugged country which on its eastern extremity breaks into the splendid Duck Mountain ridge, a world of lake and hill and forest, part of which comprises one of the pleasantest and best-equipped parks in the province. The complete rejection by the Doukhobors of individual, as opposed to communal, responsibility led almost at once to difficulties. They were reluctant to supply the government with vital statistics – it was enough, they said, that their numbers be known unto God; they refused to send their children to school, to register homestead ownership, or – crime of crimes – to pay taxes. In short, they followed a course that almost completely ignored all existing government machinery and drove government bureaucrats half out of their minds. Inevitably government pressure mounted; just as inevitably Doukhobor resistance stiffened – resistance which on the part of the extreme conservative element culminated in the first nude parade on the prairies, held in 1903 in Yorkton, in the presence of a considerable concourse of bemused and incredulous Anglo-Saxons.

Four years later the government, determined to enforce the letter of the law, offered the Doukhobors the choice of conforming to the requirements of the Homestead Act (including payment of the registration fee and registration under individual names) or forfeiting their homestead claims. Lest those refusing to conform should be left completely destitute, the government agreed to allot them fifteen acres per capita for communal living. Most of the Doukhobors refused to conform, with the result that two-thirds of the land they had originally settled on was thrown open to the public.

Inevitably the government action brought to the fore the more radical elements among the Doukhobors. Happily for Saskatchewan Peter Verigin, the Doukhobor leader (assassinated in 1924 by a time bomb placed in a railway carriage), acquired in his own name a promised land in British Columbia to which in the years from 1908 to 1912 he led most of the fanatical Sons of Freedom, leaving behind in Saskatchewan those elements who in the long run were prepared to accept the authority of the Canadian government and conform, with some reservations, to its laws.

It is a matter of regret that most Canadians outside Saskatchewan identify the Doukhobors with the Sons of Freedom lunatic fringe rather than with the hard-working, law-abiding, and in many ways progressive citizens who make up ninety per cent of the Doukhobor population.

What has happened over the past half-century in eastern Saskatchewan is generally true of the province – and indeed of the west – as a whole. Some communities have managed to preserve a degree of ethnic integrity; but Canadianization, in the sense of acceptance of Dominion laws and, up to a point, the conventions of a cosmopolitan society, is everywhere a clearly definable process. Long-sustained isolation from one's fellows is possible only when the dedication to a different way of life is – as in the occasional Hutterite colony – total. For the rest, overlapping of interests and landholdings, increased mobility, the mingling of nationalities in the schoolroom, the curiosity of the young about their fellows in the next township – these and a host of less obvious factors have broken down the barriers of speech and custom and belief that once kept the colonists apart. So it is that today a town bearing the wholly Anglo-Saxon name of Wroxton is dominated by an onion-domed Ukrainian Orthodox church; a few miles south on the outskirts of Stockholm the Church of Our Lady of Vienna rises in colourful splendour; and a University of Saskatchewan class-room, whatever the subject being taught, is sure to be filled with representatives, most of them drawn from the province itself, of at least a dozen ethnic groups.

Among the community names of eastern Saskatchewan – Rhein, Verigin, Mikado, Thingvalla, Churchbridge, Bangor, Tantallon, Stornoway, all within a radius of a few miles, there is one – that of a village hardly more than a pinprick on the enormous prairie face – which more effectively than any other explains the nature of the pull that drew men, almost from the ends of the earth it seemed, to a new land far away from their native hearths. The name is Runnymede. Perhaps the fight for freedom begun more than eight hundred years ago in a Thames meadow has reached as successful a culmination as men can hope for on the prairies of western Canada.

11. Temperance Town

The city of Saskatoon is unique in its origins; it was founded by whiskey-hating zealots from eastern Canada who dreamed of creating a teetotallers' paradise far from the corrupting influences of civilization. (To dispel misgivings on the part of prospective visitors it should be emphasized that the only surviving evidence of the city's temperance origins is to be found in the name of a single residential street.) The temperance men, most of them Ontario Methodists, applied for and received a government land grant of 200,000 acres on and about the site of the present city – even-numbered sections only, the odd numbers being left by law for free homesteads, thus leaving the way open for the infiltration of imbibers. The sober-eyed advance agents of the colony, headed by Commissioner John Lake, saw clearly (allegedly from a point now marked by a stolid, ill-proportioned cairn) and chose well. They located their townsite in the year 1882 on the high east bank of the South Saskatchewan River – flats below for the convenience of ferry and steamboat traffic – in almost the precise centre of the Saskatchewan plains country, thus establishing a pivotal distribution point for the settlements which by the turn of the century had filled up nearly all the vacant spaces on the prairie map.

John Lake didn't do so well when he chose a name for the settlement. Upon being told that the Indian name for a certain purplish berry growing in abundance along the river bank was *saskatoon* he exclaimed in a moment of unfortunate inspiration, 'Arise, Saskatoon, Queen of the North!' By itself the name is perhaps acceptable, but the combination of Saskatoon Saskatchewan outsiders find difficult to take seriously. As for the berry itself – for years now a campaign has been under way to convince the world that the saskatoon is a distinctive and delicious fruit, and particularly tasty in pies. (Distinguished visitors to the city seldom escape without having a pie or two thrust upon them.) The saskatoon is indeed edible, even tasty, when combined with other fruits whose flavours dominate the mixture. Served by itself it is filling.

Most of the early settlers came to Saskatoon over a prairie trail from Moose Jaw, the nearest point on the C.P.R. Newly disembarked prospective settlers usually struck north in caravans of a dozen or more horse- or ox-drawn wagons, some canvas-covered but most open to the sky. Nearly every settler brought with him up the trail two or three horses or oxen, a cow or two, a dog, essential household goods, and odds and ends of farm machinery. Wisely, for local supplies were scarce and prices high. It was a long hard haul from Moose Jaw overland to Saskatoon, and many of the newcomers from the Old Country or eastern Canada – especially the women – must have suffered at times terror and heartbreak, coming, as so many of them did, from an environment of friendly hills and sheltering trees and clear running water into a wilderness of such dimensions that even today it can startle and at times appal all except the most insensitive. From the summit of a mile-long hill at the elbow of the South Saskatchewan the newcomers looked ahead over a great waste reaching to the horizon, with not enough bush growing on it 'for a gopher to hide behind'. No firewood and no water for forty miles or more. The end of the journey – eight days on the average for a caravan with livestock, four days without – found the horses exhausted, the women frequently in a state bordering on shock, everyone tired and dirty, and some ill from drinking brackish water. The men suffered a good deal less than the women; they were buoyed up by sight of those vast open spaces over which in imagination they were already grazing great herds of cattle, or running ploughs preparatory to growing forty bushels to the acre of number one hard wheat.

Late in the year 1883 the first substantial supplies of lumber reached the townsite, having come down river by raft from Medicine Hat, and modest frame buildings began to replace the tents and sod huts of the first comers. But Saskatoon in the years of its infancy was no boom town. The railway ran 150 miles south; few trails led into the settlement, and river traffic was slow and spasmodic. Moreover, any community that depends for its existence on agriculture must over the long stretch pace its growth to that of the agricultural community as a whole; and Saskatoon, in spite of one or two wild boom-or-bust aberrations, followed the orthodox pattern.

Saskatoon's early history, like that of most western Canadian communities, is sober to the point of dullness – entirely lacking the colour and violence associated with the American frontier. No hard-eyed gunmen ever stalked one another along Second Avenue; no rustlers swung from the poplars lining the riverbank. The Mounties and the missionaries who preceded the settlers either jailed the bad men or converted them; church 'sociables' took the place of lynching parties; debating societies resolved disputes with words instead of bullets. None the less the early Saskatoon settlement was at times on the fringe, if not at the centre, of stirring events. In 1885 the village imagined itself under threat of attack from the Sioux Indians (long-time refugees from Minnesota) of the Moose Woods Reserve a few miles south; but the settlers, about seventy all told, presented a resolute front to Chief Whitecap, whose intentions appear at worst to have been no more than mildly hostile, and no scalps were lost on either side. Shortly thereafter General Middleton, who had been encamped at Clarke's Crossing a few miles below the village, advanced with his little army of militia on the Métis concentrated at Batoche; and the realities of warfare were brought home to the settlers with the setting-up in Saskatoon of a military hospital to care for the forty or more soldiers wounded at Fish Creek.

In 1890 the railway reached Saskatoon from Moose Jaw, thus depriving the townsfolk of one of their most cherished forms of entertainment, that of watching the clumsy river steamers run aground on sandbars. There were, however, compensations. Numerous parties of settlers bound for the assorted utopias promised by government and land-company promotion literature brought a good deal of excitement, and occasionally a little money, to the town. Of these parties the most notable was the Barr Colony from Great Britain. The colonists camped in Saskatoon for two weeks in the spring of 1903. There they purchased supplies and plotted the overthrow of their incompetent leader, the Rev. Moses Barr. Most of the colonists moved on after the fortnight was up, but a few remained behind to become in the course of time leading citizens of Saskatoon.

Saskatoon's development from frontier settlement to city was at first painfully slow. Discouraged by successive years of drought, early frosts, and grasshopper plagues, the colonists turned more and more to ranching; and it was not until the early 1900s, when the rains fell abundantly, that the agricultural potential of the community began to be realized and the town to fulfil its role as distributing centre for a rapidly expanding agricultural domain. How rapidly that domain expanded is suggested by a lyrical editorial commenting on the filling-up of the country south-west of Saskatoon, which appeared in the Saskatoon *Phenix* (*sic*) in the spring of 1909:

> The spring of three years ago (1906) witnessed a spectacle on those prairies to the south-west which will never be forgotten. There is a point on the trail about thirty miles out and somewhat south of Delisle where a man can see with the naked eye a block of country probably two hundred square miles in extent. Winding through that area was the trail to Goose Lake, and that particular spring the traffic of the incoming settlers was so steady and continuous that it was not an uncommon sight to see an almost unbroken line of wagons and vehicles of all kinds and degrees of richness stringing out in a long snake-like caravan many miles in length. At night round every slough the campfire blazed, while in the stopping houses . . . brave men and women, weary but full of hope, rested on their way to the land which promised comfort and prosperity. And today the traveller reaching that point in the trail, reins up involuntarily and looks with amazement at the dozens of cozy farm steadings which dot the wide plain. The change suggests to the mind the Arabian Nights for it is as if some wizard had waved a magic wand or breathed an incantation and turned the wilderness into a populous country.

The exuberant overspending that accompanied expansion created problems that could not be blamed on the weather. In 1907, the year following the incorporation of Saskatoon as a city (population 4,500), city credit was so overstrained that the mayor was compelled to borrow $30,000 on personal security in order to complete the installation of an electrical plant to operate the newly laid water system. Only a year or two later the city was enjoying the greatest boom in its history, largely as a consequence of the rapid settlement of the surrounding countryside, and the certainty of being a point intersected by railway lines running in several directions. (In the early west it was an article of faith that intersecting railway lines guaranteed a community's growth and prosperity.) Frantic speculation in real estate did much to encourage wild spending and over-expansion and hastened the sudden collapse of the boom just before the outbreak of the First World War.

During the boom years the future character of the city was most profoundly affected not by business or industrial expansion (in both instances the expansion was to some extent illusory) but by the establishment on the city outskirts of the provincial university – this after the usual desperate political manoeuvring consequent upon the desire of every city, town, and hamlet in Saskatchewan to be the Athens of the prairies. The choice was a sound one; in the long run it made for a fair degree of harmony between Saskatoon and Regina (which had already grabbed off the Legislature); the location was central to the most heavily populated areas of the province; and the actual physical location of the university buildings on an ample acreage high on the east bank of the Saskatchewan and commanding a splendid view of river and city could hardly have been bettered elsewhere in the province. The Saskatoon campus is today one of the handsomest in Canada; the buildings, most of them faced with local grey stone, achieve a pleasing and dignified harmony of colour; and although ranging in design from orthodox collegiate Gothic to contemporary functional have managed, by avoiding the extremes of either, to suggest evolution rather than conflict. The almost unlimited land available has permitted uncluttered expansion; and the careful nurturing, over more than half a century, of trees and shrubs and flowers has made the university grounds a horticultural show-piece.

From the day of its foundation (April 3, 1907), the University of Saskatchewan has profited from the inclination of well-educated, ambitious Maritimers to leave their native haunts and serve in western universities at ranks rarely below that of Dean. The founding president, Dr. Walter Murray, came direct from Dalhousie to guide the University of Saskatchewan in its vital formative years and put upon it the distinctive stamp of his own character. Dr. Murray's diplomatic talents helped him, on behalf of the university, to win the confidence of government and general public, his sensitive academic antennae to seek out and gather around him a nucleus of bright young men who welcomed the opportunity to create their own individual empires in a brave new university world. Not surprisingly, the initial university emphasis was on the development of a College of Agriculture; and it is in agricultural research that the university has made some of its most notable contributions to the welfare of mankind. Hardy varieties of cereals and fruits, weed-destroying chemicals, anti-encephalomyelitis vaccines – these are but a few of the significant results of College of Agriculture research. But the greatest single contribution to the welfare of the Canadian wheat economy, the development of a rust-resistant wheat, must in large measure be attributed to the brilliant work of Dr. Walter Thompson, Head of the Department of Biology, later Dean of Arts, and from 1949 to 1959 President of the University.

Thus far the strength of the university has lain mainly in the natural sciences. Dr. J. W. T. Spinks, formerly Head of the Department of Chemistry and since 1959 President of the University, is an internationally recognized authority on the peacetime uses of nuclear energy. Immensely significant research in nuclear physics was made possible in 1948 when the university acquired a twenty-five million electron-volt betatron, the first of its kind in Canada. Four years later the world's first cobalt bomb, intended primarily for the treatment of cancer, was designed and built at the University of Saskatchewan.

In the life of the university there have been inevitably crises, scandals, discontents other than divine, behind-scenes politicking – all the concomitants unavoidable in a closely knit academic society in which the passion for learning is not the only one in evidence; but it is fair to say that the University of Saskatchewan has achieved its present impressive stature with fewer internal dissensions than most of its sister universities. The faculty no doubt feels that this agreeable state of affairs is the consequence of its presidents being distinguished by their 'teachability' – a quality not always associated with academics at the highest, or indeed any, level.

In Saskatoon, town and gown have always exhibited a fair degree of tolerance towards one another. They know each other very well for they have grown up together. The university has, happily, escaped the fate of many of our older universities – it has not been physically overwhelmed by an outrageous urban growth on all sides; nor has it, as is unfortunately true of many of our newer universities, been tacked on as a sort of novel excrescence to a city that has already established its own clearly defined independent character. Inevitably members of faculty have from time to time been looked upon with a jaundiced eye by a disturbed citizenry; the university has been accused of harbouring the orthodox raffish assortment of socialists, communists, long-hairs, atheists, free-lovers, alcoholics – and a few have done their not ineffectual best to live up to the roles in which they have been cast. In general, though, the town-and-gown relationship has been remarkably harmonious. And with reason. Half the citizens of Saskatoon, it seems, are graduates of the university; and most of the other half spend their spare time attending night classes, concerts, and theatre on the university campus, and rightly consider themselves a part of the university community.

If the growth of Saskatoon depends, as now seems probable, on industrial development financed by outside interests, it may be that the university and the city will ultimately tend to follow independent – even divergent – courses. Thus far, however, the University of Saskatchewan has been – to a degree rare in most university communities – a vital part of corporate city life.

Following the First World War the growth of the city slowed almost to a standstill. Saskatoon's role as distributing centre, widely advertised in the uninspired soubriquet 'Hub City', was confirmed; and while making for a measure of security it was hardly conducive to rapid expansion. In the years between the wars Saskatoon was essentially a pleasant university town, distinguished in outward appearance only by reason of an admirable oasis-like setting and the numerous delightful parks that are still one of her most attractive features. During the Dirty Thirties Saskatoon suffered greatly; and survivors of those agonizing dust-bowl years still speak of their experience in tones of mixed pride and horror. In the 1940s the rains returned; and in recent years a comparative abundance of moisture allied with scientific farming methods has virtually eliminated the possibility of crop failure.

During the past quarter-century the character of Saskatoon has – superficially at least – undergone a marked change. The development of huge potash resources close to the city has provided an unprecedented stimulus to industry and earned for

Saskatoon the self-conferred title – already a little overworked – of 'Potash Capital of the World'. Potash was discovered in Saskatchewan as early as 1942, and the first shaft was sunk near the town of Unity ten years later. Potash is formed from the deposits left from the drying-up of an ancient sea; in Saskatchewan the potash beds cover hundreds of thousands of acres at depths varying from three thousand to seven thousand feet and in layers up to six hundred feet in thickness. Saskatchewan's potash reserves are, in fact, so great as to justify the overworked adjective 'inexhaustible'. In the sinking of the huge shafts near Esterhazy and Saskatoon the chief problem to be overcome was that of flooding from a waterlogged soil layer about six hundred feet down; the layer was first frozen, and the entire shaft lined or 'tubbed' with huge iron rings, each ring installed in segments weighing about four tons apiece.

Ninety per cent of the huge potash product of the province (more valuable now than oil) goes into the making of commercial fertilizer, the rest for a wide variety of uses in commercial products including liquid soaps, bleaches, fine glass, rocket fuel, and salt substitutes.

The rapid industrial development of Saskatoon has inevitably resulted in dislocations and growing-pains; population (now 120,-000) has almost tripled in the last quarter-century; professors complain bitterly that the varied sounds of bursting seams inhibit philosophic speculation; and there is a strong feeling on the part of many citizens that the price of progress need not have included the really monstrous potash 'monument' – a huge tubbing-ring mounted on a thirty-foot steel-and-concrete base standing naked, floodlit, and unashamed in a new river-bank park development. Saskatoon is, in fact, no longer a well-mannered, rather sedate child, but a raw-boned, sometimes raucous adolescent with braces on her teeth, who, however, gives promise of real and lasting beauty once she attains maturity.

Things to see in Saskatoon include the Mendel Art Gallery, an architecturally interesting modern building delightfully located on the river-bank, in large part the gift of a prominent local industrialist, Mr. Fred Mendel; and for those seeking a contrast between the old and the new, the Western Development Museum which houses one of the finest collections of pioneer memorabilia and relics in Canada. Pionera, a week-long exhibition and carnival dedicated to glorifying the pioneer way of life and recapturing something of its spirit, is one of the highlights of Saskatoon summer entertainment. Pionera is a novel kind of entertainment, drawing heavily on the Western Development Museum for its exhibits. Its original altogether worthy purpose is in some danger of being lost sight of; today the emphasis seems to be less on re-creating a way of life that really existed than one dreamed up by movie-makers and writers of wild-west fiction. Certainly nothing could be more alien to the institutions of a pioneer temperance society – Methodist at that – than the chorus-girl and folk-singer bedizened saloon which is now the most prominent feature of the Pionera midway. (Advocates of the saloon hasten to point out that it upholds the temperance ideal by selling soft drinks only.)

For those of us whose memories of the prairie go back a long way, one of the most interesting of the Museum exhibits is that dinosaur of the machine age – the steam-engine. The steam-engine, like the dinosaur, is long since extinct, but in its day it commanded the respect – veneration even – of prairie dwellers to a degree not even approached by its successors, the gasoline tractor and the combine. The steam-engine was used for a variety of heavy tasks – including breaking the prairie sod with as many as twelve ploughs at once – but it really came into its own at harvest time. The steam-engine powered the grain separator; and for the old-time farmer the great moment of the year arrived when he saw the smoke-belching behemoth (owned and operated by a man who might live forty or fifty miles away) lumber on to his land and pull the separator into position for the threshing. Steam outfits cost a lot of money, hence they were few and far between. Many of them enjoyed runs lasting from early fall until Christmas or later, depending on the snowfall. (Cold was seldom a deterrent to operations.) One of the loneliest, most haunting of sounds that I associate with my boyhood is a banshee wail rising from somewhere out of the still pitch-black night – in actual fact the sound of the steam-engine whistle blown by the fireman (who had already been firing up for an hour or so) to rouse the threshing crew asleep in the caboose to breakfast and a new day.

At the Saskatoon Pionera a number of the Western Development Museum steam-engines are fired up and put through their paces. They are serviceable yet, and as powerful as ever, but like the ox teams too slow and cumbersome for modern requirements.

Around them old threshermen congregate like flies – slaves to the memory of those golden years when, in harvest time at least, they were gods not from but of the machine. Unhappy men now, I sometimes think, no better and no worse than the rest of us; and who, having once savoured divinity, can be content with the common lot?

Architecturally Saskatoon is undistinguished. The City Hall, a building of comparatively recent date, is redeemed from the merely innocuous only by reason of some admirable landscaping, and an exquisitely designed forecourt fountain, the work of sculptor Robert Murray. High-rise apartments, churches, shopping malls follow designs already tested and approved elsewhere. The one building which to an extraordinary degree dominates downtown Saskatoon physically and spiritually – and would be a standout anywhere – is the C.N.R. hotel, the Bessborough. The hotel was completed in 1931 but remained closed during the early years of the depression. It was officially opened in 1935 and ever since has been the centre of the city's social life. A massive turreted structure – 'grotesque palace from a bad fairy tale' says poet Peter Stevens – the Bessborough sits on the river-bank dwarfing into utter insignificance the puny structures huddled in its shadow. The Bessborough is not really like anything anywhere else; it is unimitated and inimitable – which may help to explain the unique authority it exercises over all neighbouring buildings and the community at large.

In recent years extensive 'modern' interior decorations have replaced the original ponderous and ornate décor – 'railway rococo' a friend of mine called it in an inspired moment. No doubt the new is more restful than the old, but it is less distinctive. A hostelry should, I feel, be a repository of history – a view shared by Old Country innkeepers for the past two thousand years or so. But ghosts haunt only familiar scenes; and when the wall brackets and candelabra and potted palms and tapestried baronial armchairs disappeared from the Bessborough the ghosts went with them.

The best time to see Saskatoon is at sunset, from almost any point on the high east bank of the river. Especially when there is no wind stirring and the river is still. The bridges cast their arches into the water; church spires duplicate themselves; and

the inverted image of the Bessborough's improbable turrets in-
vests them with the grace and magic of fairy towers recalled from
a childhood dream. There is nothing dreamlike about the Bessborough itself; it stands out against the sunset, matronly rather
than elegant; and behind it rise the modest skyscrapers of the
downtown city, and, farther off, exotic onion-domes which call
to mind names learned in poetry like Xanadu and Samarkand,
and beyond the onion-domes on the horizon's rim, outlined
against a flame-coloured sky, a huge government grain elevator,
in the light of common day cumbersome, utilitarian, but now
cast in lines that to the dreamer's eye are a temple to ancient
gods.

At such a time it is easy to believe that the merging of chateau
and spire and onion-dome and temple into a twilight harmony
is symbolic of that mingling of cultures drawn from far-off places
which has become the culture of the city. A mingling, too, of
time present and time past, so that, surveying chateau and
temple and spire and onion-dome against a now luminous violet
sky it is possible for the onlooker to feel for a fleeting moment
as James Joyce felt when he looked across from Howth Head at
his beloved Dublin – that all ages are as one.

Saskatoon celebrated her Golden Jubilee in 1956, her Diamond
Jubilee in 1966, and between times and after participated enthusiastically in the University of Saskatchewan Golden Jubilee
(1958), the Provincial Diamond Jubilee (1965), and the Centennial celebrations (1967). Inevitably such a plethora of jubilees
called forth a corresponding plethora of 'tributes' in verse, prose,
and song, ranging all the way from the severely scholarly to the
outrageously sentimental and the blatantly boosterish. Of all the
tributes to the city of Saskatoon that I have read, I like best one
written by a twelve-year-old boy, Don Sylvester, who, observing
the world about him with clear-eyed unsentimental detachment,
caught in a few lines of verse the essential character of his environment and the people who are a part of it:

> *Here's Saskatoon with sixty years of growing,*
> *And sixty years of snowing.*
> *The wind it blows and bites*
> *And the city council fights and fights.*
> *The people always yell*
> *About the stockyards' funny smell.*

The Civic Centre in Saskatoon
Will raise our taxes every full moon.

I like Saskatoon despite my remarks,
Because of its beautiful streams and parks.

12. Battles Long Ago

There are many roads out of Saskatoon that lead to the battle-fields; but the best one of all follows the river downstream from Fish Creek to Batoche through some of the loveliest scenery in Saskatchewan. The countryside is at its most moving and dramatic in autumn, when the scarlet and gold splashed against the long valley slopes recall the colours of regimental uniforms once seen against this identical background; and the great flights of birds southbound over denuded fields touch all things with a hint of melancholy and remind us – appropriately since we are on our way to the battlefields – of our own mortality.

We follow Highway No. 5 east for eighteen miles to its junction with No. 27. At the junction we turn north and follow No. 27 through Strawberry Valley to Clarke's Crossing. From Clarke's Crossing the road turns briefly east, then north again through the small town of Aberdeen to the Hague Ferry and an impressive stretch of river where the bluffs rise to an unusual height and command a view of a vast expanse of prairie flowing away to the west. From Hague the road turns east a mile or two, then north past a substantial Ukrainian Orthodox church and so back to the river and Fish Creek.

The Riel Rebellion is now sufficiently removed from us in time to have acquired something of that aura of romantic melancholy which surrounds the deeds of desperate men when the consequences of those deeds do not affect us personally. But not yet far enough removed, perhaps, to permit us a clear view of the chief protagonist – the man who in 1870 was guilty of a sordid murder, who in 1885 was hanged for high treason, and who today is the most controversial figure in Canadian history, viewed by honest men according to their lights as either a lost soul or a martyr, but hardly ever as anything in between.

Louis Riel was a Métis born in the Red River country of Assiniboia in 1844. The Métis were a people of mixed Indian and French blood who roamed the great plains all summer long in pursuit of the buffalo and wintered in settlements along the Red River Valley where each man occupied a small land-holding. Riel was educated in Montreal, where he trained briefly for the priesthood. In 1869 he formed a provisional government to administer Assiniboia at a time when the Government of Canada, without consulting the Métis population of Assiniboia, was arranging with the Hudson's Bay Company for the transfer of the entire Northwest Territories from Company to Dominion rule. It was Riel's contention that he legitimately formed his government to fill a vacuum; no other administration was functioning in Assiniboia at the time, the Company having surrendered its authority, the Government of Canada not yet having taken over. Unfortunately his treatment of those who opposed him cast him in a more sinister role than that of disinterested servant of his people. Some of his opponents he imprisoned; one he shot. A military expedition was despatched from eastern Canada to restore order and enforce the authority of the Canadian government in Assiniboia; and on the appearance of the soldiers outside the walls of Fort Garry Riel slipped away from his stronghold and fled to the United States.

Fourteen years later the call reached the exile to come once more to the aid of his people – this time those Métis who, hoping vainly to escape beyond reach of the white man, had fled from the Red River Valley and settled along the South Saskatchewan River between Saskatoon and Prince Albert. For now in 1884, just as in 1869, white surveyors were moving in on the land which the Métis, true to their French inheritance, held in the old seigniorial fashion (each farm a long narrow strip fronting the river), and redividing it into the square sections the Métis hated.

Riel answered the call. All through the summer and early winter of 1884-5 he bombarded Ottawa with pleas for a just recognition of Métis rights to the land they had settled upon and which they now regarded as their own. As well talk to the whirlwind, fight Goliath without a slingshot. The extinction of minority rights which frustrate the majority will is, even in a democracy – perhaps particularly in a democracy – a frighteningly inexorable process. The Métis way of life was wasteful; it demanded a vast land area to support a small population. To prospective white settlers, hungry for farmland, it was an intolerable injustice that a handful of French half-breeds should be allowed to claim squatters' rights to the rich lands of the Saskatchewan River valley. And to the Government of Canada it was unthinkable that the Métis would actually fight to defend those rights. Even if the Métis were joined by all the hungry, restless Indians in the whole of the North-west, a revolt must inevitably be crushed with ease; for the combined forces of the malcontents could never number at the most more than a few thousand ill-armed, untrained fighting men.

What the Government of Canada failed to realize was that the mental processes of the leader of the Métis were not logical. It did not occur to the government that God might be on Riel's side. Riel knew that He was. And having God on your side more than compensates for any trifling deficiencies in manpower and fire-power.

The outcome of the Rebellion was inevitable, but the casualty list on the government side would have been much longer had Riel trusted less to the guidance of his supernatural voices and more to the military talents of his field commander, Gabriel Dumont. Dumont was an uncomplicated man, a skilled hunter and crack shot who knew how to lay cunning traps for wild animals and white men. Given *carte blanche* in the field he would have made life miserable for the government forces. But Riel, in spite of that one dark deed committed in 1870 when he shot Thomas Scott against a Fort Garry wall, was no man of blood. At almost every turn he overruled his aggressive field-general and waited for the sign from heaven which never came. But in spite of being burdened by an indecisive and inconsistent superior, Dumont managed to do damage to the militia out of all proportion to the size of the force he was able to lead against them – never more than two hundred men, most of them armed with ancient muzzle-loaders.

The government forces in the field were commanded by General Fred Middleton, a veteran of the Indian Mutiny and a very brave man, whose courage was generally more in evidence than his intelligence. The troops under his command consisted of untrained, inexperienced militia units from eastern Canada and Winnipeg supported by a stiffening of regulars, two batteries of artillery, a machine-gun which the Canadian government generously permitted an American army officer to try out on the Métis (there being no Indian wars going on at the moment in the American west), and two small bodies of mounted volunteers recruited mainly from among Old Country men of the Qu'Appelle Valley and Moose Mountain districts. The Mounted Police, to their chagrin, were assigned by Middleton to routine garrison duty at a number of key points throughout the west.

Middleton advanced from Fort Qu'Appelle, where he had spent a week or two drilling his green troops, to Clarke's Crossing on the South Saskatchewan, fourteen miles below Saskatoon and only a little more than fifty from Batoche. Almost simultaneously two other government forces moved up on trouble spots – General Strange from Calgary to Edmonton and Fort Pitt in pursuit of Big Bear and his insurgent band, and Colonel Otter from Swift Current to the relief of Battleford, which for three weeks had been under desultory siege. At Clarke's Crossing Middleton foolishly divided his force, which now numbered eight hundred men, sending half to the west side of the river. On April 22, 1885, both columns began the advance on Batoche.

Two days later, at a place called Fish Creek, soldiers and Métis met head-on. The Métis, deadly marksmen at close range even though armed with semi-obsolete weapons, crouched in rifle-pits at the bottom of the steep Fish Creek ravine and shot at the troops as they appeared against the skyline above. They extended their line from time to time along the ravine bottom away from the river to forestall Middleton's clumsy attempts to outflank their position; and because they were fighting a defensive battle against green troops who were forced to show themselves before making any sort of advance, they were able to inflict casualties ten times greater than their own.

Fighting – aimless, inconclusive – sputtered off and on all day. General Middleton fretted and fumed, exposed himself recklessly to the Métis fire — one bullet, said to have been fired by Gabriel Dumont, actually ripped through his fur hat – and at the same time exhorted his men to keep their heads down and take no chances. Many of the militiamen were members of influential eastern Canadian families, and a heavy casualty list would inevitably have provoked a row. It is easy enough to sympathize with

Middleton, a tough old professional soldier who found himself cast in the entirely antithetical roles of military commander and nursemaid.

Middleton wasn't the only man who cursed and fretted and fumed during the spasmodic action at Fish Creek. On the opposite bank of the river four hundred militiamen and regulars smelled battle from afar, and figuratively pawed the ground in a frenzy of frustration, for incredibly no transport was available to carry them across the river to the battlefield. Towards evening a battered old scow was located and pressed into service, but by the time the first scow-load of eager warriors reached the east bank, the fighting was over. The Métis, whose numbers never exceeded one hundred and fifty, had run short of ammunition and slipped away with the coming on of darkness.

The Fish Creek engagement was a costly one for Middleton. He had inflicted no casualties to speak of on the enemy; but he himself out of a force of four hundred had lost sixty men killed or wounded, and his advance was delayed for two full weeks while he arranged for the hospitalization of the wounded and awaited the arrival of fresh troops and supplies.

Today the country around Fish Creek is more intensively cultivated than it was in 1885, but the ravine itself has hardly changed at all. A typical prairie stream meanders sluggishly through the ravine into the Saskatchewan River which runs only a few hundred yards from the scene of the most intense fighting. Even the most cursory inspection of the ravine makes clear the formidable nature of the task facing the green soldiers on that spring day in 1885; in order to see the enemy they had first to allow themselves to be seen; and had they been reckless enough to risk a charge they would have been slowed almost to a standstill by the dense growth of shrubbery covering the side of the ravine – hence easy marks for the Métis sharpshooters crouched in the rifle-pits below.

A rutted trail leads south from the ravine a short distance to a community park and picnic-ground. In the centre of the park stands a cairn commemorating the Battle of Fish Creek. The inscription on the cairn reads thus: 'While General Middleton was moving to capture Batoche his forces were attacked on the 24th of April, 1885, by the half-breeds under Gabriel Dumont from concealed rifle-pits near the mouth of Fish Creek. The rebels were defeated and driven from the field.' The inscription reflects no credit on those responsible for its wording; it is inaccurate and in the worst possible taste. The Métis were not driven from the field; they withdrew of their own accord after their ammunition had run out; and one would like to think that terms such as 'half-breeds' and 'rebels' as applied to brave men fighting in defence of their way of life no longer hold any place in the vocabulary of those seeking to preserve through public memorials some fragment of the history of the Canadian west.

Beside the cairn a modest headstone marks the graves of three militiamen killed in the fighting at Fish Creek. The headstone communicates far more effectively than does the cairn with its crudely insolent inscription the infinite pathos of a struggle which, like so many of the wars of mankind, affected only those who had everything to lose – their lives – and left untouched the men who, out of malice and stupidity and greed and desire for political gain or economic advantage, dug the graves of the dead gunners in the lonely meadow within sight of Fish Creek. The single economy-size headstone which bears their names encompasses within its trivial dimensions the essence of all the war memorials on earth.

The road to Batoche crosses the Fish Creek ravine and winds north along the river past the church-dominated Fish Creek settlement and the old-fashioned farm-houses which in many instances reflect Quebec *habitant* influence. At times the road adheres strictly to the convolutions of the river, at others observes the conventional municipal straight-line pattern; but in either case the scenery is of almost unvarying charm. Six miles south of Batoche the river road intersects a gravelled highway which runs down to Gabriel's Crossing, so named after Gabriel Dumont, who operated the original ferry here in 1872. The ferry still runs, and one of the pleasantest ways of returning to Saskatoon after a visit to Batoche is by way of Gabriel's Crossing (there is a charmingly located picnic site on the west side of the river) and so home on Highway No. 11 through immaculate Mennonite communities centred on the town of Rosthern.

Through this tranquil countryside Middleton's men marched from Fish Creek to the final show-down with the Métis at Batoche. Middleton had nearly a thousand men under his command now, with fresh forces coming up; and on the river his naval unit, the *Northcote*, was hopping madly over sandbars in a frantic effort to keep more or less abreast of the land forces. From the high banks of the river the Métis took occasional pot-shots at the steamer, but as usual they were short of ammunition and under orders from Dumont to save what they had for Middleton's men.

The siege of Batoche lasted four days, from the 9th to the 12th of May, 1885. The pattern of fighting at first followed fairly closely that of Fish Creek, with this difference, that Middleton tested the Métis position with far greater caution than in the earlier engagement, and the soldiers were at pains to avoid exposing themselves on the skyline above the rifle-pits. On the first day of fighting they advanced as far as the church and the new rectory which stood at the head of the long slope above the settlement. Then the Métis in their rifle-pits seaming the slope opened up with a heavy fire and the soldiers retired a short distance and lay down in the grass for the rest of the afternoon. A similar pattern of action and inaction was followed during the next two days, the soldiers advancing, deploying, lying down, occasionally firing a few rounds of ammunition in the general direction of Batoche, with the artillery making reassuring bangs in the background. About all that can be said for Middleton's conduct of the siege is that it was consistent in its indecisiveness. Each night the disgusted soldiers withdrew to what Middleton – harking back to his soldiering in the east – called a zariba, a stockade formed of supply-wagons with supporting entrenchments. The field in which the zariba stood was cultivated, the wind blew hard and incessantly, the soldiers ate hard-tack and canned beef and dust, slept restlessly or not at all, and cursed the restraints their cautious commander imposed upon them.

On the afternoon of May 12 Middleton gave his familiar order for a general advance towards Batoche. The troops pushed forward as far as the church at the top of the long valley slope, where Middleton established his headquarters and from which he ordered a 'reconnaissance in force', meaning no more than a cautious crawl by advance units to a point where they would, as usual, be pinned down by Métis rifle fire. Colonel Williams, in command of the Midland battalion of militia from Ontario, pretended to misunderstand the order and called on his men to charge. Middleton, when he saw his raw lads running helter-skelter down on the rifle-pits, firing in all directions as they ran, was appalled. 'Stop firing,' he bellowed. 'Why in God's name don't you stop firing!'

Perhaps Middleton was afraid the soldiers would shoot one another. But there was no stopping them now – particularly since the firing from the rifle-pits had died away almost to nothing. (Towards the end the Métis were ramming rusty nails, pebbles, anything that would fly and hurt, into their muzzle-loaders.) Middleton himself rode forward to direct the final stages of the action, and less than an hour after Colonel Williams had given the order to charge, the only men remaining in the rifle-pits were dead.

Two days after the fall of Batoche Louis Riel was picked up in the bush near the settlement. In the weeks that followed, the government's resolve to make an example of Riel hardened as sympathy for the doomed man mounted. The execution of the Métis Messiah – a man, it must be remembered, more French than Indian – split the Canadian nation, and the passing of nearly a century has done little to heal the rift. Riel, as is always the way with the martyr, has exercised far greater influence in death than he was ever able to do in life.

Gabriel Dumont escaped martyrdom to become a folk-hero. His daring escape on horseback all the way from Batoche across the border into Montana accords well with our conception of the frontier man-of-action, and gives Dumont a modest place in the pantheon of wild-west heroes, of whom Wild Bill Hickok, Buffalo Bill, and Wyatt Earp are supreme exemplars. It is significant that Dumont later went on tour with Cody's celebrated Wild West show, in which, however, he was assigned a comparatively minor role.

That Dumont should become a folk-hero while Riel remains merely a martyr is entirely logical. A folk-hero embodies in his character and dramatizes in his actions the simple and admired virtues and vices of a community or a people. Robin Hood and William Tell and Buffalo Bill and Gabriel Dumont conform admirably to the conventional folk-hero stereotype – simple souls who express themselves in childlike and ingenuously heroic ways. But Louis Riel moves on an altogether different level. There is something remote, alien, unapproachable about the man – perhaps because the world he lived in was so seldom the world of ordinary men and women. The folk-hero is, in mentality and outlook, essentially of the folk; deeds rather than personality set him apart, earn him that unqualified approbation which is forever denied the man whose mind works in ways beyond common apprehension.

The approach to Batoche from the south borders on the spectacular. From an immensely high bluff the view reaches back over a mighty bend in the river, across the river to rich parkland flats, and downstream to where the spire of the original Batoche church still measures itself against the sky. A general store flanks the roadside, and just beyond it signs point the way to the earthworks behind which Middleton's men sheltered uncomfortably at night. The earthworks are much overgrown now but still clearly visible. A little farther along, a parking area on the high bluff impinges on depressions that were originally miniature fox-holes dug by militiamen threatened by Métis rifle fire from below. Part way down the bluffs the grave of Gunner Phillips, the only soldier buried on the battlefield, serves as an unofficial memorial to all the men killed fighting at Batoche.

The original Batoche settlement, named after the first trader to settle on the site, has long since disappeared; but on the valley rim the church in which Middleton briefly established his headquarters still stands, and beside it the rectory in which the nuns and priests of the Batoche mission found shelter during the fighting. Both buildings still bear the scars of battle – bullet-holes carefully preserved and marked for the benefit of tourists. The rectory has been converted into a pleasant little museum filled with relics of the Rebellion era as well as typical exhibits of the pioneer way of life. Outside the rectory a memorial cairn and a judiciously worded Historic Sites marker officially commemorate the last stand of the Métis.

A few hundred yards from the church the Batoche graveyard commands a magnificent view of parkland and river. Most prairie graveyards lie bleak and desolate beside a highway or railway track – by contrast the Batoche graveyard occupies the most beautiful site in all the country round. One feels that those who chose the site did so in the firm belief that the dead see with mortal eyes and cherish familiar scenes.

The grave of Gabriel Dumont, who returned from far-off places to die in his own country, has recently been marked by a massive natural rock with an appropriate plaque attached. It is well that he should be so remembered, although in size the memorial is disproportionate to its surroundings and makes all the more obvious by contrast the neglect of that part of the graveyard sheltering the dust of nine Métis patriots who died in the fighting at Batoche. Happily their names, including that of Joseph Ouellet, aged ninety years, have recently been recorded on a modest cenotaph erected near the centre of the graveyard.

Louis Riel is buried far away in St. Boniface, Manitoba, close to the place of his birth. The headstone over his grave bears a single word, RIEL, and the date of his death. And that is all. Perhaps those who erected the headstone could think of no inscription that might make clear to the passer-by the nature of the man thus austerely honoured, or the measure of his achievement.

Today, even allowing for the softening influence of time and the accumulation of evidence that time permits, the appropriate inscription would be just as hard to find as in 1885. Louis Riel failed to save his people; he split Canada in two; he spread mourning into a hundred homes across the nation. And yet, because he made the ultimate gesture on behalf of the people he could not save, because he may have moved later generations of white men to feel at least a twinge of embarrassment when they contemplate the fate of the people they dispossessed, he is perhaps deserving of a place among those Canadians whom we honour as the heroes of our nation.

13. First Capital of the North-west

There is another battlefield of the Riel Rebellion readily accessible from Saskatoon. It is not so well known as those of Duck Lake and Fish Creek and Batoche – perhaps because, of all the battles of the Rebellion, Cut Knife Hill is the one we would be happiest to forget. The engagement was fought on the government side by green militia aided by a few regulars and a handful of policemen; on the Indian side by an inferior force of ill-armed braves who so far in the course of the Rebellion had made no overt move to join Riel. Colonel Otter said that he attacked the Cree camp in order to discourage the young warriors, in Otter's view now beyond Chief Poundmaker's control, from going off on their own to join the rebels; and there is irony in the fact that only Poundmaker's exercise of authority prevented the Indians from turning the defeat of Otter's men into a massacre.

Battleford, the town from which the soldiers marched southwest into the Eagle Hills against Poundmaker, is old as Saskatchewan towns go. There were trading-posts on or near the site from the mid eighteenth century on; for the Battle River flows into the Saskatchewan only a mile or two below the site, and in the old days the two great river valleys were rich in furs, the Saskatchewan providing the finest of waterways for their transport. The fur-traders – Independent, Nor'Wester, and Hudson's Bay – were thus ideally located, both for collecting furs and for moving them east.

From the beginning of the white invasion this was lawless country. The Cree and Assiniboine of the lovely Eagle Hills country south and west of the meeting of the waters were corrupted by rum more quickly than most of the Indians; they were soon made sullen, importunate, and bitterly resentful of their own degradation. It was natural that they should take out their frustrations on the men who caused them. An attack on a trading-post was an act of violence almost unheard of throughout the length and breadth of the Territories; but in the Battleford district several such attacks were made and one post was plundered and burned. But in the end the Company – a house built on a rock – triumphed over native hostility and white corruption. It won the confidence of the Indians and absorbed its competitors. In 1821, the year of amalgamation, the Company moved into the old Nor'Wester post and stayed there until 1885. In that year the post was destroyed by Indians.

Settlers moved into the district in 1874. A community of sorts sprang up around the H.B.C. post and almost overnight assumed a political importance that made its rapid growth a seeming inevitability. The Mounted Police arrived in 1875, the telegraph in 1876, and the Government of the Northwest Territories, earlier established briefly at remote snake-infested Fort Livingstone, in 1877. Battleford was the logical choice to succeed Fort Livingstone, since it was central to the areas of the west that were sure to be settled quickly, and lay on the route the proposed transcontinental railway was to follow. In 1878 Lieutenant-Governor David Laird opened the second session of the North-West Council in the newly-built Government House. In the same year Patrick Gammon Laurie arrived in Battleford to report legislative deliberations and local gossip in the columns of the Battleford *Herald*, the first newspaper in the North-west. Laurie brought his plant with him from Fort Garry, six hundred miles across the plains by Red River cart.

A short day's life and a long night's dying – such is Battleford's history on a pinhead. The successive blows that shattered expectations and dispersed fair dreams fell suddenly and fast; and the machinations of those who delivered them have been roundly cursed by Battleford citizens even to the third and fourth generations. The Canadian Pacific Railway, originally routed through the rich parklands country in a direct line to and beyond Battleford, changed course and cut through the arid southern plains instead. (The plains country, it had been found, grew splendid crops, contrary to Palliser's pessimistic predictions.) Overnight Pile of Bones became Queen City of the Plains and capital of the Northwest Territories. The North-West Council packed its notes and paraphernalia and betook itself to the new capital; the Confederation Table – Quebec, not Prince Edward Island, edition – which with infinite difficulty had been lugged across the plains by cart and wagon, followed the councillors, in transit breaking whatever bonds it was alleged to have established between the citizens of Battleford and the Government of Canada. Government House, barely initiated as a council chamber, was converted into a school; lots bought by speculators supported nothing but a burden of unpaid taxes; and as the poet said of another abandoned capital, hearts that once beat high with hope (of an infinity of profitable deals) now felt that pulse no more.

In 1885 the town was still, however, important enough to attract the attention of the Indians.

The ambiguities of history are the befuddlement and delight of curious-minded people – more particularly professional historians and poets. The role in the Rebellion of the North West Mounted Police, a body of men whose courage and efficiency had by 1885 been established beyond question, is oddly difficult to come to grips with, to see in a hard clear light that casts no shadows. It has become a cliché of western folklore to blame Middleton for virtually immobilizing the police during the course of the Rebellion, and there is a good deal of truth in the charge; none the less it cannot be overlooked that on those occasions when the police were free to act on their own initiative they did so disastrously or not at all. Major Crozier and his mixed force of policemen and civilian volunteers – strong in point of numbers – were bloodily defeated at Duck Lake, indeed barely escaped annihilation. Inspector Dickens and his force of twenty-five men abandoned Fort Pitt (this after the civilians in their charge had surrendered to the Indians); and from the shelter of the Battleford police fort Inspector Morris and his force of forty men, later strengthened by the addition of the Fort Pitt detachment, looked on in helpless wrath and indignation while Indian hoodlum gangs – whose behaviour bears a striking resemblance to that of our own Hallowe'en and Grey Cup mobs – plundered stores and houses and over a three weeks' period burned down most of the old Battleford settlement. At no time, however, did the Indians appear in force; at no time did it appear that their intentions were deliberately warlike in that they were mobilizing to drive the white man out or exterminate him. Restless, hungry, bitterly resentful of the white man's intrusion, they seized the opportunity provided by the Rebellion to enjoy some excitement and gather plunder at the white man's expense. No doubt the police were up to a point inhibited from taking action by the number of refugees under their protection – nearly four hundred; but most of the adult refugees were armed and knew how to shoot. The total immobility of Morris's men over a lengthy period thus remains something of an enigma.

It is of course difficult to estimate the effect of the Custer disaster at the Battle of the Little Big Horn on the thinking of the men in command of the government forces during the Rebellion. General Strange, who led the Alberta Field Force, candidly acknowledged his fear of 'committing Custer', and Middleton and Morris acted as if they shared Strange's apprehension.

Unfortunately the Little Big Horn didn't influence the thinking of Colonel Otter, who in five and a half days had marched from Swift Current at the head of nearly four hundred men to raise the siege of Battleford. The men of the relieving force were heroes for an hour; then, reinforced by a small detachment of policemen, they marched into the Eagle Hills country to teach Poundmaker a lesson. At his trial Poundmaker testified that he had attempted to affirm his loyalty to the Crown, but that the Indian agent in charge of the Battleford district before whom he sought to appear had fled to safety across the North Saskatchewan and was thus inaccessible. What is certain is that Poundmaker had succeeded in rounding up his restless young men and confining them to camp some forty miles south-west of Battleford. Whether Otter really believed it necessary to beat up Poundmaker in order to ensure his loyalty, or whether he was a small-time glory-seeker must always remain an open question. And what is even more difficult to determine is how Otter proposed to justify – after the event – an early morning surprise attack on a sleeping camp, particularly a camp of Indians who so far had refused to ally themselves openly with Riel.

It has been pleaded that the attack would have forced the Indians to 'declare themselves'. But dead men cannot stand up to be counted.

As things turned out the dead were mostly on Otter's side. An Indian lookout spotted the militia climbing out of the deep ravine of Cut Knife Creek and toiling up the long slope of Cut Knife Hill (so named after a Sarcee warrior said to have been defeated near the hill by the Cree in a great battle). Pound-maker's people were encamped on a level spot near the base of the hill; and had Otter's advance-guard charged at once, they would almost certainly have overrun the Indians, who were barely awake. But the advance-guard hesitated and waited for reinforcements to come up. The Indians swarmed out of their tents, and while the soldiers dug in near the summit they sought cover in the coulees and crevices seaming the hill-side and opened up on the troops above.

Four years before the Cut Knife engagement a strong British force, established on the summit of a South African kopje called Majuba, had been utterly routed and all but destroyed by a vastly inferior force of militarily untrained Boer farmers. The lessons of Majuba – that it is easier to shoot accurately uphill than down, that men exposed against a skyline are extraordinarily vulnerable to rifle fire – had been lost on Colonel Otter. On the summit of Cut Knife Hill, and on the long slope where the wagons and guns had bogged down, Otter's men were fearfully exposed to the gunfire of an all but unseen enemy, who with superlative skill made use of the cover provided by bush and coulee and even trivial surface irregularities in the hill-side. All that saved the soldiers from heavy casualties was the inadequacy of the Indian fire-arms – a few modern rifles among them, the rest muzzle-loaders. Some of the braves were armed only with bows and arrows.

By noon it was clear to Otter that his position on the terrible hill was untenable. One of his two cannons was out of commission, the Gatling gun (on loan from Lieutenant Howard of the U.S. Army) periodically sprayed the air with lead but never hit anything. And the Indian fire was growing hotter, the warriors were growing bolder. Mounted Police and members of the Bat-tleford Home Guard, displaying a good deal of dash and courage, chased off the Indians who had closed in behind the column, and through the gap thus created the weary heartsick soldiers straggled, bearing with them their wounded and dead. Once the retreat began the Indians did not press the attack. Poundmaker still exercised enough authority over his braves to call them off just when the time was ripe for the kill; and the badly battered little force wound its way unimpeded through the hills and back to Battleford. Eight of Otter's men were dead and fourteen wounded. The Indian losses were probably half as many.

Poundmaker, a victim of that impersonal legalistic injustice which stems from a sound knowledge of law and none at all of the human heart, was imprisoned following the collapse of the Rebellion and died soon after his release, in Alberta Blackfoot country far from his native hills. In the spring of 1967 the remains of the great chief were brought home by his own people, Cree tribesmen of the Sweetgrass Indian Reserve, and buried on Cut Knife Hill, the scene of his most brilliant victory and most magnanimous gesture.

Cut Knife Hill can easily be reached about forty miles out of Battleford over Highway Number 40, through the Sweet Grass Indian Reserve and the village of Cut Knife. It is a beautiful drive all the way; and the view from the high bench overlooking the great valleys of the North Saskatchewan and Battle rivers, with the twin Battlefords showing clearly in the distance, is one of the most impressive in the west and makes it clear that, on one count at least, Battleford's claim to be the capital of Saskatchewan was better founded than Regina's. But aesthetic considerations rarely influence politicians.

Sixteen years after the Rebellion the final crushing blow fell on Battleford town; it was decided to run the C.N.R. from Saskatoon along the north side of the Saskatchewan River rather than the south, thus not only completely by-passing Battleford but cutting it off from easy access to the railway. A new townsite, that of the now flourishing little city of North Battleford, was opened on the railway side of the river, and the original Battleford town, its commercial prospects now permanently blighted, sank cursing into oblivion. Overnight its character changed; the entrepreneurs and real-estate men folded their tents and stole away; and only a year or two after the railroad was built on the north side of the river, Battleford had become 'largely a town of old North West Mounted Policemen, veterans of the stormy times past, half-breeds and full-blooded Indians – altogether a lively town of sports, bad whiskey, bronzed horsemen and ever ready guns'. (The ever-ready guns add a pleasingly romantic wild-west touch to the picture, even though they were used mostly on coyotes and gophers.)

What survives on the south side of the river of blighted hopes and aspirations unfulfilled is invested with an odd kind of distinction not shared by any other prairie town. Several impressive public buildings – antique survivals of a day long past – dominate the wide main streets; Government House lingers on as a school; and several of the private homes by virtue of design and ornamentation look like transplants from late-nineteenth-century Ontario. But what sets the town apart at once from its fellows is the seemingly haphazard scattering of houses and public buildings broadcast over the prairie. They are set down in queer places with great open spaces between them, in conformity to no observable pattern. All this is, of course, the natural consequence of the town's having been laid out for the boom that never came. The empty spaces between buildings were lots once held by speculators. When the railway passed by on the other side, the lots reverted to the town to cover unpaid taxes, and the buildings already erected here and there were left isolated and forlorn.

But habitable. Indeed, many of the residents of bustling North Battleford prefer to live across the river in old Battleford town. It is more peaceful there – and the taxes are lower.

The official story that explains the by-passing of Battleford asserts that it was cheaper to build the railway on the north side of the river than to bridge or fill the twenty or more creeks flowing into the river on the south side between Saskatoon and Battleford. But loyal Battleford citizens, old and young, still mutter darkly of land speculation and graft, and eastern sharpers and politicians distorting the logical course of history for the sake of a quick buck.

North Battleford, the upstart usurper of old Battleford's future, is a bright brisk city of ten thousand or more, commanding along its southern front a magnificent view of the river valley and the lovely rolling Eagle Hills to the south-west. On its northern exposure the city faces the Jackfish Lake and Thickwood Hills country – pleasant, well-watered parkland through which holidayers swarm in the summertime. A distributing centre of some importance, North Battleford inevitably condescends to its shabby relation across the river; but old Battleford continues to preserve an individuality denied its one-time rival. And history, although unkind in the main, has conferred one inestimable benefit on old Battleford which is denied the new – it has made the town the site of a National Historic Park.

The old police fort, which in 1885 had sheltered behind its palisades sixty-odd policemen and four hundred settlers, was in the following year extensively remodelled and enlarged to meet the needs of a greatly expanded police force. The new buildings were of frame construction, the assumption being that they would shortly be replaced by more substantial structures of brick. But with the settling-down of the country to an era of peace and progress, the need of a strong police force lessened; gradually the men of the Fort Battleford detachment were dispersed in small units over a wide area; the automobile replaced the horse as a conventional means of transport, the stable gave way to the garage. In 1924 Fort Battleford, at one time second only to Regina in importance as a police base, was permanently abandoned.

For nearly thirty years the 'temporary' buildings stood wind-battered and empty on the prairie half a mile east of Battleford town – splendid play-houses for children, and happy hunting-grounds for souvenir collectors. But public opinion, formulated by enthusiastic local antiquarians, would not suffer these relics of a colourful past to perish utterly; appropriate pressure was applied in proper places; and in 1951 the site and buildings of old Fort Battleford were declared a National Historic Park.

One of the original buildings, the Commanding Officer's Residence dating from 1877, still stands intact, along with four of the temporary buildings put up after 1885 – Officers' Quarters, Guard Room, Mess Hall and Kitchen, and Sick Horse Stable. Three of the buildings now serve as museums.

I do not know of any spot in western Canada that more effectively captures the spirit and atmosphere of the day before yesterday than Fort Battleford. Many of the exhibits are inevitably of the kind seen in any museum devoted to western pioneer culture, and I confess I have grown a little weary of collections of old stoves, cooking utensils, chamber-pots, oil-lamps, guns, ox collars, and moulting Indian head-dresses. But in the Fort Battleford Museum there are other things besides. Fine old furniture in the Commanding Officer's Residence (the Commandant obviously lived in some style); rooms that look as if their occupants had left them only a moment or two before; and marvellous displays of photographs that bring vividly to life the men and women to whom the old Fort was once the only home they knew. Footballers (circa 1900) arrayed in splendid upswept moustaches and drooping shorts; gymnastics teams piled up in weird pyramidal formations; officers' wives – many of them remarkably handsome and elegant in *fin de siècle* and Edwardian-era costumes; shots of gala nights when the policemen in their glittering dress uniforms no doubt fluttered the hearts of the local belles; and a gallery that strikes a more chilling note – memorials of brave men who perished in the course of police duty, or who, in much larger number, exchanged scarlet for khaki and died in Flanders fields and Passchendaele mud.

Two roads join Saskatoon and Battleford. The most frequently travelled, Highway No. 5, is paved all the way and commands splendid views of the valley of the North Saskatchewan. Forty miles west of Saskatoon, No. 5 crosses the river by the handsome Borden Bridge and follows along the north side of the valley to the town of North Battleford, where narrow old twin bridges – or, a little farther on, an impressively broad and substantial new one – lead us back across the river and into old Battleford.

The second road leading from Saskatoon to Battleford is a good deal less comfortable to travel over than No. 5, but of particular interest to romantic souls who would like to follow as far as possible in the footprints and cart tracks of the original pioneers. Instead of crossing the Borden Bridge, the pilgrim should turn left just before the highway dips into the river valley and follow, in a general westerly direction, the gravel-surfaced and usually dusty municipal roads passing through or near the villages of Struan, Sonningdale, and Spinney Hill. Beyond Spinney Hill it is possible to follow almost to Battleford the exact trail used by the pioneers on their journeyings back and forth between Battleford and Saskatoon, and followed by many of the Barr colonists on the first lap of their overland trek from Saskatoon to the Alberta border, one hundred miles west of Battleford. The old trail was, for all practical purposes other than limited local use, abandoned years ago; its recent restoration to the point where it is passable to general traffic has been a highly imaginative and worth-while Battleford centennial project. The trail hugs the river; it provides many superb views upstream and down; and it crosses so many coulees and creek-beds, including the wide and beautiful valley of the Eagle Creek, as to lend some credence to the claim that it was cheaper for the C.N.R. to bridge the river itself and run the railroad along the north side than to make the necessary fills on the south.

My wife and I first drove the Pioneer Trail from Battleford towards Saskatoon on a glorious autumn day when the river valley lay before us, a wide brown and golden bed flecked with vivid splashes of red and green – the muddy old Saskatchewan a wide ribbon of unexpected dazzling blue unrolled along the valley bed. A farmer we had picked up on the road – a huge man who overflowed the back seat of our small car – showed us the way to the Pioneer Trail which we hadn't known about before. He was a man from Poland (there is a substantial Polish settlement in these parts along the south bank) and a passionate, all but inarticulate lover of the sky and the great river and the land and all living things contained therein.

'It's nice,' he repeated over and over, in a tone which combined, in equal proportions, affection and a kind of awe. 'It's nice. The trees – the birds – it's nice.'

I had never before heard that most banal of expressions, 'it's nice' sound like a passionate hymn of praise to all created things.

14. Latter-Day Moses

Isaac Moses Barr was unfortunate in his name. It gave him aspirations which his talents could not match, set him treading paths he had no staying-power to follow. Once, at least, in the course of a long life, he must have felt anticipations of fulfilment – when at the head of a band of the Chosen People he stood in sight of the Promised Land. But like that other Moses, though for far different reasons, he was not allowed to enter it. Nor could he find on the rolling prairie a Mount Nebo on which to leave honourably his bones.

There arc men who, though a good deal talked and written about, contrive somehow always to elude us. The Reverend Moses Barr is one of these. A villain with no real evil in him; a good shepherd accused of 'fleecing' his flock; an empire-builder incapable of coping with building materials more complicated than a child's set of blocks, Barr is a quicksilver character, practical and idealistic, wambling and tendentious, above all elusive – of whom one can say with assurance only that he was born neither to lead nor to follow.

In London the Rev. Exton Lloyd, an Anglican clergyman who had lived for some years in Canada (he was a graduate of Wycliffe College, Toronto), wrote a letter to *The Times* urging the desirability of settling the Canadian west with uncontaminated British stock and inviting anyone interested in emigrating to the prairies to get in touch with him. It was his intention to offer personal advice and encouragement to prospective emigrants; but the hundreds of replies he received to his letter made the carrying out of such a plan an impossibility. Lloyd was at his wits' end to know what to do, when to his office in the London Mission Society Building there came, as if in answer to his prayers, a short, thick-set, persuasive man who introduced himself as the Rev. Moses Barr. He was, he said, an Anglican clergyman who had farmed for fifteen years in western Canada and had already taken preliminary steps to carry out precisely such a settlement scheme as Lloyd had envisioned, although on a much larger scale. Lloyd, convinced of Barr's honesty and competence, handed over to him all the letters he had received and turned back to his mission work. Lloyd was forty-one years of age; he had a wife and five children, he was happy in his mission work, and he was of no mind at this time to go to the prairies himself.

Barr had in fact been negotiating with the Canadian government for a large tract of land to be set aside for immigrants of British stock. He does not appear to have himself been farther west than Battleford; nor did he impress any of the local pioneers he talked with as a potential colonizer. None the less, Barr conducted all the early negotiations on both sides of the Atlantic with a good deal of intelligence and foresight. His prospectus – which trumpeted CANADA FOR THE BRITISH in large black type – was more helpful and a good deal more honest than most of its kind; the colonists selected for the initial venture seemed ideally suited in body, mind, and pocketbook to the tasks of empire-building; and the land Barr had chosen for them, on the basis not of personal inspection but of map-reading and hearsay, was in the long run to prove immensely productive of both grain crops and oil. In fact all of Barr's arrangements, including those for the formation of a variety of 'companies' – Hospital, Transport, Co-operative Home-Farm, Stores Syndicate – into which the colonists were permitted to buy shares, were, on paper, admirable.

The main body of immigrants, nearly two thousand strong, sailed from Liverpool in the early spring of 1903 aboard the S.S. *Lake Manitoba*, a down-at-heels steamship built to accommodate eight hundred passengers, which had lately been employed as a troopship in the South African war and still bore the scars of service. Food was bad and in short supply; privacy, except for the few who had reserved first-class cabins, an impossibility; and the sanitary conveniences, in the words of one indignant user thereof, 'would have shamed a monkey-cage.'

'It speaks well for British love of law and order,' the same passenger reported, 'that only eleven fights, seven incipient mutinies, three riots and twenty-two violent interviews with Barr . . . occurred during the voyage.'

Still, health remained good, spirits for the most part high; and even the wild confusion that ensued upon disembarkation could not entirely dampen the enthusiasm of the colonists as they piled aboard the trains waiting to bear them swiftly to the west. Observers were most favourably impressed by the appearance and behaviour of the colonists, as a report that appeared in the Montreal *Gazette* of April 11, 1903, indicates:

> Four special trains carrying the Barr colonists, numbering 1,960, left here today for the Saskatoon district, where the new Canadians will establish homes and cities. The party, which is declared to be the greatest emigration from England since the departure of William Penn, arrived Saturday morning on the steamship *Lake Manitoba* whose cargo of humanity was packed like fish in a box. The colonists bring with them ½ million pounds sterling. They are probably the finest body of men, women and children that ever landed here. Lawyers, doctors, clergymen, merchants, aristocrats, artisans, domestics, tradesmen and labourers are included, besides babies by the score. . . . Rev. I. M. Barr, the organizer of the party, is a brisk businesslike man, who is full of enthusiasm over the prospects of his scheme. He says 1,500 more colonists are to follow and that 10,000 more will come next year.

At Saskatoon, in 1903 a settlement consisting of 'a score or so of glorified packing-cases', the colonists detrained – eighteen days out of Liverpool and only a mere two hundred miles from the land Barr had spied out for them. Their spirits were still high, their hopes unbounded.

Not for long. Such arrangements as Barr had made to accommodate the colonists while they bought equipment and prepared for the long wagon-trek west proved all but non-existent. Department of the Interior officials, by now experienced in handling greenhorn colonists, were on hand to offer assistance and advice. The colonists accepted the assistance. But no amount of government aid could compensate them for the loss of luggage (enormous quantities disappeared somewhere between Saint John and Saskatoon) or for loss of faith in their leader, who now, in addition to bearing the burden of his own sins and deficiencies, was made by the colonists to bear the burden of theirs.

Rumour inevitably ran wild through the tent-camp on the banks of the Saskatchewan. Barr, it was alleged, was collecting *per capita* commissions from the government and from railway and steamship companies; he was in the hire of the farm-machinery manufacturers and livestock merchants; he was making it almost impossible for the colonists to reclaim certain funds that they had committed to his care. Barr's behaviour while in Saskatoon did little to allay the colonists' fears. He had thus far consistently refused to delegate to anyone even the most trivial measure of authority, but so long as he functioned with a reasonable degree of competence this was no great matter. Now, however, it was a matter of common talk that he was making a confidant of the whiskey bottle; and he was suddenly subject, as he had not been before, to queer fits of temper and an excitability that bordered on the irrational. A doggerel verse, set to a music-hall tune and sung long and loudly throughout the camp, reflected the changed attitude of the colonists towards the man whom they had earlier followed in complete faith and blindness:

> *Barr, Barr, wily old Barr,*
> *He'll do you as much as he can;*
> *You bet he will collar*
> *Your very last dollar*
> *In the valley of the Saskatchewan.*

Barr was still in charge when the first wagon outfits pulled out of Saskatoon on May 2, 1903, and began the two-hundred-mile journey west towards the block of land that two years later was to be split by the border line running between the newly created provinces of Saskatchewan and Alberta. But further exploitation, as the colonists believed many of Barr's demands on them to be, combined with the miseries of trail travel across rugged prairie in early spring, quickly exasperated the more hot-blooded of the colonists to the point of revolt. The precise point appears to have been reached when the co-operative-stores syndicate, in which many of the colonists held shares, proved to be strictly private enterprise with Barr himself the entrepreneur. The charge is impossible to prove absolutely, but there is a good deal of evidence to suggest that Barr bought up all available supplies of potatoes and oats along the route from Battleford west and attempted to re-sell these staples to the colonists at prices ranging up to ten times what he himself had originally paid for them.

What Barr in his dealings with the colonists overlooked was the fact that they arrived in western Canada not as meek, frightened foreigners, poverty-stricken, unfamiliar with the language and customs of the country, but as the well-heeled lords of the earth. 'Why did you come to Canada?' a reporter for the Boston *Transcript* asked a Cockney member of the colony. 'To claim Canada for the bleedin' Hempire,' is the alleged retort, which there is really no need to doubt. In that retort, with its assumption that Canada 'belonged' to England and that Englishmen were therefore inevitably overlords of all other nationalities represented in the vast melting-pot, lies the origin of much of the hostility directed towards English settlers in the homesteading days. But however much such assumptions of superiority ruffled the feelings of those who were at first willing and eager to help the colonists, it stood the colonists in good stead in their dealings with Barr. In England the Englishman accepted his place in the class structure without question; in the New World, with visions of vast landed estates dancing in his head, he was subservient to no man.

Battleford was Barr's Runnymede. A mass meeting deposed him and elected in his place a committee of twelve. A new unofficial leader, the Rev. Exton Lloyd, who had joined the colony at the last minute when he learned that the colonists were going on their long journey without a chaplain, reigned thereafter in Barr's stead.

Barr was no weasel fighting in a hole. At no time does he seem to have felt himself guilty of iniquitous behaviour or considered the complaints of the colonists in any way legitimate; indeed, with what the government authorities concerned considered shocking presumption, he held a press conference in Ottawa and demanded from the government a substantial bonus for having settled two thousand top-drawer colonists in western Canada. He himself, he said, was substantially out of pocket on the deal, and, he assured the reporters, 'I was not in the work out of feelings of pure philanthropy, and would think it only fair that I have my services appreciated.'

The government, having already spent large sums providing the kind of assistance that a properly planned and executed settlement scheme should never have needed, was moved by

Barr's appeal to nothing more tangible than indignation, and so the man disappears from Canada and history. It is rumoured that some years later he led a group of American colonists to Australia and died in that country at an advanced age in 1937; but so far no one has investigated the truth of the rumour.

Perhaps the fairest judgment of Barr must be that of the colonist who contended that no one man could possibly have exercised competent supervisory authority under existing conditions over so large a party, particularly when, after reaching Saint John, it began to break up into smaller groups, which were eventually strung out across the country all the way from Montreal to Battleford. 'No man living,' the colonist wrote, 'could have made a perfect success as the leader of such a crowd as the Barr colonists . . . not unless he could have enforced a sort of army discipline with King's Regulations and sergeant-majors, and all the rest of the charming enactments devised for making rational men do what they didn't wish to do.'

Whatever Barr's end, it must have been some satisfaction to him to know that in spite of a motion passed by the colonist committee, at the instigation of the Rev. Exton Lloyd, which sought to dissociate the name of the colony from Barr's, his name is none the less indissolubly linked with the most colourful of all western Canadian land-settlement schemes. It is a pity, though, that he could not know that in death he found his real point of identity with that greater Moses, for both are buried in unknown graves.

Migratory movements hold for most of us an extraordinary fascination. On the whole, man's movements are a little more intelligible than the lemming's; reasons economic and even spiritual can be found to justify them, and the migrants do not precipitate themselves at journey's end into the sea. None the less, mass migrations appear often to be the result, in part, of the working of obscure forces, less rational than instinctive, which set man in motion towards the setting sun and the fabled islands of the west; forces which, in an odd way, involve the observer too, perhaps through that Race Memory in which stir subconscious recollections of a movement or movements his ancestral self was a part of, ages long ago. So it is that the journeyings of the Barr colonists, in scope and consequence insignificant in the sum of things, hold for the people of Saskatchewan their

own peculiar fascination, stimulated, perhaps, by the identity
of names between that of the colony leader and that of the mighty
man of God who followed the cloud by day and the fiery pillar
by night on the archetypal migration to the Promised Land five
thousand years ago.

The long haul from Saskatoon to the homestead lands (now
centred by the town of Lloydminster) was slow, difficult, and at
times dangerous. The weather was at first bad, the trail almost
impassable, the inexperienced city-bred colonists reluctant to
heed advice that would have saved them a good deal of distress.
At the end of the first week of travel 'every slough and creek
and gumbo flat from Saskatoon westwards for two hundred
miles was decorated with one or more mired wagons,' – the trail
itself littered with the carcasses of dead animals, discarded house-
hold goods, and food-stuffs destroyed by indifferent packing. (On
projecting pieces of metal such as harrow-teeth and mower
blades 'bags of flour and sugar stoically disembowelled themselves like disgraced Japanese officials.')

By the time the colonists reached their destinations, they were
a part not only of history but of folklore. Perhaps at no time in
the history of western settlement were so many 'green Englishman' jokes spawned or revived. One teamster, so the story said,
kept the harness on his horses for two weeks, knowing that if
he took it off he could never get it back on again without the
instruction he was too 'stuck-up' to ask for; another, in order
to persuade his balky oxen to move, lit a fire under them, whereupon the animals stepped forward a few paces and placidly
chewed their cuds while the teamster's wagon and household
goods went up in flames. Inevitably there cropped up among
the amused and slightly irritated old-timers the story about the
colonist who bought oxen instead of horses because you could
milk them, about the settler who planted his first cultivated
acres to bran, and the lad fresh out of Eton (or Winchester or
Harrow) who tried to buy a bag of wild oats because he had
heard that every young man was expected to sow a few. All these
and a hundred more – hoary chestnuts now, and most of them
already time-worn in 1903, but stories that clearly reflect the
attitude of the old-time settlers towards the stand-offish newcomers who, seemingly bent on preserving an integrity of blood
and custom among lesser breeds, welcomed neither friendship
nor advice.

It is significant that the curious cult of British-Israelitism, founded on the conviction that only the English could possibly be God's Chosen People, has flourished more strongly in the Lloydminster community than almost anywhere else in the west. In their attempts to convert a part of the prairie into a large-scale rural England, the colonists received support and encouragement from their clergyman-leader, the Rev. Exton Lloyd. Lloyd, who combined in himself the more obvious characteristics of Lord Baden-Powell and Savonarola, was not nearly so complicated or interesting a personality as Barr; but his knowledge of the country – he had fought in the Riel Rebellion – his enormous vigour, and his passionate belief in the capacity of the Englishman to overcome all obstacles provided the kind of practical guidance and moral stiffening the colonists badly needed. In the immediate situation his leadership was invaluable. His ideal of nationhood, however, appears to have been an Anglican theocracy, and his fierce intolerance of 'foreigners', his efforts in later years to staff schools and hospitals with British teachers, doctors, and nurses made him a nuisance to governments and a hindrance to the development of a cosmopolitan Canadian nation.

The story of the Barr Colony, following the arrival of the settlers on the land Barr had chosen for them, differs little in its broad outlines from that of almost any large-scale settlement in the west. The first winter occasioned much suffering; badly built sod or log houses provided indifferent shelter against winter's blasts, and, to accommodate some whose dwellings disintegrated, a large tent called a 'House of Refuge' was put up by the government. It was in this early and trying time that Exton Lloyd served his people best – exhorting, encouraging, comforting; at the same time sending back to the Old Country explicit denials of widely publicized stories about the hardships being endured by the colonists, thereby preparing the way for further immigration the following year. The Anglican Church of St. John, built of logs by the settlers, became the centre of the spiritual and patriotic life of the community; the House of Refuge, which served as a town hall as well as a shelter for the dispossessed, the centre of cultural activities propagated by a literary society and various choral and dramatic groups.

In the spring of 1904 many immigrants bound for the colony detrained at Edmonton 140 miles west of Lloydminster and tried

to complete the journey by floating themselves and their posses-
sions down the North Saskatchewan. But the river defeated
them; it swamped or grounded their scows, inflicting miseries
and losses far in excess of anything experienced by those who
took the land route from Saskatoon. The railway linking Edmonton and Saskatoon came through Lloydminster late the same
year; and the long journey from the end of steel to the promised
land slipped into history, became a tale told of experiences that
time would elevate from the merely arduous to the heroic.

The distinctively British character of the colony was maintained
long enough to enable the colonists to transform a bleak Lloydminster village into one of the prettiest towns in the west – this
primarily through the cultivation of numerous delightful 'Old
Country' gardens. But a physical environment so alien to that
which the colonists had known in their homeland, combined
with an influx of homesteaders of many nationalities (Barr had
been able to claim only the odd-numbered homesteads for his
people), made the preservation of a purely British identity an
impossibility. The Rev. Exton Lloyd preached against foreigners
and alcohol with equal fervour; but in the long run he was able
to keep out neither.

Today Lloydminster, a town which straddles uncomfortably
the border line between two provinces, shows little evidence of
its all-British origin. The discovery of large crude-oil deposits
in the vicinity – the earliest of such discoveries in Saskatchewan
– transformed a beautifully landscaped, leisurely paced community into a slightly frenetic boom-town, the boom being distinguished by all the benefits (mostly to outsiders) and drawbacks
normally attendant on rapid and inadequately planned expansion.

In recent years Lloydminster, like so many western communities, has developed a conscience about its past. A museum has
been established south of Highway No. 5 on the Saskatchewan
side of the border. The museum building contains the usual
collection of pioneer oddments; and the original Anglican
Church of St. John, a modest log structure, in its day the symbol
of faith in God and the British Empire (to many of the colonists
the names were synonymous), has been moved log by log to the
museum park and there admirably reconstituted.

Understandably there is no memorial in Lloydminster to Isaac Moses Barr. There should be. Whatever his faults and follies — and they were many — he was a man to whom the original colonists owed a great debt. Had it not been for him, most of those colonists would have lived out their lives in drab provincial Old Country towns, the land which they ultimately, through Barr, possessed, never anything more than the idle dream of an idle hour — the dream buried at last beneath that weight of years which crushes man's fondest aspirations.

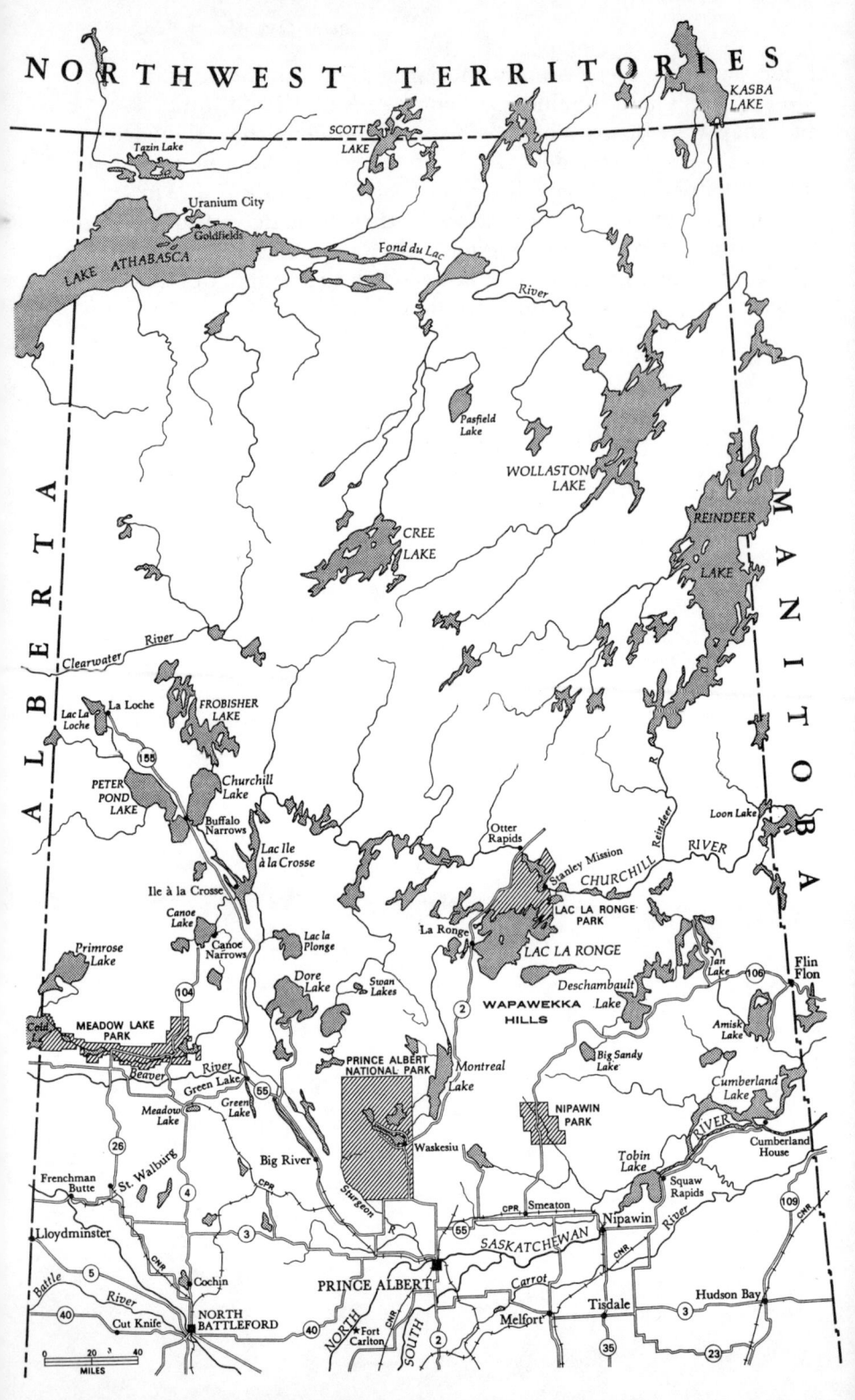

Forest, Lake, and River

15. Northern Exposure

For nearly all men – and some women – the call of the north is a trumpet-blast borne on a pine-scented wind that awakens strange longings, stirs atavistic instincts, impels many of us long in populous cities pent to rush out and buy a train- or airplane-ticket to some remote backwoods outpost, preliminary to a plunge into the forest primeval. But before buying his ticket or heading his car up a road which, according to the map, will lead him into the very heart of Saskatchewan's northland – a wild unspoiled region of lake and river and evergreen forest – the would-be escapee from the shackles of civilization had better know precisely what he is letting himself in for.

Northern Saskatchewan is simply not equipped to deal with the orthodox tourist whose pleasure it is to hustle through beautiful country, admire strange sights in passing, and find before nightfall a comfortable caravanserai in which to enjoy a night of undisturbed repose before moving on the next day. Northern Saskatchewan scenery is intermittently beautiful; there are some strange sights to be seen (many of them provided by the tourists); but such accommodations as can be reached by car are mostly primitive, comfortless, and not always clean – their distinguishing architectural feature the outside privy. The north-woods *mystique,* which exercises powerful authority here, seems to decree that comfort and honest-to-God red-blooded masculinity are irreconcilable; certainly most north-woods cabins my wife and I have sheltered in provide the bare necessities of existence and no more. In their favour it could be argued that they undoubtedly encourage outdoor living in the most literal sense; but the man who likes to read occasionally, even when leading the rugged outdoors life, will hardly find a straight-backed chair and overhead bulb adequate to his needs.

The orthodox tourist will further find – particularly if his native habitat is the plains country – that far from stimulating a sense of freedom and encouraging a feeling of expansiveness, life in the north woods is in some ways extraordinarily inhibiting. When Byron said that there is a pleasure in the pathless woods he wasn't thinking about northern Saskatchewan. Our woods are pathless all right, but whatever pleasure they might have to offer is sadly diminished by tangled underbrush, fallen trees, muskeg swamps, blackflies, horseflies, deerflies, houseflies, mosquitoes, and sometimes bears. Besides, the tenderfoot who strays a hundred yards or so into their depths had better make sure he leaves a carefully blazed trail behind him or he'll be brought out a week or so later – if at all – by helicopter.

Once, to our great delight, my wife and I came across a Department of Natural Resources sign in a northern campsite area directing us to a Nature Walk through the woods. (FOLLOW THE ARROWS the sign said.) We tightened our belts, looked to our water bottles, armed ourselves with stout staves, and followed the arrows. Five minutes and two hundred yards later we were back where we started from. Apart from this solitary expedition into the forest depths we have walked – when we walked at all – along gravelled roads or dirt trails where the dust hangs forever between green walls and agility counts for more in survival than endurance.

It is possible, of course, that hikers might enjoy themselves in the Saskatchewan north woods in their own peculiar fashion. And here I would like to make a distinction – an important one, I think – between the hiker and the walker.

The hiker wears shorts in all kinds of weather, and boots weighing about twelve pounds apiece. It makes no difference where he walks, for he buries himself under a load of paraphernalia which bows him down to the point where, if there is any scenery to see, he can't see it anyway; he simply follows his feet, and the only real pleasure he derives from his exertions, apart from a sustained masochistic thrill, is in toting up the number of miles he has covered in a week.

The walker wears conventional shirt and trousers and a pair of sneakers – or even bedroom slippers if his feet hurt and he isn't going very far. He progresses at moderate speed, pausing from time to time in an attractive spot to smoke a pipe, examine the surrounding flora, indulge in a spot of bird-watching or similar

profitable entertainment. If he is with a fellow-walker he engages
at intervals in intelligent conversation; if alone, he meditates. In
short, a walker is not content merely to cover ground; he endeav-
ours to lead a well-rounded life while on the trail, and whether
he covers one mile or ten is irrelevant.

I would compare the hiker to the dedicated fisherman who
equates the worth of a day with pounds of fish caught – and the
walker to a perambulating Izaak Walton.

The ideal walking country is of course England, with its stra-
tegically placed pubs. A walker familiar with the terrain is
usually able to average about three miles to the gallon.

For the camping enthusiast, northern Saskatchewan is fine.
The campsites are numerous; they are admirably located, ade-
quately equipped, and competently supervised. The Department
of Natural Resources men have moved in too late to be able to do
much about the early-bird private entrepreneurs whose scruffy
cabins disfigure many an otherwise beautiful shoreline, but the
camps and picnic grounds for which the D.N.R. is responsible are
beyond praise.

Northern Saskatchewan is fundamentally sportsman's country.
There, if you are passionately addicted to rod and gun, heaven
will be opened unto you. That is, if you are willing to pay the
price of admission. The best hunting and fishing spots are well
beyond the farthest point at present reached by road. They are
accessible only by plane – and the all-inclusive per-person rates
in the more luxurious of the lodges in the wilderness run as high
as sixty dollars a day. Many of these luxury camps are owned by
Americans, and most of the guests are American too. Ruddy self-
confident men, some from as far away as Texas, who can shoot
out a squirrel's eye at one hundred yards and cast into a bucket
at sixty feet.

In the fall hunters move into the north woods to shoot deer and
moose and frequently each other. It is, of course, an article of the
north-woods creed that your true sportsman should endeavour,
when big-game hunting, to live off the spoils of the chase. But
not all of those who hunt are true sportsmen. I recall vividly an
evening I spent at a dismal social gathering trapped in a corner
of the room with a stranger – a big, red-faced man who turned out
to be in all things my natural enemy. (Men I get trapped with at
parties nearly always do.) Big-game hunting, the red-faced man
said, was the sport that separated the men from the boys; if you

liked it, you had blood in your veins. If not, milk. Skim milk. Hunting, he said, did great things for a man – hardened muscles, tightened stomach, tuned up reflexes, restored virility, sharpened appetite –

'Tell me,' I said, 'do you *like* moose meat?'

'Hell no,' the man said.

'Here's what I do,' he said. 'There's four-five of us goes north in November and we camp. See? Only way to get the real feel of the woods. Camp.'

'And sleep on pine boughs?' I said.

'Sleeping-bags,' the man said. 'Pine boughs is for boy scouts. The dumb ones. Like the ones that tries to make a fire rubbing sticks together. Well, these other guys, they bring in pork and beans to keep them going till we get a moose. I bring steaks. Maybe a dozen steaks if we're in for a week. Two inches thick and a foot across. These other guys they eat their pork and beans and then we get a moose and they eat moose meat. I eat steak. Done rare. Bloody on the inside.'

He belched nostalgically. 'These other guys they eat moose meat. Tough. Stringy. Dry. And every so often they look at me and they call me sissy and a lot of names like that – and all the time they're looking at my steak and the spit's running down their chins. And they wrestle a while longer with their hunks of moose and then they say they guess they should maybe leave a few scraps for the dogs or the birds or the Indians or something and they dump the moose meat and finish up with bread and jam. A lot of bread and jam.

'Takes a lot of bread and jam to fill the hole you get in your gut when you're all day hunting,' the man explained. 'And then on the last day you should see their faces when I say, "Look, you guys, I got a few extra steaks here. Hate to waste them. How about helping me out?" '

'And they help you out?' I said.

'They help me out. After first of all yapping about how they hate to give up that last feed of good old moose meat but it'll keep all right till we get back to town (where they figure they'll get rid of it on the neighbours) and they guess they'd better help an old pal out. And this time you can bet your shirt there's no scraps left over for the dogs. They're starved, see? Steaks keep them alive till we get out.'

Something as incongruous as pity flickered in the man's eyes. 'The dumb bastards,' he said.

16. The Road to Otter Rapids

Three main highways, gravel nearly all the way, strike deep into the Saskatchewan northland. The Hanson Lake Road on the eastern side of the province links up with Manitoba Highway No. 10 at Flin Flon; Highway No. 2 runs from West Poplar on the Saskatchewan-Montana border five hundred miles north to Otter Rapids on the Churchill River; and No. 155 thrusts up on the west side as far as Buffalo Narrows near the headwaters of the Churchill, only two hundred miles from the border separating Saskatchewan from the Northwest Territories. From these main highways branch roads – most of them dirt trails – lead into several of the larger lakes (all renowned for their fishing); but for many years to come vast areas of northern Saskatchewan must remain inaccessible except by water or air. Road-building in a land of forest, water, rock, and muskeg is an enormously expensive undertaking.

For all of the roads running north, Prince Albert is the tourist's logical jumping-off spot. The city, fourth largest in the province, is splendidly located on a high bank overlooking the North Saskatchewan River, at a parallel of latitude where the parklands begin to merge into northern evergreen forest.

Prince Albert was founded in 1866; but for more than one hundred years before the building of the log mission house around which the settlement took shape, the fur-traders – Hudson's Bay, Nor'Wester, and Independent – had been familiar with the surrounding countryside and several had established posts at strategic points near by. Fort à la Corne, built as early as 1753 by the Chevalier de la Corne, stood near the river-bank some fifty miles east; in 1776 the ubiquitous Peter Pond staked his claim to a spot at the mouth of the Sturgeon River five miles west; and the Hudson's Bay post of Fort Carlton fifty miles south-east on the South Saskatchewan River was for many years the most important trading and distributing centre for the fur trade west of Fort Garry. From Fort Carlton Major Crozier and his mixed force of policemen and civilian volunteers went out that black day in March 1885 to intimidate the restless Métis with a show of firmness and strength, and were shot to pieces at Duck Lake, a few miles east of the Fort, by Métis riflemen led by Gabriel Dumont. The day following the disaster the police burned Fort Carlton – whether by accident or design is not known – and retreated to Prince Albert, bearing with them their wounded and dead. In Prince Albert there was little time for tears, even among those who had lost husbands or lovers or sons in the Duck Lake disaster. The appalled citizens aided the police in round-the-clock preparations for defence, and braced themselves to withstand a combined Indian and Métis assault. The assault never came. Once a civilian sentry mistook a distant row of poplars waving in the wind for a party of redskins in war bonnets riding into battle and almost precipitated a panic; but otherwise Prince Albert was free of war's alarms for the duration of the Rebellion.

Fort Carlton, burned by the police and thereafter abandoned, is at present being reconstructed as a tourist attraction and provincial historic monument. The Fort is well worth the time involved in a side-trip from either Saskatoon or Prince Albert. It lies squarely athwart the westward course of history on the old Carlton Trail; the reconstruction, which employs substantial twenty-foot palisades, is authentic and impressive; and the North Saskatchewan river scene at this point is one of rare and tranquil beauty at odds with the bustle and violence that must have animated the locale in the great days gone by. There are, too, subsidiary attractions in the Carlton vicinity which cannot be overlooked. Whether the traveller approaches the Fort from Prince Albert or Saskatoon via Highway No. 11 he must turn west at the village of Duck Lake (where an interesting little museum has recently been opened) and pass the Duck Lake battlefield, clearly marked by a roadside memorial, about three miles out of the village. Even the most cursory inspection of the battlefield makes clear the hopelessness of the police position – men, horses, and sleighs trapped in deep, soft snow on an open, level space surrounded by poplar bluffs and low ridges that provided ideal cover for the Métis sharp-shooters.

The visitor to Fort Carlton will also pass Canada's most unusual centennial project. It was conceived and executed by Johnny Baynton, the postmaster of Carlton village, a man of strong humanitarian spirit and much concerned about the preservation of local historic buildings. 'I wanted to do something personal,' Johnny explains. 'For Canada and Canadians. Something that would remind us of our past and likewise be useful here and now.' Beyond question he has done all he hoped to do. The Baynton outdoor privy, in the family for no fewer than four generations, has been moved from its original site and now stands stark and lonely at a municipal cross-roads a short distance from Fort Carlton. Newly painted and refurbished, adorned with the centennial motif, and advertised by a large sign in both English and French, Johnny Baynton's Centennial Comfort Station is at once an historic monument and a house of refuge for hard-pressed travellers of modest disposition who find themselves trapped in the wide open spaces with never a service station in sight.

It seems a pity that Johnny Baynton has not thus far been suitably honoured for his unique contribution to the celebration of his country's centennial year and to the comfort of his fellow men. Perhaps a seat on the Privy Council?

Prince Albert's founding father was a Presbyterian missionary, the Rev. James Nisbet, born in Glasgow and a graduate of Knox College, Toronto, who in 1866 at the age of forty-three left his parish of Kildonan and journeyed west with his family to bring the Word to the Indians of the North Saskatchewan. The mission he established became the centre of a large Indian settlement; and Nisbet, believing it to be a vital part of a missioner's work to feed the hungry and clothe the naked, worked with enormous enthusiasm to grow cereals and vegetables in a land where cultivation had never extended beyond the occasional garden-plot on the grounds of a trading-post. In 1869 the Prince Albert Mission produced one thousand bushels of grain and four hundred of potatoes. The next year Nisbet was charged by the Manitoba Presbytery, whose members obviously preferred starving Christians to well-fed heathens, with spending too much time on the bodies of his Indians and not enough on their souls. The charges were eventually dropped, but neither Nisbet – a slight, frail man – nor his devoted wife seems to have recovered from the shock of having their zeal for the faith called into question. Both died in 1874 within a few days of each other.

James Nisbet's visible memorial in Prince Albert is the log mission church, now standing in Bryant Park, which he built more than one hundred years ago.

Prince Albert has numbered among its citizens several prominent Canadians, and has been represented by no fewer than three prime ministers – Sir Wilfrid Laurier, W. L. Mackenzie King, and John Diefenbaker. Laurier represented Prince Albert briefly in 1896; King, having been rebuffed in 1925 in his home riding, thereafter chose to run in Prince Albert, known to be a Liberal stronghold, and represented the constituency almost to the end of his lengthy career. King and Diefenbaker ran against each other only once, in the by-election of 1926, when Diefenbaker, at the time a political fledgling, was badly defeated. In the eyes of his constituents King was always, however, a remote and rather chilly alien to whom they gave their votes but never their hearts. The local boy – Diefenbaker was raised on a homestead a few miles south-west of Prince Albert – eventually won both.

The tourist making his first strike into the Saskatchewan north woods from Prince Albert would do well to follow Highway No. 2 running almost directly north through the Prince Albert National Park and La Ronge to Otter Rapids on the Churchill River. La Ronge is one of the oldest and best-developed tourist areas in the north beyond the National Park. It is the best equipped to deal with visitors; it offers excellent fishing, and provides numerous admirably supervised campsites, particularly on the magnificent fifty-mile stretch between La Ronge and Otter Rapids.

Waskesiu Lake, twenty miles inside the Prince Albert National Park, is the ideal north-woods holiday spot for a man who, like myself, longs to breathe deep of pine-scented air and at the same time retain certain contacts with civilization – the type of holiday-maker who might be compared to a man standing with one foot in a boat and the other on the shore, hesitant to commit himself fully to either. So long as one is able to maintain a nice sense of balance, all is well; but let the boat begin to move ever so little and a quick decision must be made whether to go or stay.

At Waskesiu it is possible, I find, to maintain a nice equilibrium between wilderness and civilization. The forest is all around one, bears come nightly to the garbage dump to be photographed, and a splendid chain of lakes and portages leads deep into regions of almost absolute solitude. At the same time it is possible to find in the town of Waskesiu excellent food and lodging and all the standard attractions of an up-to-date resort – golf, tennis, roller-skating, cinema, liquor store, and even the occasional mild teen-ager disturbance. The fishing in Waskesiu Lake and those immediately adjoining is fair to good, although the dedicated fisherman usually seeks out colder waters much farther north, in regions into which the holidayer to whom fishing is the pastime of an idle hour rather than a Grail chase never strays.

All national parks face common difficulties, the most insistent, apart from that of providing adequate accommodation for the ever-increasing swarms of visitors, being to prevent the built-up commercial areas from degenerating into bush-league Coney Islands. The town of Waskesiu is no sylvan bride of quietness, and at times the smell of hamburger and onions triumphs over that of balsam and pine, but, on the whole, commercial development has been kept within reasonable bounds.

Of the private cottages in Waskesiu one of the most pretentious is that which belonged to Mackenzie King. He occupied it for a day or two during each election year, but never found the time or material with which to build ruins in his back yard.

Thirty miles beyond Waskesiu and accessible only by water and portage lies lovely Lake Ajawaan – insignificant in terms of size but in the 1930s the most widely publicized and best-known body of water in Saskatchewan. For to the lake in 1930 came that remarkable half-breed Grey Owl to take up his duties as conservation officer for the Prince Albert National Park. Grey Owl, who said he was the son of a Scottish father and an Apache mother, brought with him to Lake Ajawaan his beautiful half-breed wife Anahareo; a passionate belief in the need to protect the North American beaver from extinction; and a growing reputation as a writer of fascinating true stories about wilderness life and wilderness animals.

As a mere youth Grey Owl, then called by another name, had trapped and hunted in the Timagami country of northern Ontario; he had lived with the Indians and learned their lore; he had been adopted into an Ojibway tribe living on the Mississagi River and from them received the name he was later known by throughout the English-speaking world:

> A blood-brother proved and sworn, by moose-head feast, wordless chant, and ancient ritual was I named before a gaily decorated and attentive concourse, when Ne-ganik-abo, 'man-that-stands-ahead', whom none remember as a young man, danced the conjuror's dance beneath the spruce trees before an open fire. . . . The smoke hung in a white pall short of the spreading limbs of the towering trees, and with a hundred pairs of beady eyes upon me I stepped out beneath it when called on. And not one face relaxed in recognition as, absorbed in the mystery of their ritual they intoned the almost forgotten cadences. . . .
>
> The sensation of stepping into the motionless ring was that of suddenly entering a temple, devoted to the worship of some pagan deity, where the walls were lined with images cast in bronze; and there I proudly received the name they had devised, which the old man now bestowed upon me, 'Wa-sha-quon-asin' – Grey Owl.

Following his initiation into the Indian tribe, Grey Owl lived on in the wilderness, hunting and trapping as before, but with a growing distaste for the killing of animals, and especially beaver. Then came the moment of conversion, from destroyer to preserver, when the whimpering of two orphaned beaver kittens whose mother he had just shot impelled Grey Owl to swear a solemn oath never to kill another beaver. He and Anahareo raised the orphans by bottle and thereafter, became increasingly devoted to the cause of beaver conservation.

Life for the next few years was a bitter struggle to exist, for in sparing the beaver Grey Owl had cut himself off from what had for long been his chief means of support. But he persevered in the beaver cause; a few articles he wrote on the subject of conservation for an English magazine proved popular enough to warrant the publication of a full-length book, *Men of the Last*

Frontier; the book caught the eye of the National Parks Service and led to Grey Owl's appointment to the conservation post in Prince Albert National Park.

Thereafter life closed swiftly in. Grey Owl wrote more books, all of them best-sellers; he fought a successful battle for beaver conservation; he became the most widely-known Canadian author and lecturer of his day. Twice he toured England, lecturing to large and fascinated audiences. He was received by King George VI and the Royal Family, in whose presence he conducted himself with extraordinary poise and dignity. Everywhere he went, he carried himself not like a half-breed but like a great chief. He looked the part – tall, lean, bronzed, hawk-nosed. And acted it – proud to the point of arrogance, quick to resent the faintest hint of condescension on the part of the white man. (A Canadian publisher who had been deputed to introduce Grey Owl to an audience of educators in a well-known Toronto hotel still recalls with a good deal of emotion the scene that ensued when, just as he and the magnificently attired Grey Owl were about to enter an elevator, a goggle-eyed little man tumbled out of the adjacent beer-parlour with a joyous shout of 'Jeez, Mac, where'd ya get the Indian suit? C'mon in here so the boys can see ya!')

But the wilderness man adjusts ill to urban society, and the pressures mounted. Alcohol eased them, relaxed Grey Owl to the point where getting him pulled together for his platform appearances became a major concern of his attendants. Still, once on the platform he told his story well. No irrelevancies, no aberrations. Except, perhaps, that evening in Hastings on the Channel coast when he invited anyone in the audience named Belaney to come and speak with him.

The next year Grey Owl died in a Prince Albert hospital, his ravaged body unable to withstand the shock of pneumonia. Animal lovers around the world lamented the news of his death. And a newspaperman in Hastings remembered an odd word spoken – the word Belaney.

The truth, which came out piecemeal over a long period of time, shocked Grey Owl's public far more than had the news of his death. The truth – which affirmed that Grey Owl was without a trace of Indian blood, was in fact a Hastings-reared Englishman, Archibald Stanfield Belaney. He had come to Canada at the age of fifteen; he had found his way into the Ontario north

woods and had there become so enamoured of the Indian way
of life that as a preliminary step to becoming wholly absorbed
into it he had severed all connection with his own people.

Inevitably those persons most intimately associated with Grey
Owl in the time of his renown – including his English publisher
who had camped with him in, of all places, Epping Forest on the
outskirts of London, and listened to a long harangue on the
plight of the half-breed – at first refused to accept the full impli-
cations of the revelation. Others did so, but fiercely resented
having been hoodwinked. Grey Owl, whom they had loved for
his humanitarianism, his noble chieftain's mien, his romantic
aura, his fine tales, was a fake, an imposter. An Englishman
named Belaney.

On one level – the strictly factual – Grey Owl was no doubt
a fraud. It is easy now, being wise after the event, to find discrepancies in the stories he told about himself, and to detect here
and there in his usually straightforward prose, passages that could
only have originated in dim, perhaps subconscious, recollections
of sentimental Victorian literature read in boyhood – 'far overhead the Unseen Musician improvised a low rambling melody in
the many-stringed lyre of the pine-tops' – 'I buried him . . .
beneath the birches near the lakeshore, where he may hear the
singing birds trill in rippling melody their evensong in the sad
days of the Fall of the Leaf, and the north-west wind may bring
a message from the Great Lone Land beyond.'

The fact that Grey Owl was an Englishman named Belaney,
however, in no way affects the value of his achievement. His
work as conservationist, writer, and publicist on behalf of the
Indian and the half-breed is not degraded by the revelation of
identity. Only for those who can never separate the work from
the man, who damn Burns's poetry because Burns drank and
rate Shelley below Tennyson because his life was less pure, does
Grey Owl's achievement lose much of its value when the man's
life is examined in the cold light of conventional morality. For
what, after all, is to be made of an Englishman who denied blood
and birthright, and of a husband who left to mourn his loss, as
a dazed public was soon to learn, not one widow but *four*?

For many of Grey Owl's followers it was the awareness of being
deceived, led astray, that made objective judgement of his work
thereafter impossible, and with their feelings it is easy enough
to sympathize. But it should be borne in mind that, of all men,

Grey Owl was himself the most deceived; some time over the long stretch of years that he lived among the Indians as an Indian in the Ontario north woods he had crossed the border-line separating one life from another, the dream had merged into reality, the white man Archie Belaney had become in his own mind and heart the Indian Grey Owl.

Except, perhaps, for that single moment on the platform in Hastings when some obscure prompting out of a long-suppressed – indeed almost totally extinguished – past impelled him to speak the word Belaney.

When Grey Owl was buried on the shore of Lake Ajawaan near the cabin he made famous, rumours about his identity were already in the air; and it is said that the clergyman who officiated at the burial service insisted that the dead man be clad, not in barbaric buckskin, but in decent Christian blue serge lest, in Howard O'Hagan's words, 'imposter to the end, he arose in the full panoply of the wilderness to confuse his Maker.'

It is unlikely that his Maker would have been confused. And it is certain that, remembering that the dead man's life had been dedicated to the saving rather than the destruction of His creatures, He would have welcomed him – in buckskin or blue serge – as Grey Owl.

Beyond the northern boundary of Prince Albert National Park, Highway No. 2 cuts through singularly drab forest, mostly stunted spruce. The monotony of the green tunnel is relieved by occasional glimpses of Montreal Lake, a fine body of water nearly thirty miles long, and sometimes of a bear or moose, although animals tend to keep well away from the highway. Between Waskesiu and Lac La Ronge, a distance of slightly over one hundred miles, there is only one settlement of note. Molanosa's claim to recognition rests on a geographical fact – it is the approximate centre of Saskatchewan. This bit of information usually comes as a shock to travellers on the La Ronge Highway, who feel that having passed the limits of the Prince Albert Park they are well into the far north.

Paradoxically, since at La Ronge we find ourselves among the oldest rocks in the world, those of the Pre-Cambrian Shield, the country through which No. 2 passes seems new, untouched. And untouched it is. There are no historic markers to provide an excuse for a wayside stop, no smoke plumes marking the site of mill or mine, no side-roads leading into the forest, no evidence anywhere, except for the road itself, of man's presence. There is the gravel surface beneath, the long empty avenue up front, the empty sky overhead. Take a step or two off the Highway and you might well be back in one of the first ages of man.

The settlement of La Ronge is one of the oldest in Saskatchewan. A century or more ago it was a Hudson's Bay post and an Anglican mission; still earlier Peter Pond traded with the Indians of La Ronge, and was afterwards accused of having murdered his partner. Today the community is a mixed Métis and Indian settlement, and a tourist centre catering to fishermen and hunters. The town proper straggles along the west shore of La Ronge for nearly two miles; the Indian and Métis settlements huddle on its outskirts. Tourist accommodation is better than in most northern settlements; the hotel, I am told, is first-rate; the cabins built in clutches along the lakeshore or highway are clean, but designed to accommodate the outdoors man who, for the week or two he is in the wilderness, is contemptuous of the comforts he couldn't possibly live without back home. Airplanes land and take off almost by the minute, creating an atmosphere of feverish activity at odds with one's romantic notions about the lonely, silent north woods. Most of the planes are engaged in carrying sportsmen to and from hunting-grounds or fishing-waters deep in the forest where no roads go. Plane pilots, like cowboys, will go to almost any lengths to avoid walking; to get from one end of the street to the other they taxi their planes along the waterfront. They are hardly to be blamed for choosing what may seem to be a lazy man's mode of locomotion. There are no sidewalks in La Ronge, and the pedestrian who commits himself to the single long street is either enveloped in a cloud of dust or submerged in a sea of mud.

The La Ronge Anglican Church of All Saints, built four-square on a mighty slab of Pre-Cambrian rock, is modern, but the mission of which it is the centre dates back to 1845. In that year an Indian catechist from the Red River training-school, James Settee, answered the call of the Cree tribesmen living in the La Ronge district, who had heard something of the white man's God from their neighbours at Cumberland House and were anxious for more explicit information. Within five years of Settee's coming all of the Indians in the settlement clustered around the Hudson's Bay post on La Ronge were church-going

Anglicans. In the Church of All Saints, services are still conducted in Cree as well as in English.

Lac La Ronge is a magnificent body of water, island-studded,
forest-fringed, blue under a blue heaven, grey under grey. Blue
or grey, La Ronge is generous in its yield of fish — pickerel and
trout of such magnitude that not even the most ambitious of
fishermen need ever lie about the size of his catch. Or so I am
told. But for the run-of-the-mill tourist the country lying north
of Lac La Ronge between the provincial park and the Churchill
River holds attractions that surpass even those of the mighty
lake.

The road leads straight north from La Ronge to Otter Rapids,
a distance of fifty-odd miles. This is Shield country. The forest
diversifies; high ridges and even modest hills appear; and for the
first time the traveller is aware that he is on a road that insinuates
itself among and around innumerable lakes, snakes delicately
across countless narrows. There is water on every side now, nearly
always in sight. Campsites and picnic grounds too — more numerous than anywhere else in Saskatchewan and all admirably
maintained.

No man with any sense of history can look unmoved on the
Churchill River as seen from the bridge spanning Otter Rapids.
(Nor can the man with a feeling for beauty, for the river, compressed here between high narrow banks, tumbles in a mad cas-
cade towards the freedom of the lake lying a mile or two below
the bridge.) The Churchill, like the Saskatchewan, is one of the
great waterways of the early fur trade. Here upstream in 1778
came Peter Pond, that sullen, dangerous man, to give his name
to one of the two great lakes near the headwaters of the Churchill,
to find a passage north from the Churchill into Lac La Loche,
and thence, incredibly, by the Methy Portage into the Athabasca
River, thus opening up a waterway, reaching all the way from
Hudson Bay to the Rockies, over which huge shipments of fur
were soon to be carried.

The Churchill actually rises in Lac La Loche, though the
greater part of the flow comes from the two larger lakes, Pond
and Churchill, fifty miles south. It is a freakish river in that
instead of gathering its main flow from subsidiary streams over
a lengthy stretch of territory it springs almost full-fledged into
being. It is unusual in another respect, too, for until it flows

out of Indian Lake on the last lap of its journey to Hudson Bay, it is in actual fact a water-chain, linking together a series of lakes of astonishing number and varying magnitude. The general pattern of river-and-lake combination is observable at the Otter Rapids bridge, where a powerful flood of water pours out of Nipew Lake and into Otter Lake. The bridge provides the kind of bird's-eye view that helps us to understand something of the problems and hazards encountered by traders on the Churchill – fast water, treacherous rapids, and lakes offering a choice of a dozen or more channel exits, all except one being actually dead ends.

There is a substantial tourist-cabin settlement at the point where the Churchill flows into Otter Lake a short distance below the bridge. From the settlement it is possible to visit by boat the Stanley Mission a few miles distant at the south-east end of the lake. The chief ornament of the mission is the Church of the Holy Trinity, the oldest in the Saskatchewan Anglican diocese, built during the years 1853-60 under the direction of two English missionaries, the Rev. and Mrs. Robert Hunt. Architecturally the church, built of lumber sawn on the spot and adorned with stained-glass windows sent out from England via Hudson Bay, has little to commend it. It is awkwardly proportioned, graceless, in no way related to its physical surroundings; but as visible evidence of the determination of the early missionaries to make the white man's faith prevail among the heathen, it is in an odd way impressive. And by its very incongruity in relation to its physical environment, by its peculiarly Old Country appearance in this new world of wilderness, it calls most forcibly to the attention of the visitor into the Saskatchewan north country a problem of which he can hardly help being aware, and which, if his preoccupation with hunting and fishing is a little less than allabsorbing, must cost him at least a moment or two of heartsearching and embarrassment.

In some respects, particularly that of health, the Indians and Métis are better off now than at any other time since the white man first took possession of their land. The death-rate from communicable diseases, and most notably from tuberculosis, has been greatly reduced; medical services are more readily available than ever before; and well-equipped hospitals and schools are no longer a rarity. But the fundamental problem of integration is

no nearer resolution than it was one hundred years ago; if anything, it is further off, for intermarriage between Indian and
white is much less common now than in the old days. Nor has
any visible progress been made in helping the Indian to adjust
to a stable order of society. Once he is cabined, cribbed, confined, he appears to lose whatever initiative he might have
exercised in the old nomadic environment; he sinks into a kind
of sullen, hopeless apathy, and his surroundings, including his
home, reflect his mental attitude; they quickly assume the appearance, even in the wilderness, of a wretched slum. Grey Owl
pointed out as clearly as anyone the futility of attempting to
settle Indians in permanent homes patterned after those of the
white man:

> Modern influences have taken away much of the picturesque
> appearance from Indian camps, as seen on reserves and more
> readily accessible areas of the wilderness Their racial pride has
> been sapped, and, destitute and hopeless, they no longer have
> the ambition to keep up the old methods and traditions, so that
> home life is slipshod and wretched, and national character is
> falling into decay.

Things haven't changed greatly in the forty years that have
passed since Grey Owl wrote those words. The Indian is still at
heart a nomad, or else has abandoned himself to living squalidly
in the meanest of shack-towns. In an age when it is commonly
assumed that a man needs at least a B.A. degree before he is
qualified to operate a gas-pump, the Indian's education stops at
the elementary-school level. His attendance at high school is rare,
at university almost unheard of.

As in the old days those who live on the plains fare better than
the dwellers in the forest; they raise livestock, grow some cereals
– and the sun and the hot dry winds quickly sterilize the offal
which, around so many communities in the north woods, is a
permanent festering mass. Unlike the Negro, the Indian seems
incapable of adapting to urban life (he might argue that he has
never been given the chance); and unfortunately the worlds of
the herdsman and the trapper, in which he has been most at
home, are rapidly contracting.

So far about all that has been made clear to us in our dealings
with the Indians is that money, goodwill, even affection, are not
enough to bring him out of the world of his ancestors into our

own. Some of those most concerned about the welfare of the Indian argue that the transition from the one world to the other – or from a borderland between the two – can be made only when the Indian feels that we honestly respect him. 'If we ask the Indian to change we must ourselves change.' But an attitude of mind is not something to be assumed or discarded at a moment's notice; if it is to be significant, it must be nurtured and developed over a long period of time, otherwise it is merely prejudice. And mutual respect is rarely to be found existing spontaneously between peoples whose values are so radically different as those of the white man and the Indian.

So far it seems that there is only one level, the last of all, on which the white man and the Indian are to be found together and at peace. The graveyard at La Ronge makes no distinction between peoples. This unity in death, and only in death, is acknowledged in the words inscribed over the entrance to the graveyard, words which may be interpreted as an expression of utter cynicism, or – more hopefully – a humble acknowledgement of wrongs committed and hence a sign of grace.

The inscription reads:

IF WE DID NOT AS BROTHERS LIVE
LET US HERE AS BROTHERS LIE.

17. Farthest North

The long road (No. 155) north to Ile à la Crosse, Buffalo Narrows, and – if the traveller has the time and the courage – to La Loche on Methy Lake a few miles south of the portage that leads over the height of land to the Athabasca River, is most readily approached from Prince Albert by Highway 55 through Big River and Green Lake. But if he has a day or two in hand and is interested in the history as well as the scenery of the northwest, the traveller would be well advised to make Lloydminster his point of taking off. The meridian road running north from the town enters, after a few miles, a picturesque countryside dominated by splendid rolling hills, and shortly thereafter links up with Highway No. 3 running due east from the border. At Deer Creek, sixteen miles from the border, a ferry takes one across the North Saskatchewan, at this point a stream of impressive volume flowing swiftly between high, heavily-wooded banks. From the ferry a side-road leads five miles to Fort Pitt and Frenchman's Butte, scenes of some of the most exciting action of the Northwest Rebellion.

In 1885 Fort Pitt consisted of a Hudson's Bay Company trading-post with the usual semi-permanent Indian settlement hugging its flanks. Built on the flats of the North Saskatchewan River, the Fort was never meant to withstand a siege; its buildings were scattered over a wide area and the ramshackle palisade, which at one time had surrounded them, served no purpose other than to create the feeble illusion of a walled fortress. Based at Fort Pitt in the spring of 1885 was a force of twenty-five Mounted Policemen under the command of Inspector Francis Dickens, son of the novelist Charles Dickens. It was the responsibility of the detachment to maintain the peace over a wide area, and particularly in the camp of the band of Plains Cree under the chieftainship of Big Bear, who for some time now had been hanging around the Fort Pitt – Frog Lake country, spoiling for trouble. Unlike most of the Indian tribes of the north-west, Big Bear's Cree refused to live on a reservation and were thus denied the five-dollars-a-year-per-person treaty money and other fringe benefits which a paternalistic government conferred upon its adopted children who behaved themselves. In the spring of 1885 Big Bear's people were hungry, bitterly hostile to the white man's rule, and agitated by rumours of revolt on the part of their half-brothers, the Métis, living far away on the South Saskatchewan at Batoche.

On the day before Good Friday, in 1885, occurred the most tragic episode of the Northwest Rebellion. On that day Big Bear's warriors, incited to murder by their bitter, brooding war-chief, Wandering Spirit, massacred at Frog Lake nine unarmed white men including the Indian agent, Tom Quinn. When word came to Fort Pitt, brought by one of the few survivors of the catastrophe, that the Indians were on the war-path, civilians and police worked frantically to prepare the defensible buildings to withstand a siege. They built a crude stockade around the buildings, laid in supplies of food and water, armed everyone – including the young daughters of the Hudson's Bay factor – with rifles, and braced themselves for the horrors of Indian warfare.

The Indians gathered on the hills overlooking the Fort. When a three-man patrol, returning to the Fort from a scouting mission towards Frog Lake, rode carelessly into Big Bear's camp, the excited Indians killed one policeman and badly wounded another; but beyond firing a few shots into the stockade they made no hostile move against the Fort itself. It is, however, possible to understand Inspector Dickens's willingness to allow the thirty civilians huddled inside the stockade to surrender to the Indians on the promise that no harm would be done to them. Had he compelled them to remain, he would have had to assume responsibility for their safety. It is less easy to understand his subsequent abandonment of the Fort and flight with his men aboard an old scow down river to Battleford ninety miles away. True, the police were outnumbered six or seven to one; but they were armed with up-to-date repeating rifles. Most of the Indians carried old Hudson's Bay Company muzzle-loading trade guns.

Perhaps a man who has lived all his life in the shadow of another's greatness is reluctant to seek a place in the sun.

Meanwhile, moving briskly up from Calgary at the head of a motley force of local volunteers, militiamen from Winnipeg and Montreal, and a strong detachment of Mounties under the command of Major Sam Steele, came Major-General Tom Strange, a retired British army officer turned rancher, now called out of retirement to help restore order in the troubled west. Genial, eccentric, popular with his troops, and quick to recognize the fighting ability of the Mounties and the frontiersmen who had enlisted as volunteers, Strange was the one competent commander on the government side turned up by the Rebellion. At Fort Edmonton, following a remarkable forced march from Calgary, Strange embarked most of his troops and supplies on a fleet of scows which he had ordered built in anticipation of his arrival. The flotilla – first of its kind on the Saskatchewan – drifted down river to Fort Pitt, where Strange disembarked his forces and established headquarters. A few days later he ran Big Bear's band to ground on Frenchman's Butte, a lofty hill rising a few miles east of Fort Pitt. The engagement that followed was indecisive – and nearly bloodless. Most of the ammunition fired by the green lads under Strange's command thumped harmlessly into the hill-side; and Wandering Spirit, Big Bear's war-chief and a warrior of superior military talents, manoeuvred a handful of his best sharp-shooters skilfully enough to discourage Sam Steele's attempts to outflank the Indian position. The outcome of all the firing and strategic marching and counter-marching was anti-climactic; both sides detached themselves from the engagement simultaneously. Strange's men withdrew to await the coming-up of fresh supplies and ammunition, the Indians fled away into the heavy bush to fight another day – in their haste allowing eleven of the thirty-odd prisoners they held to escape.

Of old Fort Pitt nothing now remains. One building has been rebuilt along its original lines by a local antiquarian, but otherwise there is nothing to show that here until 1889 stood one of the most important Hudson's Bay trading-posts on the North Saskatchewan.

A few miles east of Fort Pitt village, Frenchman's Butte dominates the surrounding countryside. It is an impressive elevation, difficult of access, and most visitors are content to look at it from a mile or two away. For those sound of wind and limb, a climb to the summit will prove rewarding; the view is spectacular –

and Wandering Spirit's cunningly placed rifle-pits still scar the hill-side just below the summit.

Six miles south-west of St. Walburg on Highway No. 3 a large sign points the way to the Imhoff Gallery, privately owned and operated, just two miles off the Highway, and on no account to be missed by those who delight in the freakish and the off-beat. Count Imhoff was a Bavarian who came to America when a young man and lived for a time in Pennsylvania; then, because, so he said, he wanted to paint in quietness and solitude, he settled on a farm in the bush country near the village of St. Walburg. There he lived continuously from 1913 until his death in 1939. On the farm he built himself a substantial house, in design vaguely reminiscent of his native Bavaria – and a 'gallery' decorated on the outside with murals, much faded now, employing traditional Bavarian motifs. The gallery, although the size of an overblown dairy-barn, is not nearly large enough to exhibit the really stupefying number of canvases that the Count had completed before being compelled by death – and only by death – to lay down his brush.

As a young man Count Imhoff studied in Europe under recognized art masters; he was a sound enough craftsman and knew how to lay on paint. Essentially he was a copyist of almost incredible industry. Everything that had ever been painted was grist to his mill; and the walls of the enormous gallery are lined with reproductions of world masterpieces – da Vincis (including two Mona Lisas), Titians, Rembrandts, Raphaels, and a hundred more. Other works on display in the gallery include portraits – copied mostly from bad originals or photographs – of assorted members of British and German royalty, hanging side by side with Lincoln, Washington, William Penn, Napoleon retreating from Moscow, several popes, and half the saints of the Christian calendar. A visit to the Imhoff Gallery is a unique experience and in one respect at least a salutary one. It provides sure proof, if any be needed, that the creation of a work of art requires more than industry and good intentions. Whenever the Count drew for subject-matter on his own experience and imagination, all that can be said for the consequences is that they are not like anything the visitor to conventional art galleries will have seen elsewhere.

Count Imhoff seems to have loved grapes, Biblical scenes, saints, bishops, old masters, Indians, dead ducks, and Homburg hats roughly in that order. His Crucifixion, which dominates one end of the gallery, is surely among the biggest of its kind ever painted; most of his Indians, some of them done from life, bear a striking resemblance to George Washington; and his dead ducks – so a wild-life connoisseur has assured me – look really dead.

Count Imhoff's self-portraits – there are several in the gallery – almost invariably show him wearing a Homburg hat. And in the one exception, a portrait in which he has painted himself in full cowboy regalia, he has contrived to make his sombrero *look* like a Homburg.

There is a really charming incongruity about the picture our imagination frames of the dapper little Count buried in the Saskatchewan bush, madly copying old masters for his own satisfaction and decorating churches for the love of God. (He died of a stroke while working, for no fee, on a mural in a Battleford church.) He adds not merely a touch but a whole kaleidoscope of colour to the rather colourless community he lived in; and his memorial, the gallery that bears his name and houses his life's work, for that reason if for no other deserves our attention and, in an odd way, our respect. Let us hope that his reward for his labours is that promised by Kipling to all artists who, whatever their limitations, strive always and honestly towards the realization of their ideal:

> *And those who were good shall be happy; they shall sit in a*
> *golden chair;*
> *They shall splash at a ten-league canvas with brushes of comet's*
> *hair:*
> *They shall find real saints to draw from – Magdalene, Peter and*
> *Paul;*
> *They shall work for an age at a sitting and never be tired at all!*

From St. Walburg our road (No. 26 now) leads through heavy bush-country past Loon Lake to Meadow Lake Provincial Park. Loon Lake is a popular local holiday resort, and a point of interest to students of western Canadian history, for it was here that for a second time Big Bear's warriors, hotly pursued by Mounted Police scouts, turned at bay and exchanged fire with the men in red coats. Following the exchange they retreated along a peninsula jutting far out into the lake at a point called the Narrows, forded the lake, and vanished into the muskeg country to the north where the police could not follow. It later transpired that Steele's enthusiasm for shooting it out with the Indians had prevented two of Big Bear's white prisoners from communicating to Steele a request to discuss terms of surrender. A few days later Big Bear set his captives free, dispersed his warriors, and gave himself up to a policeman who found him wandering unattended in the bush.

At Loon Lake an historic marker on a high ridge commanding a magnificent view of the Narrows celebrates what is termed, rather grandiosely, 'the last military engagement' fought on Canadian soil.

From Meadow Lake Provincial Park – one of the largest and newest in Saskatchewan, heavily wooded, lake-studded, but as yet inadequately developed to cope with any considerable flow of tourist traffic – the north-bound traveller anxious to keep to the best highway should drive south a few miles to the town of Meadow Lake, then east to link up with Highway 155 at Green Lake. Green Lake is a substantial settlement at the end of a long, narrow body of water up which the wind funnels at times with tremendous force. It is the centre of an interesting experiment begun in 1952, intended to settle the Indians and Métis on the land in a government-supervised co-operative farming venture. Unfortunately the project has not fulfilled the hopes of its initiators – in part because of the apparent inability of the Indians to settle down in one spot for any length of time.

On our most recent trip to Buffalo Narrows we eschewed the regular highway route and drove out of Meadow Lake Provincial Park over a Natural Resources Department road (No. 104) to Canoe Lake, and thence on a connecting road to link up with No. 155 near Lac La Plonge. Driving for several hours over a road such as No. 104, through dense forest with clearance of only a few feet on either side, is like taking part in a marathon underwater swim. The green waves close over your head; you thrust forward resolutely through a green world that filters – at times almost shuts out – the sunlight; there is a sense of movement but nothing changes – just greenness on all sides, and even overhead, for the sky seems to absorb the colour of the forest. Then, at the moment when suffocation seems inevitable, you strike an air-hole (a lake or similar substantial opening) where it is possible to take a deep breath before once more immersing yourself in the green depths.

Friends of mine to whom the north woods are a genuine passion find my claustrophobic reactions to their green heaven inexplicable and absurd. I think, though, that I can muster some evidence to support my view that a forest environment is not only physically oppressive, but mentally inhibiting. It is surely true that the great artists and prophets have been, in the main, products of an intensely communal urban life or of far-horizoned worlds where trees grow sparsely or not at all. The best European novelists knew intimately the steppes of Russia, and at least one – Dostoevsky – was no stranger to Siberia; Thomas Hardy brooded over Egdon Heath; the greatest English novel was conceived on the moors of Yorkshire; and Phidias could see for twenty miles every time he lifted his eyes from a figure on the Parthenon. On the other hand it is safe to affirm – as a generalization to which there are few, if any, exceptions – that *no great art ever came out of the bush.* Thoreau, it is true, retreated to a grove of trees beside a pond and there meditated *Walden* into being; but he was careful to keep Concord and its congenial society within easy walking distance. It is worth noting, too, that for the past half-century or more the British Columbia woods have been full of prospective writers holed up to 'do' the great Canadian novel or epic poem. Most have come out after a few weeks, bringing with them some sheets of paper covered with grocery lists; those who haven't come out are almost certainly bushed by now and won't be heard of again.

It is here on these relatively untravelled northern trails (such as 104) that a road sign – or posted communication of any sort – becomes an object of the most passionate concern, to be studied with the intensity usually reserved for great works of art. The sign may be no more than the cabalistic scribblings of a survey party, or a label denominating a stream intersecting the trail as Skunk or Horsehide or Hanging Dog or Misery Creek – but an inscription of any sort provides a welcome human touch in a seemingly uninhabited and utterly indifferent world.

The Indian and Métis settlement at Canoe Lake Narrows sets the pattern for most of the smaller native communities scattered throughout the Saskatchewan north woods. Little attempt has been made to arrange the buildings according to any kind of preconceived design; log shacks and box-like frame houses – most of them without foundation – are scattered higgledy-piggledy over a wide area around a substantial new Roman Catholic church; cattle and horses graze among the houses and in the churchyard; fishnets hung on fence-railings dry in the sun; children and dogs play in noisy concord along paths that wind hither and yon through the settlement seemingly without direction or purpose; the young bucks cluster round the door of the log pool-room (the centre of their community life) and stare without comment at any girls who chance to pass by. When they are not busy with their nets or livestock, the elders of the settlement sit on their doorsteps and gossip. The children look happy, animated – the very old impassive, remote, as if already detached from life; their faces, and particularly those of the women, are a network of lines furrowed deep by time and tribulation. Here in Canoe Lake things are a little better than in many of the native communities (the livestock alone represents community property of considerable value), but even here living is always precarious; and death – as the inscriptions on the wooden crosses in the weed-ridden settlement graveyard indicate – claims most of the natives long before expiration of their traditional three score years and ten.

From Canoe Lake a gravel road leads east to a junction with Highway No. 155. Ile à la Crosse, one of the best-known and best-ordered of the northern settlements, is reached from 155 over a side-road that follows a long arm of land thrusting down into Lac Ile à la Crosse a distance of some fifteen miles.

At Ile à la Crosse in the year 1846, shortly after the arrival of the Anglican catechist Settee at La Ronge 150 miles south-east, the first permanent Roman Catholic mission in Saskatchewan was established. To the mission in 1860 came three dedicated Sisters of Charity whose names, Pépin, Boucher, and Agnès, hold an honoured place in the records of Canadian missionary enterprise. The Sisters opened a convent, a dispensary (later made into a hospital), and a school. The mission survived flood and fire; twice destroyed, it was twice rebuilt. The fire of 1867, so one of the fathers reported, left the missioners 'without even a handkerchief to wipe away their tears'; but Captain Butler, who visited Ile à la Crosse in 1873 in the course of a journey that provided him with material for his well-known travel book, *The*

Wild North Land, was obviously impressed by what he found at the partially restored mission station:

> The fort of Ile à la Crosse is a solitary spot. Behind it spreads a land of worthless forest, a region abounding in swamps and muskegs, in front the long arms of the Cruciform Lake. It is not from its shape that the lake bears its name; in the centre, where the four long arms meet, stands an island, on the open shore of which the Indians in bygone times were wont to play their favourite game of La Crosse. . . . At a short distance from the fort stands the French Mission. One of the earliest established in the north, it has thrown out many branches into remote solitudes. Four ladies of the order of Grey Nuns have made their home here, and their school already contains some thirty children. If one wants to see what can be made of very limited space, one should visit this convent at Ile à la Crosse; the entire building is a small wooden structure, yet school, dormitory, oratory, kitchen and dining-room are all contained therein.
>
> The sisters seemed happy and contented, chatted gaily of the outside world, or of their far-away homes in Lower Canada. Their present house was only a temporary erection. In one fell night fire had destroyed a larger building, and consumed their library, oratory, everything; and now its ravages were being slowly repaired.

In 1928 the Grey Nuns, inheritors of the original mission, were appointed to staff the newly built government hospital at Ile à la Crosse.

Boat and canoe enthusiasts anxious to follow the route of the fur brigades of a distant day find Ile à la Crosse an excellent taking-off point for a journey down the Churchill. Perhaps the most unlikely of such twentieth-century enthusiasts to embark in a canoe with the intention of spending two months on the wilderness waterways was a red-headed American novelist, who in 1924 accompanied officials of the Department of Indian Affairs on their annual expedition to distribute treaty money among the northern Indian tribes.

Sinclair Lewis was then at the height of his fame; he had written *Main Street* and *Babbitt* and *Arrowsmith,* he was the best-selling novelist in the United States, and was already spoken of as a prospective Nobel Prize winner. The fact that Lewis, together with his brother, Dr. Claude of Sauk Centre, was permitted to accompany the expedition is sure proof of his immense prestige, since officials of the Department of Indian Affairs ordinarily took a dim view of outsiders accompanying the Treaty Brigade on its annual tour. Just why Lewis undertook the trip is not entirely clear, although several reasons suggest themselves. He was drinking heavily at the time and no doubt expected to benefit greatly from a healthy outdoors life, and a period of enforced abstinence (no liquor was carried by the Brigade). It is likely, too, that he hoped to gather material for a novel which he had promised to a popular slick magazine for serial publication. But the strongest reason lay in the nature of the man himself. Satirist though he was, Lewis harboured naively romantic notions about the north woods, where, so he honestly believed, a man could demonstrate his essential worth by matching himself against, and triumphing over, the indifferent or actively hostile forces of nature. 'Mind you,' he assured reporters, in words more appropriate to the utterance of a singularly innocent Queen's Scout than a world-famous satirist, 'we won't have any resthouses at the end of the day's march, where one can get a hot bath and sleep between sheets. We'll have to pack our own kits and portage our own canoes. It's going to be bully.'

From Abercrombie and Fitch, Lewis bought enough equipment to outfit an outsized expedition looking for the Northwest Passage – most of it he had discarded long before reaching the Churchill – and in a state of near-hysterical euphoria he left New York for Ile à la Crosse. En route he addressed service clubs in Winnipeg, Regina, Saskatoon, and Prince Albert and embarked on a drinking bout of such dimensions as amazed even the hard-boiled newspapermen who tried in vain to keep up with him. From Prince Albert he and brother Claude rode by freight to Big River, covering the ninety miles in eight hours, and from the end of steel made their way by boat down Cowan Lake and the Beaver River to Ile à la Crosse where the Treaty Brigade was already assembled for the journey by canoe down the Churchill.

A little more than two weeks later, when the canoes had got no farther than the Stanley Mission, two hundred-odd miles down river from their starting-point, Lewis found that he had

had enough of healthful outdoors living. Some ill-feeling had developed between him and Dr. Claude, whose superior wood-craft he plainly resented – and besides, he badly needed a drink.

Lewis joined forces with a congenial spirit, a fur-trader named Arthur Jan (who gave his name to a beautiful lake on the Hanson Road), and accompanied him in leisurely stages and by devious waterways through Pelican Narrows and Sturgeon Landing to The Pas, where he was able to catch a train for New York. Each stop along the way provided an excuse for a party; and when Dr. Claude came out of the bush he found his brother's exit trail marked by piles of empty bottles. 'All drunk,' Claude noted in his diary, reporting what he had heard at Sturgeon Landing. 'Killed nine bottles of Scotch and played poker until daylight. That's life for Harry [i.e. Sinclair] . . . if you add a woman or two at the proper time.'

Pathetic indeed is the spectacle of a man seeking a panacea in the wilderness way of life for the ills that beset him in civilization, forgetting that whomever and whatever he may be able to leave behind, he must take himself with him wherever he goes.

The novel *Mantrap*, which grew out of Lewis's efforts to be re-born in the wilds, is one of his worst. Brother Claude (thinly disguised) plays the role of villain – a clumsy ill-mannered boor whose offences against man and nature are such that he is eventually abandoned by his party and left to his own devices; Sinclair Lewis himself (even more thinly disguised) plays the hero, a city man who, after a few false starts, comes to terms with the wilderness; and the trader Jan appears as a most admirable woodsman married to a flighty amoral wench whose blatant pursuit of the hero provides the foundation of the hackneyed plot. Only in an occasional comment on the north-woods native and the white overlord's attitude towards him does the ebullient satirist of *Main Street* and *Babbitt* assert himself over the slick commercial hack. Of the Indians he wrote: 'They did not look in the least like lords of the wilderness engaged in watching, under lean shadowing hands, the flight of a distant eagle. They looked like undersized Sicilians who had been engaged in digging a sewer.'

Of bannock, a wilderness bread that excites your true-blue north-woods fancier to outbursts of lyrical appreciation, Lewis wrote: 'Now bannock is, technically, a variety of bread. But only among the copper-stomached Woods Crees is it considered to be an edible bread. It is well enough thought of as ballast, as a missile, or an anchor; but for internal use it ranks with tripe and pemmican. Bannock is made without yeast. It is flour and water, caused to cleave together by boiling it in lard in a frying pan over a maddened fire.'

And the Rev. Mr. Dillon, a missionary, Lewis damned in a single sentence: 'He was always forgiving the Indians for being Indian.'

There are some things in *Mantrap* that make it worth reading.

For most travellers on Highway 155, Buffalo Narrows is the end of the line. The road continues after a fashion for another fifty miles to La Loche – said to be the most depressed of all the northern settlements – but it is of the kind not to be attempted except in fine weather. To reach the settlement of Buffalo Narrows one must take the ferry that plies across the short, narrow stretch of river linking the Peter Pond and Churchill lakes. There is little of interest to see in the settlement itself, although it is one of the largest in the north country. Its only industry is a fish-freezing plant to which fish are flown in from lakes scattered over a wide surrounding area.

When my wife and I visited Buffalo Narrows we didn't stay long. The road for the last fifteen miles into the Narrows was under repair; we could get no gas in the settlement because of a power failure; and rain was coming on. We decided, therefore, on a hasty retreat to Ile à la Crosse where we hoped to find the gas pumps working. The handsome young Métis ferryman recognized us when, less than an hour after he had ferried us across to the settlement side, we boarded for the return trip.

'So you didn't like the town,' he said. Not as a question but as a statement of fact.

I stammered an explanation. The weather – power failure –

'That's all right,' he said. 'I don't like it either.'

He waved a hand toward the big frame house halfway up the bank. 'I live there,' he said. 'All by myself. Maybe if I got married – '

Buffalo Narrows wasn't his part of the north; he was a stranger suffering from what must surely have been one of the commonest ills to afflict men buried in the overwhelming immensity of the north woods – the simple heartache born of loneliness. Today, with radio and plane communications reaching into the remotest parts of the north-west, the sense of isolation has been in a measure diminished. What it was like for the fur-traders, the wintering-partners of the North West Company, and the factors of the old Hudson's Bay Company has been most vividly suggested by Captain Butler, who, in the course of his wanderings in 1873, had the fullest opportunity to experience at first hand the awful loneliness of the silent woods:

> God knows their lives were hard. They came generally from the remote isles or highlands of Scotland, they left home young, and the mind tires when it thinks upon the remoteness of many of their fur stations. Dreary and monotonous beyond words was their home life, and hardship was its rule. To travel on foot 1000 miles in winter's darkest time, to live upon the coarsest food, to see nought of bread or sugar for long months, to lie down at night under the freezing branches, to feel cold such as Englishmen cannot even comprehend, often to starve, always to dwell in exile from the great world – such was the routine of their lives. . . . Who can tell what memories of the early days in the far away Scottish isles, or Highland glen, must have come to these men as the tempest swept the stunted pine-forest, and wrack and drift hurled across the frozen lake – when the dawn and the dusk, separated by only a few hours' daylight, closed into the long, dark night. Perchance the savage scene was lost in a dreamy vision of some lonely Scottish loch, some Druid mound in far away Lewis, some vista of a fireside, when storm howled and waves ran high upon the beach of Stornoway.

We cannot, however, ignore the effects of conditioning, and it may be that Butler, who loved the great plains better than any other part of earth, ascribed to those who dwelt long in the north woods his own reactions. The truth is, that for some men who grow up in the north, the forest is a womb from which they are terrified to come out.

18. The Hanson Lake Road

The Hanson Lake Road is one of the newest in Saskatchewan and among the most widely publicized. It is, unfortunately, by no means one of the best; a far greater burden of truck traffic than was anticipated, most of it bound to or from the great Flin Flon smelter, has broken the road down in many places, and it is admitted that an extensive road-building program will shortly have to be undertaken.

The road (No. 106) begins at Smeaton, a village on Highway No. 55 about halfway between Prince Albert and Nipawin, and ends 225 miles to the north-east at Flin Flon, a mining town straddling the Saskatchewan–Manitoba border. In its entire course it neither passes through nor bypasses any towns or villages; it skirts a tiny handful of settlements on the shores of several fine lakes – Little Bear, Big Sandy, Deschambault, Jan – where routine supplies are usually available, though occasionally the gas pumps are empty. These settlements harbour few permanent residents; they exist primarily for the fisherman and hunter, and the accommodation they provide varies from the tolerable to the deplorable.

On the Hanson Lake Road, perhaps more than anywhere else in Saskatchewan, a man is conscious of driving through a world untouched by history. There are no great waterways near at hand along which fur-traders might have built their posts; for the greater part of its route the road runs almost precisely between the Saskatchewan and the Churchill rivers, each from fifty to one hundred miles distant, and no traders or missionaries ever made much effort to establish contact with the few bands of Woods Cree who eked out a precarious living deep in the forest through which the road cuts its way.

There is nothing tangible on the Hanson Lake Road to suggest the past. And precious little to suggest the present, for while he is on the road the traveller's only means of communication with the world he has left behind him, or is seeking to reach, is by radio.

From Nipawin Provincial Park, as yet undeveloped, to Big Sandy Lake, a distance of forty-odd miles, the scenery is of almost unvarying splendour. The forest trees grow tall and straight and in excellent variety; and the surface of the land is broken by occasional lofty ridges – notably those of the Wapawekka Hills – darkly beautiful at a distance and from their summits providing satisfying vistas, particularly towards the south, of forest greenery and, if the sun is shining, lakes painted a gorgeous cobalt blue. But beyond Big Sandy the ridges subside, the road sinks far below tree-top level, the lakes withdraw from the roadside, lose themselves beyond sight in the forest – and the green tide washes over one.

Not all the way. Few roads anywhere in Canada provide more depressing evidence of man's folly in the woods than the mile upon mile of trees standing blackened and naked, with no undergrowth as yet to lighten the somber hues of death, for the fires that destroyed the trees are nearly all of recent origin. Between Deschambault and Jan lakes, a distance of fifteen miles, the destruction along the roadside is almost total. Here one is apt to be overwhelmed by a sense not of history but of prehistory; for now the rocks of the Pre-Cambrian Shield hump their grotesque forms out of sand and swamp and water and loom up through the inadequate curtain of dead trees as sentient beings – the monstrous creations of the first age of the world.

Or perhaps, to the fearful of heart, the burnt-over landscape may suggest not the first day but the last, when a disillusioned Creator shall blast the works of His own hand – the earth in ashes ending. A combination of rock and swamp and dead forest can play queer tricks on the over-active imagination. Especially at twilight.

There is compensation of a kind for all this destruction. Jan Lake, deep in woods once more green and stately (at least they were the last time we were over the road), full of fish and boats, and fringed on its southern shore with all the appurtenances of the Outdoors Life, benefits by contrast, makes on the traveller who has just come through the dreary, burnt-over waste an even greater impact than its very real charms merit.

The Hanson Lake Road ends at Flin Flon, a Hudson Bay Mining and Smelting Company town sitting on, and among, great rocks of the Pre-Cambrian Shield. There is water everywhere – so much of it, indeed, that some houses actually cluster on rocks which form minuscule islands. Few of the houses, being built on rock, boast basements, and the laying of sewer-pipes has proved an enormous expense. The mine, which is the town's *raison d'être*, produces gold, silver, zinc, copper, and a number of lesser minerals to the value of some sixty million dollars a year.

If popular tradition is to be believed, Flin Flon was so named in a moment of sheer inanity. A prospector is said to have found a tattered copy of a preposterous science-fiction novel, *The Sunless City*, by J. E. Preston-Muddock, on a Churchill River portage. The story recounts the adventures of Professor Josiah Flintabbaty Flonatin, who discovered in the depths of a mysterious lake (via submarine) a city of gold ruled over by a formidable matriarchy. Terrified of the women, the professor fled from the city of gold and made his way back to the earth's surface through the cone of an extinct volcano. The prospector read the novel with great enjoyment and passed it around among his companions. Shortly afterwards, when he and his party came across a curious cone-shaped hole in the ground near the site of the present town, he is reported to have said, 'Boys, I guess we've found old Flin Flon's mine.'

The story of the naming of the townsite is, in fact, so absurd that it compels belief – no one could possibly have invented it. We academics are naturally anxious that the story be given wide circulation. After all, Flin Flon is the only town in western Canada to be named after a professor.

Flin Flon town is neat and clean and, if the wind is right, comparatively free of smelter smog – although there is enough hanging around most of the time to prevent the growth of lawns and gardens adequate to satisfy the ambitions of even the most lackadaisical gardener. By way, perhaps, of compensation for the destruction it has wrought within the town limits, the Company has gone all out to develop a northern Eden on the shore of Phantom Lake, a mile or two south of the town on the Saskatchewan side of the border. The development features an elaborate spread of greenhouses, and flower gardens of a luxuriance and variety of colour hardly to be matched elsewhere in Saskatchewan. In addition to the gardens the development boasts a golf course, a marina, and a fine sand beach artificially created and conscientiously renewed every spring. Piped-in music provides a dash of canned culture – and opposition to the privately operated transistors. The entire beach area is characterized by a well-groomed look which may offend devotees of the rumpled way of life but which, I confess, I find infinitely pleasing to the eye, particularly by comparison with most of the 'developments' I have encountered elsewhere in the north woods.

My wife, who was born in Cobalt, Ontario, was delighted with Flin Flon. She said it looked just like home.

From Flin Flon the logical, indeed the only, return route for the traveller who is reluctant to retrace his tracks is the Kelsey Highway No. 10, which runs down on the Manitoba side of the border to The Pas and beyond. From The Pas a good municipal road leads across country to the Saskatchewan border, where it links up with Saskatchewan Highway No. 109, a gravelled road ending at Hudson Bay, a town about eighty miles south-west of the border point of entry.

Some of Canada's finest northern scenery lies along the forty-mile stretch between Flin Flon and Cranberry Portage. This is Shield country at its most dramatic. The road is a twister, fast time an impossibility, but the landscape is of such extraordinary beauty that to speed through it is an offence against nature. Between Cranberry Portage and The Pas the scenic attractions rapidly diminish; the road once again runs down that never-ending avenue of stunted evergreen, and the rocks of the Shield give way to swamp and muskeg and reed-fringed shallow lakes.

The Carrot River, an innocent-seeming stream of no apparent consequence by comparison with such lordly flows as the Saskatchewan and the Churchill, joins the Saskatchewan near The Pas. Highway No. 109 to Hudson Bay is at first content to follow the convolutions of the Carrot upstream through heavy woods for twenty miles or more before breaking away and heading off on its own almost due south for Hudson Bay. But the Carrot, though of demure appearance and modest volume (most of the time), is no stream to be trifled with. Unlike most Saskatchewan rivers it has carved out no deep valleys for itself; for the greater part of its course it flows, as do most of its numerous tributaries, between perilously low banks. So low, indeed, that flooding is an ever-present springtime threat. Along its lower reaches the Carrot is dyked, and the traveller driving over the first twenty miles of No. 109 is likely to harbour the curious impression of actually running below the surface level of an all but invisible stream. Floods over past centuries have inevitably caused a good deal of damage; but they have made the broad tract of land vaguely referred to as the Carrot River country into a delta of immensely rich farmland.

Twenty miles north of Hudson Bay the Pasquia Hills thrust up from the forest floor to form one of the most clearly defined elevations in Saskatchewan. The picnic site at the top of the steep road ascent provides one of the best views of northern Saskatchewan forestland that may be obtained without use of an airplane. Far below the observation point, the silent forest – sadly marred along the base of the Hills by fire – reaches away to the horizon, the mottled green interspersed at frequent intervals with threads and patches of blue, the surface unruffled by any elevation except the extension of the Pasquia range on either side. Here, too, among these Hills, so I am assured, are excellent trout streams; which leads me to suggest that the sportsman who prefers to hunt or fish among scenes that are a delight to the eye and allow for the taking of as many deep breaths as one feels the need of, could hardly do better than to make the Pasquia Hills his hunting-grounds. Even though the game should prove elusive and the fish indifferent, the Hills in themselves offer compensations of a kind not always to be found in northern Saskatchewan.

The Pasquia Hills are at present a game reserve; but so far no attempt has been made to develop them beyond the provision of the usual excellent D.N.R. picnic and camp sites. There is, however, adequate motel and hotel accommodation at Hudson Bay only an hour's drive away.

Personally I have seldom enjoyed any travel experience in Saskatchewan more than that of rising suddenly from the forest floor to the height of the Pasquia ridge and surveying from a superbly located lookout-point the limitless wilderness of trees in which for days we had lived and moved and somehow survived. So must an ill-conditioned submarine-crew member feel when his ship, after long submersion, at last breaks surface and he is able to crawl through a hatch into fresh air and sunshine and see the element that lately covered him over spread out below eye-level all the way to the horizon. So too must the long-entombed miner feel when brought to the surface of a mine from which for some time past he has had grave doubts about ever escaping.

From Hudson Bay town the splendid Carrot River country runs as far as Melfort, one hundred miles to the west. There are parts of Saskatchewan with a far greater grain-production potential, notably the Regina plains and, in a good year, certain areas of the extreme south, but nowhere is there a region more sugges-tive of authentic opulence, more varied in its fruits, more abun-dantly overflowing with the contents of nature's cornucopia. In truth the Carrot River country is a land overflowing with milk and honey. Great dairy herds are nurtured here – and the udders of the cows, like everything else in the land, seem always full to the point of bursting. The bees are here too. Tisdale is the centre of Saskatchewan's flourishing honey industry – and delicious honey it processes. I have eaten the fabled honey of Hymettus in the very shadow of the mountain from which it takes its name, but not even under such ideal conditions was its flavour a patch on that of the Carrot River product.

The wealth of Carrot River soil is reflected in the homes of its owners. Indeed, it is true to say that all over Saskatchewan in-creased prosperity is manifest in the number of new farm homes that have sprung up since the end of the Second World War. I remember clearly the time when the step upwards from the frame or log shack was inevitably to the two-storey frame house with dormer windows, a wide porch running along the living-room side, the house painted white with green trim and sur-mounted by a pair of lightning conductors guaranteed to carry off all except the biggest bolts harmlessly into the ground. The two-storey farm home is now an anachronism, and so is the green and white paint job. Today rainbow-hued ranch houses and cot-tages, infinitely more convenient for the housewife to manage and more appropriate in design to a land of high wind and dust storms, crouch comfortably behind windbreaks which, over the years, have in many instances grown into miniature forests. The huge hip-roofed barn, in its day a status symbol, invariably painted red, is an anachronism too. It was built on an ample scale to accommodate not only milk cows but the horses which have long since given way to tractors; and the immense loft beneath the hip roof sheltered the loads of hay which are now compressed into neat, easily-stacked bales. The modern barn is a modest, unobtrusive affair, often yielding pride of place among outbuildings to the machine-sheds which house the vast array of complicated machinery essential to the conduct of modern farming operations.

It is to be noted that everywhere deserted farm homes – many of them two- and even three-storey structures which in their heyday were evidence of prosperity and large families – blacken and crumble into dissolution. They are symptomatic not of the decay of farming, but of its changing nature; of the shift, made easy by machinery, from the small farm to the large. Overhead costs of farming have increased enormously in relation to returns, and only the large farm is today economically sound. And even where farms have remained approximately the same size for the past few decades the farming population has been drastically diminished. In a day of rapid and easy transportation many families prefer to live in town and commute to work. The elimination of the one-room country school in favour of the large centralized unit has encouraged the migration off the land.

The Carrot River Valley towns, particularly the two largest, Melfort and Tisdale, are well-treed, well-preserved, and set in some of the handsomest farming country in the west. And close at hand, only thirty miles south-east of Tisdale, is a charming provincial park, Greenwater, set in an outlying spur of the far-ranging Pasquia Hills. Greenwater Park is centred around two deep, forest-fringed lakes which are said to be full of hungry fish and which, except in occasional seasons when the algae is troublesome, provide excellent swimming.

The visitor from eastern Canada who is made apprehensive by an environment of empty plain and empty sky with no hiding-place from the eye of God or battering wind or the loneliness which – particularly if he is a gregarious soul – is sure to oppress him, would do well to hurry to the Carrot River country. The wind blows even there, but less ferociously than on the great plains; and there are trees and running water and fine pastoral landscapes which, except for the huge grainfields, are not unlike those of rural Ontario. And to stimulate the romantic sensibility with which even the most practical and prosaic of mortals is in some degree endowed there is the knowledge, made all the more dear by the comfort and familiarity of one's immediate surroundings, that only a few miles north the Saskatchewan River flows towards Hudson Bay, and that just beyond the river begins the mighty wilderness stretching uninterrupted to Arctic seas.

19. Cumberland House

There are places of the earth whose names alone – Samarkand and Bokara and Xanadu and the Outer Islands and the High Pamirs – emanate an aura of high romance and kindle the poetic imagination, particularly of those of us who have never actually seen any of these places and indeed may have only the haziest notion of where they are. Time and distance are the elements which, when compounded, work the essential magic. In Saskatchewan, regrettably, neither element is operative. Time, instead of preserving and enhancing, has in most instances obliterated; and those places that have survived time's ravages have done so because they have become easy of access, hence deprived of whatever romantic attractions physical remoteness might have conferred upon them.

There is one notable exception. Cumberland House stands apart from all other Saskatchewan settlements. It is very old – for the Canadian west – and although located south of such settlements as La Ronge and Ile à la Crosse it has until recently been inaccessible to the ordinary tourist because no road led into it. Until 1966 Cumberland House could be reached in summertime only by air or water. Now all is changed. A road, which will no doubt be steadily improved over the next few years, follows the Saskatchewan River from Squaw Rapids to a point opposite Pemmican Portage. Two miles or more beyond Pemmican Portage Cumberland House stands on the shores of Cumberland Lake. It boasts nearly two hundred years' continuous occupation, the longest of any settlement in Saskatchewan. Until recently isolated, remote, to most of us a name rather than a physical reality, it is now open to all comers.

The road to Cumberland House properly begins at Nipawin,

a town built near the site of an early trading-post whose founding anticipated that of Cumberland House by several years. Fur-traders out of Montreal built a post near the rapids a few miles above the present townsite as early as 1768, and intermittently did a flourishing business with the Indians, for they had not only the Saskatchewan valley but the adjacent White Fox and Carrot River countries to draw on – in those days regions immensely rich in furs. Matthew Cocking, a highly intelligent, well-educated Hudson's Bay emissary, who came down to Nipawin from York Factory in 1772 to try to draw the Indians of the interior back into the Company orbit, was much impressed with the business acumen of old François Le Blanc, the trader at that time in charge of the Nipawin post. He was less impressed by the Frenchman's manners, although it is reasonable to suppose that his unfavourable reaction was in part an expression of resentment felt by the thus-far unsuccessful trader towards the successful. In particular he was offended by François's failure to 'keep a proper distance from his men'. He even permitted them to come into his apartment uninvited and 'talk with him as one of themselves'.

Cocking, who later enjoyed a distinguished career in the service of the Company, had, in 1772, still much to learn.

Dr. Arthur Silver Morton, late Chairman of the Department of History at the University of Saskatchewan and one of Canada's best-known historians, was largely responsible for the discovery in 1938 of the chimneys of the early Nipawin posts and for their subsequent preservation; and in more recent years archeologists from the Provincial Museum of Natural History have carried out fruitful excavations on the old sites.

The country around Nipawin was settled by homesteaders shortly after the turn of the century, but the original community was abandoned when the railroad bypassed it by a mile or more. The present settlement sprang into being overnight, immediately following the end of the First World War.

The modern town of Nipawin sits on a high bank commanding a fine view of the Saskatchewan River, which here is a majestic stream running deep and swift, for the two great branches, North and South, after pursuing their independent ways for a thousand miles or more, have at last joined forces some fifty miles above the town. The approach to the town from the north must be made over an horrendously narrow bridge;

but it is worth while making the crossing several times for the sake of the superb up-and-down-river views which almost any point on the bridge provides.

The business section of Nipawin could be interchanged with the business section of almost any other town of comparable size in Saskatchewan and no one would notice the difference. The main street is wide, windswept, lined on both sides with conventional small-town shops and business places – a bit drab in the daytime, neon-lit, gaudy at night. It may be, though, that more of the frontier spirit, the old genial pioneer *bonhomie*, survives in Nipawin than in most Saskatchewan towns. Although we consider ourselves inured to the strange sights and shocks one encounters in Saskatchewan small-town restaurants, my wife and I were a little taken aback when our Nipawin waitress, a not unattractive creature in a loosely assembled sort of way, sat down at our table with us – her feet hurt she said – and smoked a cigarette while we wrote out our order. The restaurant is, we admit, entirely justified in describing its atmosphere as 'friendly and informal'.

The residential part of Nipawin is the town's chief charm. Nipawin is young even for Saskatchewan, but the houses, oddly enough, are reminiscent of an earlier ampler day. Many of them are two-storeyed; nearly all are set in spacious well-treed grounds encompassed by splendid lawns and gardens. Nipawin is, in fact, a town that enjoys the best of two worlds. The forest is here unobtrusive, unoppressive, providing natural windbreaks and shelter belts; and the great plains begin to assert themselves just across the river. Plains that grow some of the finest wheat in the west – evidenced in the large-scale production of seed grain, one of Nipawin's most profitable enterprises.

The road to Cumberland House runs north-east from Nipawin forty-six miles to the Squaw Rapids Hydro Station before heading downstream along the south bank of the Saskatchewan. The building of a water-diversion dam at Squaw Rapids has created Tobin Lake, a body of water forty miles long and ten miles wide. There is talk of developing Tobin Lake into a resort area, but it seems unlikely that such a project would be widely popular. Tobin Lake, particularly in its lower reaches, is surrounded by a singularly dreary and desolate swamp-and-evergreen desert, and only morbid-minded holidayers, resolute to get away from it all and brood in solitude and discomfort, are likely to find much pleasure along its shores. Indeed, one of the reasons why Squaw Rapids was chosen as a suitable hydro-station site was that the flooding of a large area would involve no human factors, since virtually none of the land flooded was settled on.

Tourist facilities at the Squaw Rapids Hydro Station, other than overnight accommodation, are admirably developed and supervised; and every provision is made to acquaint the visitor with the complicated details of the station layout.

My wife and I drove over the road from Squaw Rapids to Cumberland House in the summer of 1966 when almost all of the traffic, apart from ourselves, consisted of assorted items of road machinery of appalling dimensions and power – great impersonal monsters able and willing, so we thought, to crush us and our car, if we impeded operations, into the roadway. (When I am thus harassed by road machinery on a road under construction, with rain threatening and no place of refuge within forty miles, I am also plagued by the recurring suspicion that probably half the missing persons in Canada have been made a part of our roadbeds by these behemoths into whose paths they have had the misfortune to wander.)

The road surface was fair most of the way except for the occasional soft patch – rutted to Grand Canyon depth by the wheels of mighty bulldozers – through which our car dragged itself along on its belly, an aging experience for both car and occupants. Happily the forest on either side of the road provided some compensation for the occasional muddy stretches through which we bucked and wallowed; it was easily the handsomest, the most varied, the most companionable, and the least obtrusive of all the forests we have driven through in northern Saskatchewan. The evergreens grow straight and very tall here, side by side with fine stands of balsam and tall slender birches and aspen; and Manitoba maples have spilled over in abundance from their home province to enrich the Saskatchewan scene. Unlike the trees farther north, those flanking the Cumberland House road do not crowd in on the motorist or on one another; at times, indeed, they grow in a manner reminiscent of an Old Country or southern Ontario woods, each tree with ample standing and breathing room, uncluttered by any tangle of undergrowth. And close at hand and often visible through the forest screen flows the river – a broad, dark, and splendid stream, a little subdued, to be sure, by the Squaw Rapids Dam, but still an impressive spectacle in a world where all things are shaped to a godlike scale.

And it is here that, to the man who has wandered widely over Saskatchewan, the omnipresence of the great river at last strikes home. Omnipresent is the right word to describe a river which, like a deity, is everywhere and at the same time isolated, remote, non-involved. For no matter where one encounters the Saskatchewan — even in Saskatoon where it splits the city in two — or on what terms, it seems to have little concern with the affairs of men. It goes its remote and lonely way, drawing farther and farther away from all settled places, until, out of an almost uninhabited wilderness, it empties at last into the vast reservoir of Lake Winnipeg more than twelve hundred miles from its source.

Cumberland House is a settlement built on the south shore of Cumberland (formerly Pine) Lake, about two miles north of the river. To reach the settlement from the new road it is necessary to cross from the south side of the river to a tiny community named Pemmican Portage, and from the Portage make one's way overland the two miles or more to Cumberland House. A road construction man whom we had consulted briefly in Nipawin had told us that since no ferry was in operation at Pemmican Portage we would have to leave our car, providing we ever got that far, on the south side of the river and cross over by boat. We had, in our innocence, assumed that some sort of regular water transport would be available, but all we found at the end of the road was an unfinished ferry landing-stage with no water transport in sight. Not even a raft. (The ferry was put into operation about a month later.)

We huddled forlornly on the bank, looked across the river at Pemmican Portage, cursed the construction man, and wondered what to do. Yell for help? Send up smoke signals? My wife, a resourceful woman, did better than that. She spotted a canoe lurking under an overhang a short distance downstream and waded through six inches of mud along the bank to solicit the canoeist for a ride. He was a singularly villainous-looking Indian, and his canoe was a battered filthy wreck, but he and it were our only hope.

He looked us over and nodded. 'O.K.' he said, and prepared the way for our boarding by throwing a dozen suckers from the canoe to the bank. My wife sat gingerly on a broken thwart amid-ships, her feet straddling a still-squirming catch of pickerel and gold-eye, and I perched on the bow and longed passionately for a life-preserver, for the river flowed deep and swift here and the water in the bottom of the canoe was rising fast. Our Charon grinned, showed a few broken yellowed teeth, and held up a broken yellowed paddle – a handle with two frayed edges at one end to show where the blade had been.

'Bust,' he explained, superfluously I thought. 'I get a new one. Some time.'

He didn't need a new one – he handled the stick and the canoe with superb skill and insouciance. In no time at all he had carried us safely across the river and deposited us in the mud of the north bank. I paid him a large enough fee for his services to make reasonably sure he'd be on hand to take us back again; then we scrambled up the bank to Pemmican Portage and braced ourselves for what we knew would be a mosquito-ridden walk to Cumberland House.

We hadn't reckoned on the degree of civilization achieved in this remote outpost. A public 'taxi', no less, was at our disposal – a battered little old bus, brought in by winter road in some long-bygone year, that shuttled back and forth between the two settlements, most of the time packed to overflowing with pas-sengers. Indians and Métis are gregarious folk who love visiting and public transportation.

Rejoicing, my wife and I wedged ourselves into the bus, which banged and ground its way over an horrendous two-mile trail to Cumberland House.

Cumberland House was built in 1774 by one of the greatest of Hudson's Bay Company men, Samuel Hearne. And none too soon, for by 1774 the posts of the Montreal traders ran all the way from the Head of the Lakes to the forks of the Saskatchewan and beyond, thereby effectively intercepting the trade that formerly the Indians of the interior had carried all the way to the Company posts on or near Hudson Bay. The failure of the Company to match the pedlars in the opening up of the west can be blamed only partially on lack of initiative or unwarranted assumption of superiority. Historians point out that the logistics problem confronting an organization operating from a base on Hudson Bay was infinitely more difficult and complicated than that for men trading out of Montreal. The Montreal pedlars started their long journey in huge, superbly constructed canoes manned by voyageurs born with a paddle in their hands; they were able to carry up to four thousand pounds of trade goods in each canoe, for they obtained from the Indians along the way nearly all the food – corn and wild rice were the basic items – necessary to keep them alive while on the journey. And once they reached the plains country they found buffalo meat in ample supply.

But for the men of the Hudson's Bay Company seeking to penetrate inland to the great plains there were available neither canoes nor the paddlers needed to handle them. No birch trees grew around York Factory to supply the needed birch bark, and the only paddlers available to man such canoes as were eventually brought down from the interior were Orkneymen better accustomed to handling row-boats. When Samuel Hearne left York Factory in 1774 to build an inland post for the Company, he had no choice but to travel upstream in small Indian canoes so laden with food supplies – the country through which he had to pass being almost devoid of game – that there was room in each canoe for only two or three hundred pounds of trade goods, a puny cargo by comparison with the two tons or more carried by each canoe out of Montreal.

With eight white men to assist him Hearne built a post on the site where the community of Cumberland House still stands, and lived in it during the winter of 1774-5. The experience was not a happy one, the survival of the party something of a miracle. The woods were almost empty of game, and the white men were at times solely dependent for food on the Indians, who occasionally brought moose-meat to the post to exchange for trade goods. The cold was intense, morale among the men inevitably low. Spring and the return of huge flocks of geese and ducks to Cumberland Lake – still a popular stopover point for migrant birds – lifted the threat of starvation and brought hordes of mosquitoes which, in alliance with the blackflies, tormented the white men almost to distraction.

At year's end Hearne was able to despatch to York Factory only a single canoe-load of furs, and a small one at that. When he left Cumberland House for good late in 1775 he must have done so with mixed feelings of intense relief and bitter disappointment, for he had failed signally to capture the trade he

coveted. He seems to have suffered, too, from a feeling of inferiority in the presence of the dashing, self-assured Montreal
pedlars who snatched furs from under the very noses of the Company men and associated with the Indians on terms of good
fellowship that Hearne and his associates were unable to match.
Company men were, so Hearne wrote in great bitterness of
spirit, 'the laughing-stock of every trader from Canady'.

The sense of failure and inferiority was unjustified. Whether
Hearne sent a small catch or large to York Factory was, in 1775,
of little importance; what really mattered was that in Cumberland House existed the visible proof of Company determination to move inland and fight the Montreal traders on their own
ground. And Hearne had learned much about the weapons with
which the battle must be fought. Big canoes. Trained paddlers.
Trade goods in abundance – mostly rum. His immediate successors at the new post, Matthew Cocking and William Tomison,
benefited immeasurably from Hearne's suggestions and their
rapid implementation by the Company. Within ten years Cumberland House was a flourishing trade centre, and for a long time
thereafter the most important Hudson's Bay post on the
Saskatchewan, commanding as it did the approaches to the vast
Saskatchewan and Athabasca fur countries, and staffed as it was
by men who, while never as gregarious as the Nor'Westers, were
their equals in courage and superiors in honesty – two facts
which the Indians were quick to recognize.

Cumberland House enjoyed its finest hour from 1818 to 1821
when Governor William Williams made the post his headquarters. In 1820 Sir John Franklin and the members of his first
expedition spent part of the winter at the post, and so, nearly
thirty years later, did the men of the first search party sent out to
try to solve the riddle of Franklin's fate. The fortunes of Cumberland House declined rapidly from the mid nineteenth
century on as a result of the opening up of more convenient
trade routes farther south, but it has precariously survived to
the present day as the administrative centre of a small Indian
and Métis community, and as a supply depot for sportsmen,
trappers, and commercial fishermen.

My wife and I unashamedly toured Cumberland House by bus.
Rain was threatening, and we knew that if it caught up before
we had escaped back across the river and covered the fifty miles of

road under construction we might not get out for a week. For part of our ride we enjoyed the company of the local chief, John Settee, a man of portly and dignified bearing whose status the bus driver acknowledged by swerving off the road and running the bus right up to the chief's front door and indeed, because of the precarious state of his brakes, almost through it. The chief's house is a modest two-storey frame structure – one room to each storey – in which he and his wife have raised sixteen children.

All the institutional buildings – school, churches, police barracks, hospital, H.B.C. store – that form the core of the larger northern settlements are to be found in Cumberland House, and in addition there is a first-rate lodge which provides the only public accommodation available and for which it is essential to book well in advance. But the most interesting object in the settlement is an old boiler now rusting on the beach of Cumberland Lake only a few hundred yards from the centre of town. The boiler is the last surviving relic of the steamer *Northcote*, which went aground for the last time in 1886.

The *Northcote* was the clown among Saskatchewan river boats, and the one best remembered, for she was pressed into service during the Riel Rebellion and carried troops and supplies downstream from Swift Current to Clarke's Crossing, where General Middleton had pitched camp prior to his advance on the rebel stronghold of Batoche. The *Northcote* stuck on nearly every sand-bar between Swift Current and Clarke's Crossing and had literally to be lifted over them on winch-operated stilts; her crew nearly mutinied and her captain threatened to resign. None the less, when the time came for the final push on Batoche the *Northcote* was ready and eager to lend naval support to the land forces and share the glory of the great day. Flags flying, marine soldiers (all thirty-five of them) cheering, bulwarks reinforced with bags of oats, smoke belching from her twin smoke-stacks, the *Northcote* trundled bravely downstream intent on opening up a devastating flank attack on Batoche, which would coincide with Middleton's frontal assault by land. Unfortunately for the *Northcote* the Métis most unsportingly dropped a ferry cable across her bows just as she drew abreast of Batoche. Her smoke-stacks and part of the deckhouse swept away, the steamboat swung hind end to and drifted helplessly downstream, while the soldiers huddled behind the bags of oats and listened to the thud of Métis bullets against the *Northcote*'s ribs.

The crewmen repaired the damage after a fashion and the *Northcote* continued downstream to Hudson Bay Crossing near Prince Albert to pick up fuel and supplies. She returned to the scene of the action towing a sister ship, the *Marquis* (which had broken her steering gear), and reached Batoche just after the Métis surrender.

The *Northcote* continued to ply the waters of the Saskatchewan until the following year, 1886, when she was beached for good at Cumberland House and left to rot. Hers was the fate of nearly all the Saskatchewan River steamboats. They enjoyed a brief hour, from the early 1870s to the mid '80s, if not of glory at least of some importance, freighting lumber and foodstuffs and settlers' supplies on a run extending from Grand Rapids near Lake Winnipeg to Medicine Hat; but the coming of the railway spelled their swift extinction. It cannot be said that the river trade ever prospered; the settlements it served were too few and insignificant, and the river itself too shallow and treacherous for comfortable navigation.

It is regrettable, though, that the end of the steamboats should have been, in nearly every instance, an ignominious one – beached and abandoned. What a pity the *Northcote* couldn't have gone down opposite Batoche, her lone gun blazing away (in actual fact it jammed almost the first time it was fired), flag flying, Captain Sheets, who hailed from Missouri, cursing his enemies and calling for more steam as the muddy waters closed over his head. At the very least, instead of being left to rot like unburied corpses in full public view, the steamboats might have had provided for them in some remote place a final harbourage to which, when their time came, they might have gone off – like the elephants, whom in size and grace of movement they greatly resembled – to die in peace and privacy far from the sight of men.

The destiny of Cumberland House is difficult to predict. From time to time grandiose schemes are projected for draining the Cumberland delta, clearing away the forest, and converting the native population into industrious farmers. Such talk may be reassuring to the talkers but it doesn't mean much to anyone else. The delta land is peaty, unsuitable for the growing of cereal crops, and the Indians of Cumberland House are no more likely than their brothers elsewhere to embrace enthusiastically the arts of husbandry. All that can be forecast positively for Cumberland House is a marked increase in the tourist trade with all its attendant benefits and drawbacks. Perhaps, had the ferry not been installed, the natives could have done well for themselves operating a canoe taxi-service between road's end and Pemmican Portage.

We found our Indian canoeman waiting for us in front of his squalid shack. His numerous progeny, several of whom were playing in a fly-infested refuse heap near by, left off their games to gather round and observe us with shy, unsmiling curiosity. One of the small boys wore a T-shirt with the name CUMBERLAND HOUSE showing in faded letters across the front. The T-shirt didn't fit him very well and I don't think it ever will.

Epilogue

Earth Abiding

There are parts of Saskatchewan where, as far as the eye can see, oil-pumps dot the fields and perform twenty-four hours a day their monotonous ritualistic task of drawing wealth from the depths of the earth; other parts where the great inverted cones of the potash mines hold the sky itself suspended; and still others where the sounds of the contractor's bulldozers and pile-drivers herald the coming to the province of a vast new industry – pulp and paper – and for at least one city a rebirth of expectation. But the man who has lived a long time in Saskatchewan, in city, town, hamlet, or country, and who has moved elsewhere, never asks about oil or potash or uranium or lumber; the question he invariably asks, and by which he invariably betrays his origins and his heart, is simply, 'How are the crops?'

The association between the Saskatchewan man and the earth around him – whether one of love or hate – is intimate, intense, and he can never break it. Elsewhere the association is more comfortable, because less passionate. An Ontario or an Old Country farmer is aware of the earth about him and loves it after his fashion, as he loves all familiar intimate things. To leave it is a wrench which hurts for a time but makes no permanent mark. But when the Saskatchewan man shakes the dust of the province from his person and departs for far-off places where the air is warm and the wind is quiet and there are hills and trees and water on every side, he finds himself, more often than not, still bound in spirit to that great and strange and savage land that shaped him – as he might in another context be bound to a capricious and sometimes cruel mistress whom he had escaped from in the flesh, only to be haunted thereafter, consciously or otherwise, by an awareness of his infidelity.

Saskatchewan, to a far greater degree than either of her sister provinces, is still a countryman's world. Half the population of Manitoba is concentrated in a single city; in Alberta, in two; but in Saskatchewan the two largest cities absorb less than a quarter of the total population of the province. So it is that, no matter what the Saskatchewan man's occupation or where his dwelling-place, his association with the land is intimate and enduring. From the centre of our largest city a twenty-minutes' drive leads him away from the heat and the smog (an innocuous dilution not to be mentioned in the same breath with the full-bodied blends of our eastern cities) into that silence and solitude which in a world daily more and more dedicated to the unholy end of keeping itself in togetherness and noise are all the more dearly to be cherished.

Silence and solitude – the finest gifts Saskatchewan has to offer bedevilled modern man. On the great empty plain, in the forest depths, when the wind is quiet and no birds sing. Nowhere, I think, is it possible for man to know better his littleness and greatness – that is, to know better himself. For this is a world which objectifies the great words, birth and love and death and God and eternity, casts them in a scale that exalts their grandeur and diminishes their terror. (It may be only a comforting fancy, but it seems to me that the man who all his life has lived close to the earth is not often afraid at the end to lie in it.)

The sage old councillor of King Edwin of Northumbria, when called upon to consider the merits of the strange new faith called Christianity, described the life of man in a striking simile:

> The present life of man, O King, seems to me, in comparison to that time which is unknown to us, like unto the swift flight of a sparrow through the room wherein you sit at supper in winter, with your commanders and retainers, and a good fire in the midst, whilst the storms of rain and snow prevail abroad; the sparrow, I say, flying in at one door, and immediately out the other, whilst he is within, is safe from the wintery storm; but . . . he immediately vanishes out of your sight, into the dark winter from which he had emerged.

Once I saw a flock of wild geese caught in the lights of the city. They hung suspended far overhead, gleaming white shapes patterned into an almost flawlessly symmetrical V, before passing at last beyond the range of light into darkness. In the vast world of

Saskatchewan's earth and sky it is possible to feel that a flight of wild geese suspended for a moment of time in a great white light is a truer symbol of man's passing from birth to death than the flight of a fear-crazed sparrow through a dim-lit room.

In the great cities, in the crowded places, the man-made world is too much with us; it blurs our responses to anything except the immediate, compels us to accept its values, shapes us in the long run to its ways. The Saskatchewan prairies are a world that enables man to see himself clearly in relation not only to his fellow men but to those values that are inherent not in the Many but in the One. It is a world that persuades him to accept the fact of his own curious duality – that he is at once nothing and everything, at once the dust of the earth and the God that made it; a world that permits him to come to terms, perhaps subconsciously, with that duration which, in Sir Thomas Browne's mystic previsioning, 'maketh pyramids pillars of snow and all that's past a moment'.

Certain it is that in the autumn days when the skies grow pale and the most haunting music of earth, the cry of the wild goose, sounds the requiem of the dying year, the truth is borne home to him of the words of the wise man of old – a truth not of negation but of affirmation: *One generation passeth away and another generation cometh; but the earth abideth forever.*

Appendix

The visitor to Saskatchewan who plans to stay any length of time should provide himself in advance with three excellent government publications: *Saskatchewan Tourist Accommodation, Camp Grounds in Saskatchewan,* and *Guide to Historic Sites and Points of Interest.* The first two may be obtained from the Tourist Development Branch, Department of Industry and Commerce, Power Building, Regina; the third from The Saskatchewan Diamond Jubilee and Canada Centennial Corporation, McCallum-Hill Building, Regina.

Saskatchewan Tourist Accommodation gives 'a complete picture of the tourist accommodations available in Saskatchewan' from the near-luxurious to the ultra-primitive. Not the smallest of small-town hotels or the remotest of wilderness cabins appears to have been overlooked. Unfortunately, no attempt is made to grade these accommodations by the popular star system, and tourists are hereby warned that the price charged is not always a guide to quality. To the uninitiated it should be pointed out that the distinction between Modern and Non-Modern accommodation is, broadly speaking, that between inside plumbing and out; and that Semi-Modern signifies running water somewhere on the premises.

The booklet also provides valuable information on such topics as Transportation, Vacation Trails, Provincial Parks, Regional Parks and Museums.

Camp Grounds in Saskatchewan lists all available camp sites in the province with full information on the facilities provided by each.

Guide to Historic Sites and Points of Interest is precisely what its title says it is. An altogether admirable production, it describes succinctly and accurately the province's regions of historic importance and marked historic sites. Accompanying maps indicate the most convenient routes by which the regions and sites may be reached.

The illustrations, most of them provided by the Provincial Archives, are well chosen and add much to the interest and value of the booklet.

Brochures describing the Provincial Parks (with rate structures) and the Vacation Trails have been prepared by the Department of Natural Resources and the Saskatchewan Centennial Corporation, and are obtainable from the Tourist Development Branch or almost any local Tourist Information Bureau. Occasionally the descriptions of the natural beauties of the parks get a little out of hand, but they in no way diminish the value of the practical information that the brochures supply.

Saskatchewan Parks

National

Prince Albert National Park: Contains 1,500 square miles of lake and forest land. Entrance sixty miles north of Prince Albert on Highway No. 2. Town of Waskesiu on Waskesiu Lake twenty-five miles north of entrance provides essential services ánd a wide variety of amenities including an 18-hole championship golf course. Hotels, motels, cabins to rent at a number of points throughout the Park. Facilities include tent and trailer grounds (with electricity and sewer connections at Waskesiu Lake and Waskesiu Narrows), campgrounds, picnic grounds, beach houses, etc. Swimming, fishing, canoeing readily available. (For detailed description of the Park see Chapter Fifteen.)

Provincial

Cypress Hills: On Highway No. 21, twenty-five miles south of the Trans-Canada Highway via Maple Creek. Restaurant, coffee shop, golf course (sand greens), heated swimming-pool. Limited boating facilities on pint-sized lake. About forty government-operated L.H.K. cabins, some fully modern. (For reservations write to Commercial Manager, Cypress Hills Provincial Park, Maple Creek.) Extensive camp-grounds with kitchens, running water, electrical connections for trailers. (For detailed description of the Park and surrounding country see Chapter Seven.)

The Battlefords: Twenty-five miles north of North Battleford via Highway No. 4. Swimming, fishing, boating. Government-operated camp-grounds two miles north of Cochin. Privately operated, modestly equipped hotels, motels, and cabins at Meota and Cochin.

Buffalo Pound Lake: Thirteen miles north of Moose Jaw on No. 2 Highway and six miles east on access road. Tent, trailer, picnic, and bathing facilities still in process of development. A few privately operated L.H.K. cabins available near by.

Echo Valley: Twenty miles north of Trans-Canada Highway on No. 35 to Fort Qu'Appelle, thence six miles west on access road. Located on narrow neck of land between Echo and Pasqua Lakes in the Qu'-Appelle Valley. Picnic areas, tent and trailer parks, swimming, fishing. Hotel and motel accommodation in Fort Qu'Appelle. Cabins on Echo Lake available for rent.

Katepwe: A small park, unpleasantly crowded on week-ends, seventeen miles north of the Trans-Canada Highway via Indian Head on No. 56. In the Qu'Appelle Valley, thirteen miles east of Fort Qu'Appelle. Swimming, boating, picnic grounds. Ample parking space except on week-ends. No camping. Privately operated cabins, stores, camp-grounds outside the park. (See Chapter Nine.)

Good Spirit: Twenty-two miles north of Yorkton on Highway No. 9, eight miles west on No. 229. Camping, swimming, fishing. Store, café. No cabins.

Duck Mountain: The park centres on Madge Lake, fifteen miles east of Kamsack on No. 57. Tent, trailer, and picnic facilities. Electricity. Excellent swimming and fishing. Golf course. Privately operated cabins for rent. The park is located on a high ridge, heavily wooded, which commands splendid views of the surrounding countryside.

Greenwater Lake: Twenty-eight miles north of Kelvington on Highway No. 38. Government-operated L.H.K. cabins, modern and non-modern. (For reservations apply Commercial Manager, Greenwater Lake Provincial Park.) Store, restaurant, tent and trailer facilities. Good fishing. Golf course. (See Chapter Eighteen.)

Lac La Ronge: One hundred and seventy miles north of Prince Albert on Highway No. 2. Located in rugged, sparsely populated Shield country, Lac La Ronge is one of the largest provincial parks in Canada. Not intended for comfortable family holidaying, but popular with sportsmen from all over the continent. Provides excellent fishing and hunting in season, and is a jumping-off place (by plane) for points farther north. Privately operated hotels and cabins in the town of La Ronge and at various points throughout the park. The quality of accommodation is still, in the main, fairly rough, but is steadily improving. Camp-grounds adjoining highway to the Churchill river are numerous, and admirably maintained. (See Chapter Sixteen.)

Meadow Lake: A large lake-and-forest area twenty-five miles north of Meadow Lake on Highway No. 4. Camp-grounds, modest tent and trailer facilities. Privately operated cabins (most of which are for the hardy) to rent at several of the larger lakes. Food supplies, gas available at several points. The park is still fairly raw, but facilities are being gradually extended and improved. (See Chapter Seventeen.)

Nipawin: On the Hanson Lake Road, thirty miles north of Smeaton. A lake-and-forest natural recreation area, as yet largely undeveloped. Fine fishing, hunting, swimming. A few privately operated non-modern cabins for rent on the Upper and Lower Fishing Lakes. Adequate, modestly equipped camp-grounds.

Moose Mountain: Forty miles south of the Trans-Canada Highway via Whitewood, on Highway No. 9. One of the handsomest and best-developed of Saskatchewan's provincial parks, set in country of unusual historic interest. Government-operated facilities include a chalet and thirty-five cabins (some modern). Trailer grounds with water and electrical connections. Playing-fields, and a challenging 18-hole golf course. (See Chapter Two.)

Pike Lake: Twenty miles south-west of Saskatoon on No. 14. A park created around a Saskatchewan River backwater, designed primarily for the use and amusement of Saskatoon citizens. Tent, trailer, picnic, and beach facilities.

Rowan's Ravine: One of the most ambitious of the Provincial Parks projects, located sixty miles north-west of Regina on the east shore of Last Mountain Lake and reached via Highways No. 20 and 220. A spacious development with impressive beach, camping, and picnic facilities. No cabin accommodation.

In addition to the Provincial Parks there are about fifty regional parks – joint provincial-municipal ventures – scattered throughout the province. Although intended primarily for local use they are open to visitors and tourists. Many feature swimming-pools. Standards of attractiveness and upkeep show wide variation. The locations of the regional parks, and the facilities they afford, are described in the *Saskatchewan Tourist Accommodation Handbook*.

The building of the Gardiner Dam on the South Saskatchewan River and the creation of Diefenbaker Lake and adjacent substantial bodies of water inevitably will result in the establishment of many more provincial and regional parks in the near future. Work on several of these parks is already (1968) well under way.

Index